Tell Me a Story, Grandpa

West Virginia Stories About
Farm Life
One-Room Schools
Logging
Hunting
Civil War

By

Thomas Bryan McQuain

1897-1988

Edited by Miriam McQuain Looker

Formatted by Tiffany Schmieder

HERITAGE BOOKS
2008

HERITAGE BOOKS
AN IMPRINT OF HERITAGE BOOKS, INC.

Books, CDs, and more—Worldwide

For our listing of thousands of titles see our website
at
www.HeritageBooks.com

Published 2008 by
HERITAGE BOOKS, INC.
Publishing Division
100 Railroad Ave. #104
Westminster, Maryland 21157

Copyright © 2008 Thomas B. McQuain

Other books by the author:

To the Front and Back: A West Virginia Marine Fights World War I

International Standard Book Numbers
Paperbound: 978-0-7884-4683-2
Clothbound: 978-0-7884-7266-4

ACKNOWLEDGEMENTS

I wish to think all who helped me get this book ready for the printer. Special thanks go to Tiffany Schmieder, who took care of scanning and inserting all the drawings from my father's originals and for other computer work. We also thank our editor at Heritage for her patient instructions.

Miriam McQuain Looker
2007

iii

INTRODUCTION

Do you know how to make a whistle out of chestnut bark?

Did you ever put your hat in front of the fireplace for Santa to fill? Or have your very own branch of the Christmas tree to trim?

Did you know that sleds aren't just for snow?

Can you remember how cold the one room schoolhouse was except right by the stove?

Did your grandpa fight in the Civil War? Grandpa McQuain's did and he tells stories his grandfather told him.

Can you imagine long evenings at home before radio, TV and electricity?

Grandpa McQuain recounts these things for his grandchildren. He also includes many stories his father and grandfather told him on those long evenings at home.

- - - - - - - - - - - -

Thomas Bryan McQuain was born on the family farm near Troy, West Virginia in 1897. This book covers his growing-up years from then until 1918 when he went off to serve in World War I.

This account was written during the winter of 1976-77 when Dayton, Ohio had a month-long blizzard. The next summer he and his wife Opal Morrison McQuain moved to Ft. Myers. He died in 1988, aged 91. They were the parents of four children, Miriam McQuain Looker, Jesabel McQuain Linscott, Thomas McQuain and David McQuain and eleven grandchildren, for whom the book was originally written.

"TELL ME A STORY, GRANDPA"

"Tell us a story, Grandpa."

"What kind of story would you like to hear?"

"One of olden times when you were a little boy."

"I remember a story Pa used to tell me and my brothers and sisters when we were about your size. It is about his father and brother when they were little boys, about four and three years old. They were your Great-great-grandfather and your Great- great-great Uncle."

"Why all the 'Greats,' Grandpa?"

"Because this is something that happed in olden times, and the 'Greats' help keep the generations straight . . ."

THE PANTHER STORY

Pa's father's family moved from Randolph County, which was then Virginia to Little Cove Creek in 1821. The trip was about 75 to 100 miles and took 3 or 4 days. They used pack horses to carry their belongings over the steep narrow roads, fording the streams.

People then did not have as much to move as they do now. They would take only what they could get along with and leave the rest behind or sell it to their neighbors. Pa's family had a wooden clothes chest, one or two beds, a trundle bed, three or four chairs, a 'mess pot' and a few other kitchen utensils, salt, flour, meal and clothes all tied on the two horses they rode, or loaded on

1

pack horses which they led. The two boys rode the horses, one each behind their Pa and Ma. Probably all of them walked at times to rest. Their two dogs walked, following along behind, in front, or on either side to protect the family and horses. In those days, there were bears, panthers, wildcats and wolves that, when hungry, would attack people or animals such as cows or horses.

Their journey came to an end when they got to a little log house which stood at the rock pile just behind where Uncle Perry's house is now located. This rock pile was formerly the chimney and fireplace for the small log cabin, which probably had only one room and was about 20 x 24 feet. The boys slept in the trundle bed which could be pushed under the big bed when not needed. The two dogs slept under the house when they were not out hunting or barking. Everyone got used to hearing the dogs barking, wildcats growling, and panthers screaming in the woods round about, together with the hooting of the owls nearby.

One night things took a little different turn. The dogs were out in the woods hunting and got into a fight with one or more hungry panthers. The panthers were too much for the dogs! Closer and closer to the house came the dogs, attacked by the panthers. When not far from the house, the dogs broke and ran for protection under the house. Just as the dogs went under the house, the panthers lunged for them and one struck the bottom log with his claws just as the dogs went under the house to safety. The panthers let out blood curdling screams of pain and disappointment as they turned again toward the forest. Two little boys jumped from the trundle bed into the big bed with their Pa and Ma for protection and reassurance.

Except for two scared dogs and boys, no one was hurt but the panther's claw marks could be seen for years on the outside of the log where the trundle bed and the two frightened boys had been.

Their pa took the gun and went out to see if he could get a shot at the 'painters' as they called them, but they had gone back into the woods. The dogs kept near their master in fear of the vicious animals lurking somewhere out there in the woods. None of them entered the woods to continue the search for panthers have been known to climb trees and lie on a limb and wait until their prey comes near, then jump on it and tear it to pieces. Neither the dogs nor the boys' pa wanted that to happen to them so they soon came back to the house.

2

The next morning all of them went out to see where the panther clawed the log when it struck at the dog. Their sharp claws had made deep scratches. The boys were glad the strong log was between the panthers and their bed!

The next evening, two scared little boys had to be reassured of the safety of their bed before they were willing to get into it for the night. After all had been quiet for awhile, a small voice inquired,

'How long will we have to wait for it to get here?'

'Oh! Come and get in bed with us for awhile. It won't be back tonight, though!' Their parents reassured the little boys and soon they got used to sleeping in their bed again but often their dreams waked them up. They never forgot the night the panthers chased the dogs under the house.

- - - - - - - - - - - -

"And over and over this story has been told to boys and girls just like you!"

"Grandpa, did that really happen?"

"Yes, I am sure it did. Pa told it to us the first time about 70 years ago."

"We've been to Uncle Perry's farm but no one pointed out the rock pile to us. We climbed the hill behind his house where the Indian grave is."

"Their trip took a lot longer then than it would now because there weren't good roads or bridges."

"Are pack horses much different from riding horses?"

"They are heavier and are trained to carry heavy loads from place to place. Remember there weren't any cars or trucks then to help people move."

"Tell us another story, Grandpa."

"Later. Get your homework done now."

- - - - - - - - - - - -

TOM and JESSIE

"Grandpa, what did you call your father and mother when you were little?"

"We called them Tom and Jessie."

"Didn't you call them Father and Mother, or Papa and Mama?"

"Later we called them Pa and Ma, but not to begin with."

"We call ours Mom and Dad. How come you used their first names? And then why did you quit calling them that and start calling them Pa and Ma?"

"I am not sure whether I know exactly just why or how it came about but maybe we can figure it out..."

- - - - - - - - - - - - -

'Tom and Jessie' is what they called each other when they were talking around the house or in the yard. After all, those were their names, just as ours were Bryan, George, Eunice, Lois and so on. We all used our first names when we worked, talked or played together. We lived on a farm about 1/4th mile away from our nearest neighbor and had to cross Big Cove Creek to get to their house. In the other direction our nearest neighbor was about one half mile away and the creek to cross twice. Since there were no bridges, this was some hindrance to visiting. Everybody in the neighborhood was busy working through the week and did not visit any. Sometimes people visited on Sunday but not every Sunday. Our visitors used first names when talking. Other children may have used 'Pa and Ma' in talking to their parents but since visiting was so seldom, we did not learn much that way.

We had a man hired to help Tom hoe corn, cut 'filth,' put up hay and help with other farm work. His name was Sherman Flesher and we called him Sherman, the same as everyone else. He played with us evenings and talked to us a great deal. We all liked him. One evening he asked us the same question,

'Why do you call your mother and father Jessie and Tom?'

'That is their names!' we replied.

4

'Don't you think it would be nicer to call them Mother and Father or Pa and Ma?'

'We don't know.'

'Don't you think they would like for you to call them Pa and Ma instead of Tom and Jessie?'

'What do you call your father and mother?' we asked him.

'I call them Pap and Mam and sometimes Pa and Ma.'

'Do they like for you to call them that?'

'They seem to like it all right.'

'Do you like to call them Pap and Mam?'

'Yes.'

'Why?'

'I think it shows that I like them and have more respect for them. Why don't you try it on your father and mother and tell me how you get along?'

'Well, we'll try,' we promised. We tried that very evening. I am not sure which one of us ventured first. It went something like this,

'Will you spread butter on my bread, Pap?'

'What did you say?'

'Will you spread my bread, Pap.'

'Who told you to say that?

'Sherman.'

'Now why would he tell you a thing like that?' We could see that both Tom and Jessie were pleased, not angry, so things went a little easier.

'He says that he calls his father and mother 'Pap and Mam' and they seem to like it and, besides, he says it shows he likes them and has more respect for them. How do you like it?'

'It sounds too flat.'

'How about Pa and Ma?'

'That sounds better.' So Pa and Ma is what it was from that day on. Now it was not that simple for we had to work at thinking and remembering to say 'Pa and Ma' instead of 'Tom and Jessie.'

We told Sherman how we got along that first evening and from time to time thereafter. He seemed pleased and interested in our new project. He said,

'You will have to try and it will get easier as you keep at it.' He was one of the best hired men who ever worked for Pa.

5

THE MESS POT AND HOPE CHEST

"The other day when I told you the panther story, I mentioned a mess pot and a wood clothes chest. Stories have been told about them as often as the panther story has been related."

"Is the mess pot the same one Uncle Perry showed us when we were out at his farm?"

"Yes, that's the one. Perry left it with your Great Uncle George at Clarksburg, when Perry sold his farm and moved to Tennessee. The legs had been knocked off to use it for a flower pot for awhile. It was in good shape when captured at Yorktown. . . . . ."

Our Grandfather, Alexander McQuain was in the Battle of Yorktown during the Revolutionary War. The British soldiers, led by General Cornwallis, were in trenches facing our soldiers and were believed to have a lot of provisions of all kinds. Our soldiers were very scarce of supplies. It was thought it might be hard to capture the British and their provisions so our officers told our soldiers they would divide the supplies they were able to capture among the officers and men in equal shares.

Our soldiers defeated the British but found they did not have as much as they were reported to have. However the things that were captured were divided as equally as possible. That old mess pot was part of our Revolutionary War Grandfather's share. He also got some food and ammunition which he needed, as well as an overcoat and a blanket, equally as badly needed. The mess pot still survives.

The old chest was probably used as a 'Hope Chest' first, although we used it for storing blankets. It had also been stored in the attic for many years. This is the chest that the first Alexander McQuain used to bring his things over from Scotland when he came to fight in the Revolutionary War.

The way the chest is put together embodies different phases of furniture-making, including Make-Do tactics. To start with, wide poplar boards were used since poplar is easy to work with and is strong, long-lasting with, or without, a fine finish. It is also light-weight. The outside of the chest shows hard usage, without formal finish, while the inside is plain, smooth natural wood, with no finish at all. The hinges were originally buck-skin, the present metal ones are later additions. It is roughly put together with a few mortises and tendons but mostly lap corner joints secured with cut square nails that were probably hand-hammered from the black-smith shop. Corner posts help secure the upright corners, with 5 inch turned extensions through the bottom at the four corners as legs. The legs also keep a space below the bottom to prevent moisture from coming up into the chest. The board from which the top was made was 17 inches wide − that was a very large tree!

- - - - - - - - - - -

"Grandpa, is that old chest the same one Aunt Miriam has in her living room? And is it the same one they brought on the pack horses?"

"Yes, that's the same one. The reason we let Miriam have it is because it has been handed down to the oldest child in the family of each generation. The oldest have been boys until it came to Miriam. She uses it as an end table now."

"Tell us about Christmas when you were a little boy, Grandpa. Did Santa Claus come down the chimney back then?"

"Yes, we had an old Santa who always remembered us, but Rudolph is a later addition. We never heard of him."

"You must have had a Christmas tree, because you could have cut it from your own woods. Some years we go out with Dad to a tree farm and cut our own."

"Let me tell you about some of our Christmas celebrations. These took place from 1903 until 1912 when I was from 6 to 15 years old.

- - - - - - - - - - - - - -

CHRISTMAS, 1903-1912

Many things were different from what they are now. We had no fuel except wood and coal. We had kerosene which we called lamp oil since we used it only in the lamps for light. It was scarce and cost money. Candles and grease lights were also used but our main light was from oil lamps, used when we wanted more than the light from the fireplace. Electric, gas, and carbide lights may have been used at the county seat or in a small mining area in one edge of the county but not in our part of the county where there were no big coal mines. Also remember there were no cars, trucks, radio, television or aircraft to disturb us.

We had wood fireplaces in our house but these fireplaces had been remodeled to burn coal by setting in steel or cast iron grates about 24 inches wide and 8 or 10 inches deep, with a space of 6 inches under the grate for ashes. The extra width was taken up with rock jamb-stones, one at each end of the grate. We used this jamb-space on either side of the grate to dry green wood for the cook stove or to use in starting fires. It was a good place to keep hot water in a bucket, teakettle or coffee pot. A back wall of stone behind the grate took up the extra depth that had been necessary when wood had been used. This extra depth was not needed for coal, although we mixed wood with coal a lot of the time. We children were not long in finding out that some green wood exuded sweet sap at the ends of through knots, as it got hot in burning. Sugar maple, apple and hickory were particularly good. This sap was too hot to scrape off with our fingers so we found flat splinters were good for this. Each of us had a splinter and certain logs or knots for each to collect sap from. This splinter-licking of sweet sap was part of our evening activity when we had the right kind of wood on long fall or winter evenings.

We also found that the burning lumps of coal played little tricks when they got hot. Blisters containing black oil would form and then a bright flame would spew from the coal which would just as quickly turn to spewing black smoke into the room if not quickly put out with the poker. Hickory wood, after it was reduced about to coals, would throw sparks in all directions when it was stirred. All this was fun, but also dangerous and might set the house afire, and therefore, had to be watched carefully.

8

Our Christmases were lighted by the burning fire in the fireplace or, if we needed more light, the oil lamp was set on the stand and lit.

In our earliest Christmases that I remember, we would hang a clean pair of stockings by the chimney. We used nails driven in the mantle to hang stockings. The longer stockings were hung nearest to the ends of the mantle. That kept them away from the fire. Then the shorter stockings belonging to the smaller children were hung. They thought this was better since Santa would be certain to see them when he came out of the chimney and start filling them first. He wouldn't be so likely to get short of gifts that way, before he got to them. We wanted to encourage Santa, so we set our hats on the stand (table) in front of the fire. The smaller children set their hats nearer the front of the stand, again so they would not be missed. We had Ma and Pa set their hats too.

These were exciting evenings. One night after the stockings and hats were all in place and we were sitting around the fire, George was by the stand looking at things. He burst out crying. Ma said,

'What are you bawling about, George?' He kept on crying but could not answer.

'Tell us what's the matter. Are you sick?'

'N----No.'

'Well, what's wrong?'

'It's too little?'

'What's too little?'

'That little old hat? It won't hold anything.'

'I hadn't noticed that,'

'Just look at it!' He was still half crying.

'It isn't very big, is it?' It was smaller than my hat and also smaller than Pa's. So Ma said,

'Maybe we can get Tom's old hat and set it out for you and put your name on it.'

'That would be better,' said George, much happier now.

That was done and it worked out all right but the same situation came up later with others and adjustments had to be made about stockings, hats and limbs on the Christmas tree when we got a tree in later years.

After things settled down and everything was in readiness, we children had to go to bed and get to sleep so as not to scare old

9

Santa away. After seemingly endless lines of thoughts in equally numberless situations, sleep came to all excited, restless children.

After a period of dream-mixed sleep, which seemed as active as no sleep, it was disturbed by an early whisper or peak at stockings.

'I wonder if Santa has come yet.'

A cautious peak at a stocking or hat brought forth a loud excited exclamation, 'Santa has come!' 'There's something in my stocking!' 'My hat has a big poke in it.' 'Ma, can we get up now?' This was hardly necessary as nearly all of us were already excitedly running here and there in our night clothes.

'Yes, you might as well,' Ma answered.

'Can we open something?' Sometimes this question was too late. Something had already been opened.

'Get dressed first so you won't catch cold.' We knew this really meant to do it now. If you have never tried to put your clothes on in a hurry under such excitement, you have missed a lot of Christmas! It takes an age: The shoe string gets in the wrong eyelet, the button in the wrong button hole, the shirt or stockings wrong side out, the shoe or stocking lost, or one britches leg inside out. You name it. It happened. I suppose it didn't really take long, it just seemed long. Someone was already getting to open something.

How long it took to get things out of a stocking or to unwrap things! Does this bag have candy? It had candy and was tasted immediately, or maybe nuts which were not so easily tasted.

'I got an apple and a striped candy cane!'

'Mine has a pencil in it besides the apple and cane!'

'Mine has a pencil too!'

'Hey Pa! I have a little boy on a cart driving a little iron horse,' said George.

'I've got one too,' I said. George and I kept our iron carts all these years. They were sturdy toys and we kept them sitting on a shelf in our bedroom when we weren't playing with them or showing them off. Mine is sitting over there in your Grandma's china cabinet right now. I think George still has his with him at his home in Clarksburg.

It did not bother us much that the apples in our stockings were like the ones we were eating the evening before however they were probably bigger and redder. They had been brought by

Santa! What did matter was that each of us got about the same number and quality of things. Santa was supposed to treat everyone alike in this respect. Our Santa was good about this even before we learned, later on, who Santa really was.

'Oh Ma! There's a big doll in this poke tied to my hat!'

'I've got one in this poke tied to my hat too! Why did he put the pokes under the stand?'

'Maybe he didn't have room to put it on the stand,' Ma answered.

'There wasn't enough room on the stand, Ma, but why the string?'

'If it hadn't been tied to your hat, how would you have known who it belonged to?'

'Old Santy knows a lot! What is this printed on the doll under its dress, Ma?'

'There is something on mine too.'

'Let me see yours, Eunice. That says 'Made in Germany.' Lois, yours says, 'Made in France.'

'What does that mean?' the girls asked.

'That is the name of the country where your doll was made.'

'I'm going to call my doll Germany!' said Eunice.

'And I'm calling mine France,' echoed Lois. These dolls with china heads, hands and feet, were very well made. The girls took good care of their dolls. There was another doll that probably belonged to Edna. These are the same dolls that your Grandma dressed in new clothes and gave to Jane, Gloria and Mary Ruth one year for Christmas. She told them some of the dolls' history and asked them to take good care of the dolls. They are really antiques now!

We were still opening presents.

'What is this?'

'That's a top!' (Whirligig)

'There is no way to spin it.' We were used to tops made of spools cut in two and sharpened to a point, with a stick thrust through the hole, and coming to a point on the sloping end to spin the top on. The stick extended above the flat end far enough to take hold of with our fingers and give it a twist to make the whirligig spin.

'This doesn't stick up enough to get hold of!'

11

'Try pressing down on the stem in the middle while you hold it a little off the floor.' We did that and the bottom flew off and started jumping about and spinning on the floor.

'What makes it spin?'

'See that spring in the hole in the top piece? And the hook on the bottom of the top piece? It hooks on that nail sticking up a little in the bottom piece. Now twist the top a little. Now hold it a little off the floor and press like you did before.'

'It works! I can't spin it that fast with my fingers!'

'This looks a little like a top, but it won't work!' This was a colored round metal top about six inches tall and about the same diameter through the biggest part, with a spiral center.

'Try holding it on the floor by the top and work the spiral center up and down until gets going. It should spin.'

'It barely goes.'

'Try pumping it a little longer and faster before you let go.'

'Oh, that's better. It hums this time.'

Such was the usual excitement and the activity accompanying Christmas when we were small and even when we were larger. I am sure it is pretty much the same wherever Christmas is celebrated.

We nearly always had nuts of various kinds, as we have today, and some extra fruit such as dried peaches, apricots or raisins, a little something extra for Christmas. 'Boughten' toys were not as plentiful or as costly then, as those that children think they must have now. Even though things did not cost as much then, money was a lot scarcer and we had to get along with less. I've heard Pa say that one Christmas morning we had broken every toy or plaything we got, before breakfast, except one horn, and that, as we went in to breakfast, the one with the horn struck at the cat and broke it too. A lot of things were pretty flimsy, but that year must have been an exception since we were warned to take good care of our things.

Our Christmas breakfasts were about as usual, but at dinner we always had something extra, a 'company' dinner. Ma always killed an old hen on such occasions, made stuffing and gravy, opened a jar of berries or other canned fruit, baked a cake, had biscuits or light bread and maybe a pie. I remember the gravy on light bread, or biscuits, more than the chicken, however nothing went begging. Any leftovers were taken care of at supper.

12

Our first one or two Christmases were without a tree, but later we had evergreen trees. Hemlock and white pine trees grew on the bluff just across the creek in front of our house. We had one picked out long before Christmas. George and I went out and cut the tree a few days early. We were small then and the tree was bigger than it looked from the house so it was quite a load for us to get to the house. We cut enough off the bottom so we could get it into the back part of the living room and fasten it to the wall. Each of us picked out his limb. The smaller children got the lower limbs and the bigger ones took the higher ones. We tied the limbs to the trunk of the tree if we thought they needed tying to keep them from breaking under our trimmings and Santa's presents.

The next few days were used to trim the tree and make it look pretty. We made our own decorations. We strung popcorn, and also made it into balls to hang on the tree. Bright paper was cut into various shapes or made into strips and chains. Since there was no electric, no lights were used. A not-too-perfect cardboard star was cut out and covered with bright paper for the top of the tree.

Ma had made each of us a stocking from bright mosquito netting. All stockings were about the same size so as not to give one any better chance to get more than someone else. Santa was supposed to treat everyone alike. These stockings were put on each of our tree limbs. This added more color. That is about the way our trees were trimmed every year. The tree was always beautiful!

The branches of our first tree were long and limber and not nearly as thick as it had looked from a distance. We were able to get better shaped white pine, pitch pine or yellow pine in later years but none more vividly remembered than this first hemlock tree.

The first tree trimmings were continued with additions of 'store-bought' trimmings from year to year. Santa often brought articles of clothing and books suitable to our various ages. Over the years many books accumulated. Ma was a good reader and read to us quite a lot from such books as <u>Robinson Crusoe,</u> <u>Treasure Island, Leather Stocking Tales</u> and other stories that were of interest from the youngest to the oldest. Even Pa listened to many of them. When Ma got tired of reading, Pa would tell his deer stories.

There was one Christmas morning when we got up too early and thought we caught old Santa. Someone was in the front bedroom standing near the door in the dark. As we opened the door, a little something red could be seen. It turned out that Uncle 'Oll' (Oliver) McQuain had come in during the night and had gone to bed. He had gotten up when we did. He had a red bandana about his neck. We were relieved that we had not bothered Santa.

I remember talking to Grandpa Lewis about Santa Claus one evening when he was visiting us. We asked where Santa stayed through the summer and where he lived. Grandpa told us older kids there was no Santa, and that it was our Ma and Pa who pretended there was a Santa but they really put the presents on the tree for us. We were sort of disappointed but not much surprised as we had seen some extra things about the house as we grew older. We were glad that they had gone to so much trouble so that we could all have such beautiful thoughts and things to look forward to as well as memories that stayed with us through the years that followed. I am sure that all of us were benefited by the Christmases we enjoyed together even if there really was no such person as Santa.

- - - - - - - - - - -

"We never set out our caps for Santa to fill, but we still hang up our stockings. And I never thought of having my very own branch of the Christmas tree."

"I almost forgot to tell you that we always got books for Christmas presents. The younger children received nursery rhyme books, Cinderella, or Jack and the Beanstalk while the older ones got Rip Van Winkle, The House of Seven Gables, Tale of Two Cities and The Scarlet Letter. We still have a beautifully illustrated bird book that Lois received from Santa one year."

"Grandpa, what kind of a little boy were you? Were you a good boy, or did you get into trouble?"

"I'm afraid you are asking a hard question for me to answer. You don't expect me to say that I was all good or all bad either, I'm

14

sure. Maybe the best way I can answer is just to say that I was an active boy. I'll tell you some stories that are very clear in my mind, or else they've been told to me so often that they're as clear as if I remember them. Then you can decide what kind of boy I was and I hope you won't be too hard on me!"

- - - - - - - - - - - -

EARLY BOYHOOD

When I was very young, in a long dress and wearing diapers, Ma wanted to show my grandparents what a fine baby I was. She rolled my dress back so they could see how big I was. I was not at all cooperative. My diaper was full to overflowing and a general clean-up was necessary before the showing off could continue. A lapse of memory prevents further details.

When I was a small boy, we had an old yellow cat that I played with a lot. We called him 'Old Yaller.' He was so gentle that I could take him by the tail and throw him over my shoulder and carry him around that way without getting scratched. One morning we found him dead in the wood box under some wood.

One time I was in the kitchen with Aunt Edna Lewis who was only a few years older than I. She was watching some things cooking on the stove. I was playing with a corn cob, which I threw in the air and it came down in one of the kettles. She gave me a slap or two that made me cry. Ma asked her what happened. Aunt Edna said I had thrown that cob up and it came down in the kettle and she just slapped me. Ma asked her what she thought Tom would think about her slapping his boy around. Aunt Edna seemed a little concerned about that, but I did not get any sympathy from Ma for my part in the matter. So that was where it ended.

A whip-poor-will would come and sit on the end of an old log near the paling fence under the pine tree in the front yard. We could see it dimly in the moonlight that came through the branches of the tree. He must have come regularly for some time as we looked forward to seeing him in the evening. Later Pa hauled this log to the creek and rolled it in where it floated away in the muddy water. He used a yoke of big red long-horned oxen to pull it.

A house wren's nest was built in a hole in one of the house logs near the back door to the old log kitchen. It was too high for me to see at first. I remember being lifted up so I could see the eggs and later the baby birds. We would watch the old birds bring worms to feed the little ones. We were cautioned not to touch the hole, the nest or the little birds since the old birds might not come back and feed the little ones who would then starve. We were careful not to disturb the nest. Wrens built here nearly every year and when I was tall enough to see into the nest, I lifted littler brothers and sisters up for a look. We played around this door, partly to watch the birds and partly because it was shady there after early morning.

An old cut stone chimney had been built up the outside of the log kitchen near where we played by the door. The stones in the chimney were crumbling and some stones had been removed from the top to prevent them from falling. We were eating dinner after a rainy morning when we heard a crashing noise. The old chimney had fallen full length across part of the area where we had been playing. It frightened all of us to think what might have happened if we had been out there when it fell.

When Pa went to Troy or Conings to the store or to the mill, Ma and I would watch for him and talk about when he would be back. One time when I was about three years old, Ma was busy and I got out of her sight. I climbed to the top of the gate post and was standing on top of it when Pa came into sight down the road. This was a paling fence in which the posts were cut off at the top railing to which the palings or pickets were nailed. The sharpened tops of the pickets stuck up 10 or 12 inches above the posts and railings to keep chickens from lighting there to get into the yard. These sharp pickets made it dangerous for me to be standing there. Pa did not call to me but rode up to the gate and dismounted quietly, came over and lifted me from the top of the gate post. A paddling would have been in order and was no doubt administered but due to some mental block, these details have escaped me. The top edge of the brace on the gate was later sloped on the upper edge which made it harder to get a toe hold to climb.

Our old dug well had a wood curb about four feet square and the same height, except on the front side where they stood to draw water, where it was a foot lower. A wide board to set the water bucket on, extended across the inside of the curb about 2 ½ feet up and stuck out far enough on the outside to set the bucket on. Sometimes this bucket was left sitting on the board inside the curb, full of water. One day, Pa or Ma found me standing on this board dipping water from the bucket with a tin cup and pouring it into the well. I was watching in the well, 8 or 10 feet below, as it hit the water and sent waves out in all directions. This was no place for a kid to be. The end of that board was immediately sawed off and the crack stripped in the curb to keep me from climbing. The low side of the curb was built up as high as the rest and a cover put over the top. This made it safer but also harder to draw water. Again I am not sure whether a spanking accompanied this episode but it would have been very appropriate.

Later this well was further protected with a pump that completely covered the well top. It was the type with a thin galvanized pipe extending down into the water and was equipped with a chain with rubber stopper attached. When pulled up through the pipe, the water was lifted from the well to a spout from which to fill a bucket. The endless chain ran on a sprocket wheel inside the pump housing. This wheel was turned with a crank handle that came to the outside of the wooden pump housing. A boy or girl as young as 6 or 8 years could turn this crank and pump water. Besides making the well safe, if gave us children an endless chore of keeping the water bucket full. This was progress!

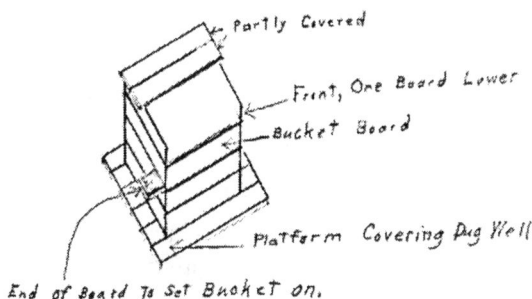

Old Well Curb

17

Our corn crib was built behind the granary and sided with 3 inch wide lath nailed on with an inch crack between them so the corn would get air to dry. These cracks made it easy to climb up the side of the crib. I don't know how many times I had climbed up and could not get on top and then had to climb back down. On this particular day, I was up 8 or 10 feet, under the edge of the roof that stuck out beyond the side of the crib. I could not reach around the roof or climb on top. Pa came looking and calling for me. From under the roof eave, my answer came,

'I can't get on top!' He came over on the ground under me and urged me to hold on tight and climb back down until he could lift me to the ground. This was the end of this play area.

Our log kitchen was very roughly finished with the ceiling laid on top of joists and the chinking between the logs showing, as well as the logs themselves. It kept out the wind and snow pretty well. The ladder to get up into the loft over the living room was kept lying on the floor, leaning on edge against the wall so that none of us kids could climb upstairs and fall and get hurt. Occasionally we were allowed to climb up and peep into the loft. This was a privilege and allowed only when someone could set the ladder up and watch us. There was room to crawl between the bottom part of the ladder and the wall which I was doing one evening. Ma said,

'Look at that big rat behind the ladder.' I screamed in fright, thinking only of a big rat. I knocked the ladder over in getting out from behind it. Ma said,

'There was no rat, I was meaning you.'

'You oughtn't to scare the boy that way,' Pa said.

'I didn't think of scaring him,' Ma replied. I am not sure this was bad behavior on my part, but they must have been kept busy taking care of all eight of us.

This next story would come under 'Parental Guidance' or some such heading as used now in television viewing. We had some harvest hands helping put up hay. They were in the shade under the pine tree resting. One older man was standing to one side talking to Pa. He had on a pair of pretty well worn-out leather boots that stood out loosely from his legs.

I remarked, as children sometimes do,

'I want to go somewhere and pee.' One of the men said,

'Just go right over there and pee in Lieu's boot!' It seemed a good idea at the time and I was in a hurry so I marched right over and cut loose into his boot. I got pretty well along before he discovered what I was doing since I was just the right height, and he was busy talking to Pa.

He stomped about but he was too late.

'Tommy,' he exclaimed to Pa, 'The little whelp has peed in my boot!' The other men burst out laughing and told Lieu,

'Well, your feet need washing anyway!'

Pa could see I had been put up to do this but it was made plain to me later that this wasn't just the right thing to do even if grown-ups had told me to do it.

Children have always been taught little rhymes, memory gems or verses to rehearse for visitors or relatives as a sort of way to show off. I remember one which I learned when very small that seemed to bring laughing approval every time. It went like this:

'The June bug has the golden wing,
The lightning bug, the flame.
The bed bug has no wing at all,
But he gets there just the same.'

As I came to the word 'there' I would brush at my ear two or three times with my hand as if knocking off a bug.

Pa had a man by the name of Mace helping chop some dry trees down and cut them into logs so they could be rolled off the cleared ground into the brush, or pile them up so they could be burned. Some logs rolled over the brush and bluff into the creek with a big splash. Mace and Pa had 'hand spikes' to use in prying and lifting the logs into position to start them rolling down-hill. These hand spikes were cut about six feet long from small black gum poles about three inches in diameter. One end was sharpened to gouge under the log or into the ground to shove the log to one side or to start it rolling. The other end was smoothed off so as not to hurt their hands as they worked with the spike. They made me a small hand spike about one inch in diameter and as long as I was tall, maybe three feet. I was about 3 or 4 years old then. They let me help them with my spike to do the same thing they did with theirs in getting these logs to roll. We were getting a big log ready to roll which we were expecting to go over the bluff into the creek with a big splash. This log was ready and I stepped back to watch it roll. I was anxious to see it go, but it took longer than I thought it should. I yelled,

'Damn it, Mace! Get in there and get it rolling!' He did and it made a big splash in the creek and floated down the creek around a turn out of sight. The creek was muddy and higher than usual. I remember this incident vividly, perhaps because it has been retold in my hearing several times. Burning the brush heaps and log piles, trimming the lower limbs from a big chestnut tree and splitting posts are less vividly remembered.

During this work or soon after, I became ruptured in the right groin. Pa and Ma thought I might have strained myself with the hand spike, but no one knew. I was evidently unable to add anything to help determine the cause. I was put in bed and kept there until the doctor came and bound me up as well as he could. He said I would have to be kept quiet as possible until he could order a truss for me or have one made. Nowadays, one would be taken to the hospital and operated on, the rupture sewed together to heal in a week or two, but not then.

A knotted cloth, or one doubled many times, was put under this cloth binding so as to bring pressure on the right groin and hold the rupture in place. The truss was finally made with a two or three inch wide belt to buckle around me, having a two or three inch round knob fastened to the inside, so as to bring better pressure and support to the right groin. An extra strap fastened to the belt, went around my right leg to be tightened to hold the belt and pressure knob in position. The truss was made so I could walk and run with a fair amount of safety but I was supposed to be careful. Imagine keeping a boy that age 'careful' when there was so much playing to be done!

I wore that truss a long time, although I do not know if it was six months, a year or two years. It became a painful chore before I could ease up on wearing it. The doctor had to make some adjustments from time to time. My right side where more pressure and joint movement was involved became galled and later the left side also. Salve and medicine were used, as well as soft cotton pads, trying to ease the trouble. Both sides became raw and scabs had to be protected. I was put to bed at times and kept there while the truss was taken off, to ease the pain and let the hip sores heal. Later the truss could be removed for awhile, but put back on if any groin pain developed. After a long time the truss could be left off

20

entirely and my hip sores healed completely, leaving scars which can be seen to this day. As for the hernia, it healed with a little extra scar tissue that can be felt by the fingers pressing on the spot. It was tender for a long while but has never bothered me at all since I grew up, even though I have done all the kinds of strenuous work that a man could.

- - - - - - - - - - - - -

"Maybe these incidents will help you to answer the question about what kind of boy I was."

"And I can also understand why parents get gray hair raising their kids!"

"Ma managed to raise all eight of us kids and retained her chestnut brown hair. When she died at 91, her hair was thinner but the natural color remained."

- - - - - - - - - - - -

THE OUTHOUSE

The outhouse was down a path from the house about 75 or 100 feet. This building was about 5 by 8 feet and made of rough boards, with a rough board door. A seat was built across the back of this building about chair height. A wide board covered this platform with comfortable holes cut into the board to sit on. When the pit below filled up, the house was moved a few feet and a new hole was dug. No regular toilet paper was available. Instead, newspapers or a catalog nailed to the wall was used as needed. If no paper was available, a bucket full of red and white corn cobs was kept handy to take the place of paper. It was always wise to check to see what was available first thing. You might have to get a handful of leaves or grass to take in with you. A smaller hole was cut into the seat board just for small children.

Sometimes the menfolk would go out about the barn where they were out of sight but regular use of the barn area was frowned on almost as much as if using the living room in the house. To cure this, the barn shovel was used and emptied into the manure

21

pile. The top rail of the post and rail fence behind the barn out of sight was also a favorite place. A lower rail furnished a convenient place to rest your feet. It was always wise to provide yourself with paper, corn cobs or leaves with which to complete the operation, before mounting the rail fence.

The little house described above was variously known as 'privy,' 'backhouse' or 'outhouse.' These houses were sometimes dressed up a little inside by wall-papering them with ends of wallpaper or newspapers which helped keep out the wind. These were the only facilities available, unless you wanted to use the slop jar, used in time of sickness, and then take it out and empty it.

Now before you start to feel too sorry for us, I wish to hasten to say that we were not the only ones having these crude ways. Everybody in the country, small towns or mining towns had no more and some did not even have the privy. Modern bathrooms were available in large cities and even in smaller cities but privies were used almost everywhere else.

The kitchen served as our wash room in which to take our baths, during periods between preparation of meals or after the supper dishes were washed. The kitchen stove warmed both the room and the water used to bathe with. Our stove had an 8 or 10 gallon tank fastened to the side in such a way that the fire for cooking heated the water and assured a supply of hot water all the time, if the tank was kept filled. A teakettle holding about one gallon of water was set on top of the stove to quickly heat water needed in cooking. This tank and teakettle had to be filled from the well by carrying water in a bucket. We had no running water unless one ran from the well to the tank while carrying the water!

In place of a bath tub, we used one or two 15 to 20 gallon wash tubs, depending on whether one or two bathed at the same time. The heating tubs on the stove were filled and heated while the first two bathed. In this way, little time was lost waiting for water to heat. When we children got big enough, we had to keep the wood box full of wood and water in the teakettle and hot water tank. It seemed to us that if fire ever broke out, it would be sure to start in the teakettle or hot water tank, since they seemed always to be dry and the wood box empty.

Bathing and putting on a complete change of clean clothes took place at least once a week, Saturday afternoon or evening. We lived on a creek which had holes of water big and deep enough to swim in. This simplified the bathing chore during the summer when this water was warm enough to swim in.

Instead of a lavatory, in which to wash our hands and faces before meals, we had a wash pan which would hold about the same amount of water as your lavatory. This was a portable pan that could be moved about from place to place. We had a shelf fastened to the kitchen wall for the wash pan which we used in bad weather. In good weather, the pan was outdoors where a stake was driven into the ground with a board nailed on the top. This was in a convenient place near the kitchen door. In either place, the pan had to be filled from the water bucket and warm water brought from the kitchen stove, if one wanted it warmer than well water. Since warm water was more trouble to get, cold water was used more often.

Clean hands were required at each meal. After a few times having to leave the table and wash hands before continuing eating, it became a habit to wash hands before going to the table. We had both homemade laundry soap and store toilet soap.

Terry cloth wash cloths and paper towels were not heard of then at our place. We had towels made from regular cotton toweling and a few good wash cloths. Too often our wash cloths were 'wash rags' as we called them. They were just that. The good ends of the worn out-towels or pieces of worn-out clothing served the purpose well. We also made towels from meal sacks when the sack got too bad to use as a meal sack any longer.

So you can see that we had a lot of improvements to be made before we were modernized. You can be sure we appreciated each one as it came along.

- - - - - - - - - -

"So don't complain when you are asked to take a shower. Just think how nice you have things now, compared to what some kids had seventy five years ago!"

"Sometimes when we're camping, we find those old fashioned outhouses. But they always have real toilet paper. I don't think I'd like those corncobs much."

"What would you like to hear about next?"

"What about your schools, Grandpa. We have seen pictures of some of them."

"It was usually a one-room school. . . ."

- - - - - - - - - - -

THE ONE ROOM SCHOOL

In many ways our schools from 1907 to 1916, and later, were different from schools of today. The general objects of learning, reading, writing and arithmetic, and how to become better citizens were not too different. It was the buildings, books, methods and conditions that varied.

Many more people lived on farms and in small towns then than in the cities, therefore more children went to school in one room country schools. There were no busses to haul pupils to school either in the city or in the country. Two miles was then about the greatest distance children were required to walk so the schools were about 3 to 4 miles apart. The number of pupils attending a one room country school ranged from 20 to 45 or 50. All children in the neighborhood attended the one room school which was taught by one teacher. When all eight grades were in school, grades had to be combined in some subjects. The reading classes were generally separate. The recitation periods were short and took up about all of the teacher's time with very little time for individual pupil assistance at other than the recitation times.

In our county, Gilmer, in West Virginia, each one room school had three trustees who hired the teacher and had some supervisory control over the school. The teacher's paycheck came from the district board of education, to which all teacher reports were sent. A county superintendent usually visited each school in the county at least once during the school year and had general supervision of all schools for the whole county. The free public schools were in use nearly everywhere at this time and were supported by taxes collected in the district or county.

Before tax supported schools, each neighborhood took up a collection in the neighborhood to hire a teacher for whatever time they could get the teacher to teach for the money they could manage to collect. Subscription schooling was very uncertain. I have heard Pa tell of attending such subscription schools shortly

25

after the Civil War until tax supported free schools became available.

The free school had been increased to a six month term about the time we started to school, except when the money was used up and teachers could not be paid for the full term. Later the school term was increased to nine months which is still the length of the term in most places.

Our schoolhouse stood on a lot about 150 feet wide by 200 feet in length along the road. We used the neighbor's meadow back of the schoolhouse yard and his garden, as an additional space for play and games. We got our water from the neighbor's drilled well in his yard. His garden was between his yard and the schoolhouse lot and about the same size as the school lot. Thus, you see, the well was near, and in plain view of the school. The well casing extended above the ground about 30 inches, inside the well curb, and was equipped with a hinged cover. The water was pulled from the well in a bailer attached to a rope, running through a pulley, fastened to the well curb roof and around a windless at the back of the curb. This was turned with a crank operated by hand to lower the bailer into the well and draw the water. This was a safe water supply even though the water had a slight sulfur taste which some did not like.

An open 3 gallon tin or zinc bucket was kept with drinking water in it, sitting on a shelf about table height at the right side of the front door. This bucket also served to carry the water from the well. A dipper was kept hanging by the crooked end of its handle, to the edge of the bucket. This made it handy for anyone to use in getting a drink.

A wash pan was kept near the water bucket, hanging on a nail in the wall. When it was used, it was set on a step or the platform just outside the front door. This completed the school's water supply system.

Each one who wanted a drink was supposed to get it before school time in the morning, at the morning or afternoon recess period or at the noon hour before school took up. However, during the hot fall days or when all played up to school time, a crowd would form around the water bucket, to take turns at the dipper. To avoid this crowding and assure that each got a fresh drink, two pupils were permitted to get a fresh bucket of water from the well and then pass it around after the pupils were seated.

26

These two started for the water at the time the teacher started to the house to ring the bell. This was a popular job among those who were large enough to do it, and they had to take turns at it. Sometimes it was hard for the teacher to keep track of the turns.

By the time the two got back with the water, all were quietly seated and at work with their studies. Some were already reciting lessons and had to be given water on returning to their seats, unless the bucket had already been returned to its shelf, when they were permitted to go to the bucket, one at a time, and get a drink. One of the two carried the bucket and other dipped a drink from the bucket in the dipper and handed it to each pupil in succession until all got a drink. This took a little time for the two passing the water but was better than all crowding about the bucket since the rest were busy with school work in the meantime. This was done only in hot fall weather when everyone played outside. In cooler weather, less water was needed and all were supposed to get their drinks at the two recess periods or at the noon hour.

The wash pan was used only in emergencies.

Seldom was permission given to get a drink during study periods. Some children hesitated to drink after others. The open water bucket and common drinking cup continued for two or three years after we started school. Then the board of education finally decided this was too much of a health hazard to be permitted to continue. It banned further use of the common drinking cup and open water bucket. Covered 5 gallon stoneware water coolers with faucets were bought and put in all the schools in the county. It was ordered that each pupil should have an individual drinking cup or at least one for each family. A variety of cups made their appearance. Some were from dinner buckets, some were ordinary tin cups and some were of the folding type with lids. There were no paper cups except when writing paper was folded for that purpose if one had forgotten his own. This was progress!

As you can see by this time, we had the same type water facilities at school as we had at home that I told you about a few days ago. You are right: We had the outside privy too! Two of the 'two-holer' type, were located about 100 yards back of the schoolhouse and about 150 feet away from each other, one for the boys and the other for the girls.

The seating arrangements in school were different from what they are now. There were two rows of double seats, one row on one side of the room and one row on the other. Boys were seated on the right side of the room and girls on the left, in this particular school. The higher seats were at the back of the row while the smaller seats were toward the front of the room, where the smaller pupils were seated.

A desk was attached to the back of each two seats for use of the two pupils sitting on the double seats behind. A covered glass inkwell was in a hole near the front middle of the top of the desk. A plowed half-round ditch extending on either side of the inkwell held pencils or pens and kept them from rolling off the desk which was slanted toward the pupil.

Three double-hung windows on each side of the building and one on each side of the door in the back furnished light. The inside of the building was painted white with the exception of the blackboard, which was the same type of smooth ceiling boards painted black. The blackboard started about 2 feet above the floor and was 7 or 8 feet high. It extended from the front window on one side of the room, around the corner, across the entire front of the school and to the front window on the other side of the room. White chalk was used except on special occasions and the joints between the boards formed straight lines to write on, much the same as in ruled tablets. Erasers were used then as now.

The heating system was simple and consisted of a round pot-bellied coal burning stove located in the middle of the room. A smoke pipe extended to a stone flue located in the ceiling immediately above the stove and extending through the roof, about 2 feet. Windows were raised to cool the room on hot days and fire was kept burning in the stove to heat the room in cool or cold weather.

Two or three recitation benches about 8 feet long, with backs, were used. They were constructed of 3 inch wide slat type boards. Part of the teacher's desk slanted and was on hinges so it could be raised to get into a storage area for teaching supplies. This could be locked and was so kept most of the time. A swiveled teacher's chair completed the furnishings except for a row of hooks along the wall to hang wraps on. A broom, coal bucket and shovel were also available. Your mother and father used the same type desks, but for a single pupil.

These buildings, seats and benches were the result of an extensive modernizing program which began not long before we started to school. I shall tell you more about how these improved facilities were used, in a later story.

The work of building fire, carrying in coal and keeping the fire going through the day as well as cleaning and sweeping the room after school, was let out by the trustees through competitive bidding each fall before school began. It was given to the person who was able to do it, and who would do it the cheapest. It usually went to the teacher if he or she wanted it at a certain price, or to someone else at that same price. If there were two or more wanting it, a decision was made through competitive bidding.

The fire was banked with ashes or slack (fine) coal to try to keep it from going out before morning. The fire was to be stirred up, or started anew if it did not hold over, before school time so the building would be warm when the pupils arrived. The water cooler was emptied each evening to keep it from freezing and bursting during the night when the building got cold. It was filled each morning with fresh water.

In zero and lower temperatures, the room would cool off at night until it was only a little warmer than the outside temperature. In such cold weather it was impossible to get the schoolroom warmed up so that pupils could get warm sitting in their seats, except for the ones nearest the stove. In such weather, one of the recitation benches was set crosswise between the two rows of desks close in front of the stove and another behind the stove so children could stick their feet out toward the stove to thaw the ice off their shoes and warm their feet. Turns had to be taken when there wasn't room enough for all who needed to warm up at the same time. Children took to the bench with them whatever book they were to study at that time. Pupils whose desks were near the stove were allowed to sit sideways on the edge of their seat and stick their feet out toward the stove. Sometimes they changed seats with the one sitting on the end farther away from the stove. In real cold weather, overcoats and wraps were kept on until each got warm enough to take them off. Sometimes it took until morning recess or even until noon, before the room got warm enough to take them off and sit comfortably in regular seats. Those in the back of the room might have to sit by the stove for short periods to warm up even after that. In these surroundings, study conditions were still pretty good. Whispering, shoving or horseplay was not permitted.

On some very cold days I have seen that old stove red hot all over and the metal stove pipe red hot halfway to the ceiling. Then the damper would be shut off to let it cool. It would get so hot that the benches would have to be moved back and pupils would hold books up before their faces to protect them from the heat. At the same time, their feet might not yet be warmed.

Remember, most of us walked long distances to get to school. At least this gives you an idea of our school.

- - - - - - - - - - - -

"Grandpa, you must have had to wear a lot of clothes if you walked so far."

"And were the subjects any different than the ones we take?"

"Did you have ball teams and cheerleaders?"

""We'll get to that another day. Grandma has dinner ready now so we'd better go!"

- - - - - - - - - - - - - -

OUR CLOTHES

"Grandpa, we have been wondering what kind of clothing you wore to school in those days. You got so cold and it took you so long to warm up. Would you tell us about that before you start on the classes and games?"

"I can understand why you might be concerned about our clothing, but there are some other things to be considered along with clothing which make it a little harder to explain. But I'll try."

- - - - - - - - - -

To begin with, the weather then was about the same as we have now. Some fall and winter days were beautiful and sunny while some were rainy, disagreeable and cold. Some winter weather was extremely cold and snowy with temperatures sometimes below zero.

30

A heated bus picks you up in front of your house and lets you off in front of the school building in sunshine, rain or snow. It makes little difference and you go into a warm school, scarcely knowing what kind of weather is outside.

In those days, children had to get up earlier than you do so they would have time to walk perhaps 2 miles to school. Then they went into a schoolroom not yet warmed up. In rainy weather there would be wet clothing to be dried out by the stove while in snowy weather, ice and snow needed to be thawed out from shoes and coats. Sometimes frozen boots or shoes had to be taken off to get feet warmed up before they, too, became frozen.

At times we used cold water or snow to wash cold feet and hands to draw out the cold. Often the same treatment was applied to hands, cheeks and ears when they had not been sufficiently protected. The teacher and older children had to help the smaller children get wraps off and warmed up of mornings. The same help was needed in the evenings so they would be as warm as possible on the long walk home. Frost-bitten heels, toes, sides of feet, noses and ears were common in winter weather.

Now as to the clothing. Grown people as well as school children wore many more and heavier clothes then, than now, for the simple reason that homes as well as school buildings had no extra insulation to keep out the cold, and were not heated as warmly as now. Our home had just the fireplace and the kitchen cook stove. In real cold weather, ice would freeze in the water bucket. Sometimes, the teakettle on the stove would have ice in it when the fire was started in the morning. We never kept fire in the cook stove during the night after supper was over and the dishes were washed. Frost would gather on the wallpaper, over the nail heads on outside walls, in that very cold weather. So you see, we needed heavy clothing at home as well as at school.

Much of our winter clothing was made at home from homespun cloth made from wool yarn from our own sheep. It was spun at home into yarn which was then knitted or woven. I have seen Ma knitting socks, stockings, mittens, sweaters, caps and toboggans using whatever size and number knitting needles needed for the job at hand. When this clothing would get holes or worn places, she would repair them by darning. Ma had gourds she called 'gourd eggs' in two or three different sizes which she used, to put into the sock to darn around, which prevented puckering so that the sock wouldn't fit. We liked to shake the gourds to hear the seeds rattle in them. She had straight and crooked darning needles which she used. These needles were run over and under, over and under, then crosswise in all directions, until the hole was mended. The darning yarn had to be extended out into the area around the hole to reinforce it and make the repaired part strong.

While I wore knee breeches, my stockings came up above my knees the same as those worn by the girls. When boys started wearing long pants, our stockings came up to or above the calf of our legs and were called socks, the same as now. In either case, the hand knitting process was the same for boys, girls, men or women. These long stockings coming above the knee were held up with garters made of elastic to fit around the leg above the knee. The knee breeches had some elastic to fasten them securely above the knee so as not to need the garters to hold the stockings.

- - - - - - - - - - -

"Making all those clothes must have been a lot of work, Grandpa! But how did your mother make wool yarn from the sheep's wool. It doesn't look anything like yarn."

"Spring is the time to shear the wool off the sheep. We have a pair of sheep shears at the lake cottage which your Grandma and I use now to trim the grass along the walk and flower beds that the lawnmower misses. You may have seen those."

"Do they have wide sharp-pointed blades that spring open after you use them? I tried them once, but not on sheep."

"There is another bent type which some think are better to keep from gouging the sheep as you shear. . . "

- - - - - - - - - - -

MORE ABOUT CLOTHING

We always made a picnic of shearing since we kept our sheep a quarter of a mile from home. We took dinner and the whole family went along. We older kids had to mind the baby and small kids while Ma helped Pa with the shearing. Both sheared and we children helped hold sheep and do other things to help. The sheep were tied and laid on a table to shear. Later, when we had more sheep, we hired some help who would set the sheep up on the ground and start shearing around the neck and shear downward. They did this with shears and later on, with clippers. When I got big enough, I took my turn and could do a pretty good job but never used the clippers. Three to five pounds of wool from a sheep was a good fleece.

The next step was to wash the wool. I have tramped about on the wool in a tub of warm soapy water to help in this work. After washing and drying, the wool was ready for carding. Two brushes similar to horse brushes were used, except that wire teeth were used instead of bristles. The wool was rubbed backward and forward and in circles between the two brushes to straighten the wool and to remove any burrs, etc, that were not removed in the washing. When the carding was finished, the wool was in loose, straight soft rolls about one inch in diameter and a foot long, ready to be spun into yarn. Sometimes wool was sent to a carding machine where the washing and carding was done, making it ready for spinning.

Two spinning wheels were used. The small one was used while sitting on a chair and operating the pedal, the same as on the foot-operated sewing machine. The three-foot in diameter wheel had a belt that turned a spindle that twisted the wool as it was fed into the spindle from the carded rolls. The quality of yarn was controlled by the skill of feeding and twisting in spinning. I never operated either the small or big wheel, but I'm telling you the way I have seen my mother and others operate them.

The large spinning wheel was about five feet in diameter and mounted in much the same way as the small wheel, both of which turned the spindle which did the spinning and rolling the yarn or thread into balls ready for use in darning, weaving or knitting. The operation of the large wheel was done while standing, by giving the wheel a push with the hand, then feeding the wool into the spindle. I have seen the operator step back a little and then toward the spindle again in this operation.

Another method of using yarn was to weave it into cloth which was then used for making clothes. The weaving was done on a loom operated by hand. We had no loom and our weaving was done by a neighbor, Becky Scott. Her loom was made of wood and took up a lot of space in the room. It was 5 or 6 feet high. Weaving is a complicated skill requiring considerable time and practice to learn and become good. Part of the operation of shoving the shuttle from side to side was done while sitting on a bench which was part of the front of the loom. We were at the loom often and I remember watching Becky working it. She wove good cloth for making clothing, and also made rag rugs. One of the coverlets woven by Becky of red, white and blue wool in an intricate design that shows she was excellent at weaving.

I have told you a little more in detail about home spinning and weaving of woolen materials because it was going out of use at that time. By the time I was about eleven years old, Ma began buying socks and stockings at the store. Darning the knitted materials continued to be a big chore. Clothing made of cotton, wool, linen, silk, leather and rubber was becoming plentiful in the stores. Ma could buy already woven fabrics for making our clothes as readily as you do now.

My winter footwear was the same as Pa wore, heavy cowhide boots coming up a little below the knee. My first pair had red tops with brass toe-pieces to keep the toe from wearing through. High-top shoes strung snugly to the same height were popular in the neighborhood. Six and nine inch high shoes were also widely used and all were of heavy strong leather that would stand hard wear. Women's shoes were made in various heights, also of strong leather. Your grandma wore homemade leather shoes as her first school shoes. She remembers being taken to the neighborhood cobbler who measured her feet. She had to go back later to get the finished shoes. Wooden pegs were used to fasten shoe soles on, in both homemade and factory made shoes. Sewing and tacking was also used and wooden pegs went out of style. I remember the pegs in my boot soles although later sewing and tacks or metal brads were used exclusively.

It was popular to have a lightweight, neat, highly polished pair of shoes for Sunday use or for visiting. Some people had more than one pair of such shoes. Later, rubber overshoes were used over light shoes. The overshoes were taken off in the house. Some men wore heavy felt boots or socks, over which they wore heavy rubber overshoes which were also removed in the house.

These felt boots were warm and were extensively worn by many people. Gum or rubber boots were also worn with an extra cotton moccasin over the socks. These were not as handy as were the high 4 or 6 buckle gum overshoes which were worn over lightweight shoes. Feet kept warmer without sweating with the overshoes. Heavy warm footwear was available in the stores and so was finer, better looking footwear for dress-up and show-off purposes.

When I was small, up age 10 or 11, I wore warm serviceable homemade clothing. Later such clothing was bought in the store ready-made, or made at home from materials available. Overcoats, pants and dresses were made over or altered to keep in style or to fit smaller children.

Your grandma says she and the other girls at school wore, for a few years, long-sleeved calico aprons that covered their woolen dresses, to keep the dresses clean and also for warmth. The gingham and calico aprons were easily washed, making it unnecessary to wash the woolens so often.

We wore underwear called union suits, because top and bottoms were made in one garment, from neck to ankles. The two piece underwear was also available.

The shoe problem in spring, summer and early fall was eased by nearly all children going barefoot. A few men and women went barefoot part of the time. Lighter shoes, or winter shoes that were too worn for winter use, were worn in summer. Thinner and lighter clothing was worn in summer. Straw hats were useful and popular.

Wooden shoes were never worn much in our neighborhood but had been used in the Dutch settlement on the head of Cove Creek although, even there, they were going out of use. We found one, now and then, lodged in drift piles along the creek.

- - - - - - - - - - - -

"You can see, from what I have just been telling you, that it was not so much the kind of clothing children wore when we were in school that made us so cold, as it was being exposed longer periods outside, and in poorly heated homes and schools. Children nowadays

would have to wear more clothing if their schools and homes were also as cold!"

"Yes, they kept our school colder that year we had the Energy Shortage. We all wore sweaters. Are you ready to tell about your classes at school now?"

"Yes, and this would be from 1906 until about 1915 when we were pupils, and perhaps some later experiences as teachers. . . "

- - - - - - - - - - - - - -

SCHOOL DAYS

George and I attended our first day of school at the beginning of the term in the fall of 1906 when I was 9 and he was 8 year old. Our Aunt Edna Lewis went along with us to school and introduced us to the teacher and helped us give the teacher whatever information was necessary for registration. The teacher said we could go out and play with the other pupils until the bell rang. Aunt Edna helped us get acquainted with other children and get started playing games with them before school, at morning recess and at the noon hour. Then she left and went home. We missed her that afternoon.

We ran races with the other children, played base, draw-ball, Ring-Around the Rosie and whatever other games may have been played that were suitable for our size and age.

Learning began with ABC's, writing and counting. We knew these things as far as we were supposed to, for our ages. Ma had taught school and saw to it that we learned these at home, even if we did not start to school as young as we should have.

We took whatever books to school with us that Ma thought we would be able to use. Our teacher tested us in these books and was surprised that we knew our ABC's, could read and count. She assigned us to the group she thought we should be with.

I don't recall much about the actual class activities this first day of school other than things went along smoothly without any disturbances. I am sure we did not know more than 2 or 3 of the 30 or 35 children who were present that day.

The next morning we were sore all over and could scarcely get out of bed. We did not want to go back to school, of that I am sure. We could scarcely walk and perhaps that soreness may have been concentrated about my previous rupture area. What other reasons may have been considered, I do not remember but that one day was our first and last day of school for that school year!

We did not escape school that easily after our first day of school that year. Ma and Pa made a table similar to our picnic tables with a seat on each side the length of the table top. A wide board was used on each side of the top, to make it better to write on. Another board was used in the middle to complete the top. This was our school for that year and a place to do homework in later years. Eunice and Lois joined us at this table and all our schoolwork continued under Ma's direction with daily regular hours assigned for this purpose. Two or three could sit at each side of the table. We even had morning recess, noon hour and afternoon recess, the same as at school. This table was set not far from the fireplace by the window in the living room.

We lived a half-mile farther down the creek from school than any other family and had to cross Big Cove Creek three times to get to school. That was two more crossings than any other family. A fairly good foot-log or foot-bridge was usually maintained at the third crossing for all to use but we had to make the first two crossings on our own as best we could. We could have taken a longer route around the hills, avoiding the first two crossings, and using the third crossing with all the other down-creek children. This was too long a route, too dangerous and was never used regularly by us.

Another route which we used was to cross the creek near our house on whatever crossing we could build, operate and maintain. After this crossing, we followed a path around the hill, on the same side of Big Cove Creek that the schoolhouse was on. Except in the fall of the year, while the dirt road was good and the creek easily crossed, this was the route we walked to school.

Crossing Big Cove Creek was always a problem since it was 40 or 50 feet wide at the narrow parts where a foot-bridge could be built and maintained. In rainy weather, the creek would rise and wash the foot-log around and it could not be put back again until the creek ran down. We later helped this crossing problem by making and using a boat to cross, but in high water, this was too dangerous and school had to be missed. Later a fairly safe foot bridge was built, high enough to be out of high water, except when the water got so high that it ran around the end of the bridge and we couldn't get to it. Then we would miss school again. All of these were part of our experiences in going to that one room school. And we did go again, the very next year!

The teacher hired for the 1907-08 school term was Dee Lamb, a son of John and Maria Lamb, who lived on Little Cove. We knew Mr. and Mrs. Lamb pretty well, and met Dee before school started. He assured us that we would all have a good time and get along fine in school. So all of us children looked forward to the beginning of school and found his predictions to be true. All four of us, George, Eunice, Lois and I started school the same day. When the weather got bad, about Christmas, Eunice and Lois stayed home and had classes at our home school bench. George and I continued attending school, except in real bad weather, when we joined them at our home school. This home study kept us up with the work at school and sometimes ahead of it. I realize now that this teaching, together with all her other work, was a big chore for Ma.

I can remember the teacher asking my age that first morning at school. I said loudly,

'Ten years old!' I was teased about answering so loudly by the rest of the family, that I never forgot my age at the time of starting school.

When we first started to school, a great emphasis was put on teaching the three R's (Readin, Ritin and Rithmetic.) We had to learn the ABC's in both print and writing and recognize words by spelling and by association with pictures. If one did not know a word, he was told to spell it and then to sound it out himself. The alphabet was printed in capital and small letters, side by side, on the top line of the blackboard, across the front of the room so we all could see and learn each letter both ways. The standing of a person in school was determined to a large extent by his reading ability, such as primer, first reader, second, third, and so on through the eighth reader. Reading, spelling, writing and arithmetic are the tools needed for school progress in all subjects. There was no such thing as grouping by grade level in a one room school when we started. There was no time. Of course, McGuffeys was the reader we used.

Students were taught and studied in groups with progress from one group to the next determined by individual ability to do the work of the next higher group. For instance, one might stay two years in the first reader before he could read well enough to go into the second reader. Some years a pupil might do two readers in one year.

The individual progress was best illustrated in teaching arithmetic which was usually taught in three groups, Numbers Class, Primary Arithmetic and Advanced Arithmetic. In the Numbers Class, beginning exercises such as how many eyes, toes, legs and ears one has, counting to ten and 100, simple addition, subtraction, multiplication and division and the signs for each. This material was both oral and in writing and included simple problems.

Primary arithmetic was the continuation of numbers and included the multiplication tables and the use of larger numbers in adding, subtracting, multiplying and dividing. An easy primary arithmetic book was used which took up weights, measures, simple percentage, decimals, interest and problems involving use of these various procedures.

Advanced arithmetic was a continuation of the various number skills to involve more difficult skills. In this class, the tables of addition, subtraction, multiplication and division should be as automatic as the alphabet. Other more difficult tables and procedures had to be learned exactly. It was either right or wrong. 2+2=4 is still exactly the same as in the numbers class. It had to be that and nothing else.

The individual progress was well illustrated in these classes by lesson assignments which were 'Work as far as you can for tomorrow.' Those working on page 40, 60 or 200 had no trouble knowing what to study. The recitation included repeating tables by memory, for those learning tables or rules, or writing them on the blackboard without the book. Since no two were likely to be working on the same page, the board work of each was different. Often students, having no difficulty with their own work, were assigned to help another who needed assistance. This gave better students an incentive to know his subject, so he could show others how. The books used were Ray's Arithmetic and Milne's Arithmetic. A few more advanced pupils used Ray's Higher Arithmetic. I was better in Arithmetic than in any other subject I had in school. I worked every problem in Ray's and went on to Milne's and Ray's Higher Arithmetic and worked all the problems in each of them.

Mental arithmetic was taught to the more advanced part of the arithmetic group involving short cuts and methods not stressed in the regular arithmetic study.

Spelling was taught in connection with reading in all grades by learning to spell and pronounce new words as they came up in reading lessons. Definitions, pronunciations and meanings of unusual words were given at the beginning or end of each reading exercise and also in a glossary at the back of the book. Formal spelling was taught, beginning about the third reader. Pupils were grouped in two or three groups according to their abilities, not according to age or the length of time they had been in a group. The average time might be two years to a group, yet some might complete the work in one year, others in three. If a student found the work in a particular group too hard, he was put back in an easier group.

In addition to arranging the letters in their proper order to spell the work, it was necessary to pronounce the word properly before spelling it. This required learning the diacritical letter markings and letter sounds as part of the spelling process and also the rules for use of capital letters. Thus, if the teacher pronounced for spelling, the word 'Columbus,' the pupil would repeat 'Columbus,' then spell 'capital C-o-l-u-m-b-u-s-.' If it were a written lesson, the word was not pronounced by the pupil, but written using capital letters as needed. Sometimes it was necessary for the teacher to pronounce the word a second time if there was difficulty understanding the pronunciation.

In written lessons, papers were exchanged and incorrect spelling checked, then graded by percentage. Ten or twenty words were used to make grading easy. A list of names of the group was put on the blackboard and the grade written after each ones name. The same list might be used for a record of several lessons, if there was room on the board to keep the list there that long.

Another spelling recitation method used extensively was: Have the class line up in a single row facing the teacher at the front of the room. The end of the row to the teacher's left was the head of the line, the other end the foot. The spelling started at the head of the line. If a student misspelled a word, the teacher would say 'next' which gave the next in line a try until the word was spelled correctly. The one who spelled the word correctly would move toward the head of the line, with those who missed it moving toward the foot. If no words were missed, no change in position was made. In order to give all a chance at the head of the line, the one at the head when each recitation finished was given an honor mark, called a 'head-mark' and he went to the foot of the line for the beginning of the next lesson. Any who were absent for this lesson went below him in line. To determine the other positions, they numbered, beginning at one for the person next to the head-mark person and numbering toward the foot with the one at the head numbering last. This number order was the order to line up for the next lesson. The teacher kept permanent record of all the names of the group together with the number of head-marks made by each.

If capital letters were left off proper names, the word was missed. In this way poor spellers worked toward the foot of the class and no special recognition while better spellers advanced toward the head of the line and head-mark honors.

In 'spelling bees' those missing words took their seats and spelling continued until one side had no spellers left standing. Primary, Intermediate, and Advanced were the usual spelling groupings for study and recitation.

WRITING CLASS

Writing materials available for use when we started to school were:

> Steel-point, dip-pen and ink
> Lead pencil, slate pencil
> Slates in wood frames
> Tablets
> Copy books of various types
> Blackboard, white and colored chalk
> Crayons and colored pencils became available later.

The slate was used extensively for all types of temporary writing and practice such as problem solving, writing and spelling lessons, sentences or for making copies of the teacher's blackboard work. Your work could be shown to the teacher for corrections or suggestions and erased so you could try again in an effort to improve your skill. The slate was easily cleaned for a new start by wiping with a dry rag, or, if a cleaner surface was desired, just spit on the slate and wipe off with your slate rag, hand, corner of your apron or by rubbing your sleeve across or round and round on the slate surface. This gave a beautiful dark writing surface, but an application of soap and water was necessary from time to time to remove surface build-up. The slate could be used almost endlessly at no expense except for new slate pencils which cost little to replace and lasted a long time.

The slate was the writing workhorse of the early one room school. Pen, ink, pencils and writing paper were more expensive and hence, used less. Some pupils threw away paper used only partly or on one side and would have none when paper was needed. At times, teachers would allow no writing paper thrown into the stove or coal bucket without permission which was not given if there was open space on either side to use. This helped prevent waste and borrowing paper became less of a nuisance.

At regularly scheduled writing periods, general instructions were given to the whole school at once. Individual instruction or assistance was given and general observation of progress was possible while all were performing practice exercises. Copies were sometimes set by the teacher to be copied by pupils in writing period but this was little used when regular copy-book exercises became available for the various age groups. It took too much teacher time to set copy examples.

Writing legibility, form and neatness were emphasized, not only in writing period, but in all written work in other subjects.

Instruction in penmanship involved all who were above the primary group and the pen was used in most writing in the other subjects. Some students developed beautiful, legible handwriting. Others continued developing their writing to get writing certificates and became expert penmen, in the use of shading and lettering. I believe penmanship was emphasized much more then than it is in the schools now.

"But Grandpa, we have lots more things to learn than just writing. And anyway, we can learn to type. Lots of kids have calculators that they take to class. Maybe we won't even have to learn the multiplication tables anymore!"

"Yes, there are a lot of things to learn now. But do you suppose we will be so busy learning all these things and will not have time to learn to write even our names? Then we'd have to make our 'mark' the way some people did in the old days."

HISTORY CLASS

I can see little change in learning history when I was in school and in learning history now. In any event, a lot of stories, battles, great men and events are involved together with dates and places to study, remember or forget.

We studied Montgomery's Beginner's History which was well written and covered a number of interesting historical incidents and facts about the United States and its relation to other countries and lands. This gave us a base or background to build on in later group study of a more advanced history text.

Little reading was done outside the textbook in either the beginners group or the advanced history group. The method of study was to read the text and prepare to answer questions on what you had read, during the recitation period or, perhaps, to review the facts or story in your own words. Recitation periods in history were necessarily short, as were all one room school recitation periods.

West Virginia state history was studied in an upper grade which would correspond to 6th, 7th and 8th grades now. This group recited once a day or on alternate days with U.S. history since the same group studied both histories.

43

GEOGRAPHY CLASS

Two groupings were used for study in geography. The Intermediate Geography would include what would now be 5th and 6th grades while Advanced Geography would include the 7th and 8th grades. Our early geography book emphasized the location of rivers, mountains and oceans, as well as countries, continents and seasons, cities and peoples. Study questions at the end of chapters were used.

Our teachers followed the textbooks closely and included freehand map drawing during study periods. Many names of nations have disappeared entirely and new countries emerged during the past 70 years to change maps. There was plenty to keep us busy then and trying to keep up with the changing world has kept us interested ever since.

HYGIENE & PHYSIOLOGY

The Physiology and Hygiene book was studied from about the 6th grade on, in one group. We learned about the body, how to take care of ourselves, avoid diseases and protect ourselves from a number of dangerous germs. I can think of nothing particularly exciting about this.

I began studying this physiology book about the same time the school got the new stone water cooler and all of us had to have individual drinking cups. These changes were right in line with what we were learning in this class.

It was during this course that our teacher had us enter a contest sponsored by the Colgate Company for the best composition on the topic 'A Clean Tooth Never Decays.' Mine was the best entered from our school. The Colgate Company sent me a medal with my name engraved on it. This was round and bronze-colored, about the size of a silver dollar. Along with my name appeared 'A Clean Tooth Never Decays.'

We all learned how to take care of our teeth. Our first tooth brushes were made of willow sticks with one end mashed so as to act as a brush. Baking soda was used in place of toothpaste. By the time we had this contest, we had real toothbrushes and toothpaste. I had my first fillings in some back teeth when I was about 16 years old. When I entered the Marine Corps in the First

World War, all my teeth were examined and the doctor commented on what good teeth I had, and also on the good condition of the fillings. When I told this to Dr. Ewing, who had done the fillings, it pleased him immensely.

- - - - - - - - - - - - - -

"Do you still have the medal, Grandpa?"

"Yes, I saw it among some things I was looking through, awhile back. I'll hunt it up and let you see it, one of these days."

"You must have false teeth now, Grandpa. Some people put their teeth in a glass by their bed at night. I bet they'd smile at you when you looked at them in the morning!"

"No, My teeth are still firmly attached and the real thing. That's pretty good for an almost 80 year old, don't you think?"

- - - - - - - - - - - - - -

CIVIL GOVERNMENT

Civil government was taught to about the same group of students as learned Physiology & Hygiene. As the name suggests, it was about government in the various ways it affects people and the ways people take part in it. We studied different types of governments, how they operate and influence people. Our own government was taken up in more detail.

- - - - - - - - - - - - - -

"I suspect you are getting tired of hearing so much about school and are ready to hear about something else. Joe looks like he's already asleep!"

"Didn't you ever have any fun at school, Grandpa? So far it's been all study."

"Grandpa, tell us some of the games you played at school. We want to see if any are the same as the ones we are still playing."

"Oh, we played many games. Let me see how many I can name for you. Let's make a list. . . ."

- - - - - - - - - - - - - -

FUN AND GAMES AT SCHOOL

Blind Man's Buff	Ring Around the Rosie
Hide and Seek	London Bridge
Mumminy Peg	Hop-Skip and Jump
Fox and Geese	Rooster fighting
Foot races	Tic-tac-toe
Base	Simon Says
Prisoner's base	Wrestling
'Antne Over'	Shinny on the Ice
Ball	(a sort of hockey)
2 base	Skating
Baseball	Snow-balling
Tip-up ball	Sliding down the hill on sleds
Pole vaulting	Barrel stave skis
High jump	wide boards
Three Deep	bob-sleds
Draw ball	Dominoes
Checkers	Knuckle down
See Saw	Snowmen
Snow Fort	Drop the Mitten
Standing and running broad jump	

No card games of any kind were played at school, but you can see from this list that we had lots of fun at school.

"What is 'Antne-Over' Grandpa?"

Antne-Over is a modification of Draw Ball, but instead of each team lining up 50 or 60 feet apart and throwing directly at each other, as in Draw Ball, they line up on opposite sides of the schoolhouse. When both teams are ready, the game starts with the team having the ball calling, 'Antne?' The other team answers

47

'Over!' at which time the ball is thrown over the building. If the ball is caught or goes out of bounds, the thrower has to go to the other team. Both teams exchange sides of the building. Anyone who is touched or hit by the ball before they can get to the other side of the building has to join the opposing team. When the teams are ready again, the procedure is repeated until no player is left on one side, or until one side reaches a predetermined minimum number. The team with the most members wins. This may not be all of the rules, but it was an interesting game and we had fun playing it.

"But Grandpa, you said it was like Draw Ball. I never heard of that before."

"Then I guess my reference to Draw Ball in explaining 'Antne Over' didn't explain very much."

Choosing up sides was the first thing necessary for playing competitive games, spelling bees and ciphering matches. Two captains were appointed whose duties were to select good players. To decide which would get first choice, a bat or a broom was pitched up and one captain caught it near the middle and the other took hold above the first with one hand. Then it was hand over hand in turn, until the top was reached by one who then got the first player choice. The other got choice of starting position, such as bat or fielding position or throwing the first ball.

In Draw Ball, each captain lined his players up in position about 50 or 60 feet apart, depending on the size of the players. The object of the game was to draw players from a team until no player was left on the opposing team.

One ball was used in this game, with the size and weight varying according to the size of the players. Play started with both sides lined up in their respective base area, which was about 5 feet wide by 20 feet long, parallel to each other. The thrower stood in this area and threw at the other side, trying to hit one or more opposing players who had to run to his side before being hit with the ball by their own players. In the event a player caught the ball, the thrower had to go quickly to the team of the catcher. The

48

catcher could give him a little time before throwing back at the other team or else he could throw at the other end of the opposing team. If a thrown ball bounced off a player into the area between the bases, it was a free ball for either side and could be thrown at an opponent from wherever picked up. This made for close throws, and exciting, rapid plays. When the ball went back of the base line area, it could be brought back to the base line for throwing at the opponent. If this was done quickly, you might get a close throw at an opponent. A caught ball always drew the thrower to the catcher's team. A caught, bounce ball protected the catcher but didn't draw the thrower. The game continued until one team had no players or was down to a pre-determined number. We did not use a referee, but I can see how one might be used. If you were to try to play Draw Ball from these instructions, you might need a rule or two more, but mainly, this was the way we played the game.

Small children, using soft light balls, could safely play this game as a group when it was unsafe to mix in with bigger pupils. This was important since all ages and sizes attended our one room school.

We had no special playground equipment such as swings, slides and monkey bars nor did we have catcher's masks, gloves, baseballs, volley balls or footballs from the store. Our baseballs were homemade or improvised as was the other equipment used. We made balls with leather covers similar to regular baseballs. We also had one or two worn-out baseballs that had been used by the bigger students but hard, heavy balls would sting our hands so lighter, softer balls were more popular. There were not enough big boys for two teams in most schools.

A nearby school was playing with a baseball when a girl was accidentally hit on the head with a thrown ball and died within a day or two as a result. This stopped the use of baseballs or heavy hardballs in all schools in the surrounding area. We had been in school 4 or 5 years when that happened.

After the bigger boys and girls got ice skates at home, we brought these skates to school when the ice on the creek was safe. Then we all, skates or no skates, played 'Shinny on the Ice.' The ball or object we knocked around, endangered our unprotected shins as well as did the crooked sticks we used to bat it about with. This was our version of hockey.

49

We drew two lines across the creek on the ice, a convenient distance apart, for our goals, instead of hockey cages. Those without skates were stationed near these lines to defend them as a goalie defending his cage. Others were stationed near the middle of the court. Some skaters were not much better at getting around over the ice than those without skates. In all, we had fun and a lot of exercise, together with several sore shins, whether we had observed all the rules of hockey or not.

Some games could be played only outside on the playground and others were largely quiet games for inside the schoolhouse. Still others could be played either place.

'Fox and Geese' was such a game. We played this game outside when new snow was on the ground by stepping off a circle of appropriate diameter, perhaps 100 ft, around a center hub of 5 or 6 feet. Then we stepped off a bigger circle outside the first but around the same hub, big enough so one could not step or jump from one circle to the other. Paths from the hub of the inner circle to the outer circle, like the spokes of a wagon wheel divided the play circle area into 4ths, 6ths or 8ths, depending on the size of the play area. The spokes and circular paths just described formed the running tracks. The hub area was the den where the geese were penned as they were caught by the fox. One or two players were the foxes and the other players were the geese. The object of the game was to keep from getting caught. I don't recall all the rules, but it was an active game which provided both fun and exercise.

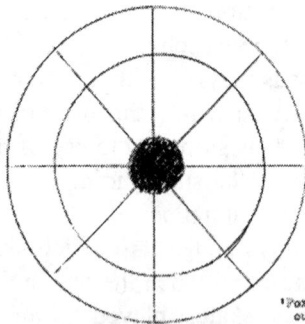

'Fox and Geese'
outdoor version

Fox and Geese, Outdoor Version

50

Fox and Geese, as played inside the house, was entirely different from the one I have just described. It was played with different kinds of grains of corn on a board which I will try to draw for you. The game began with a certain number of geese (white or red kernels of corn) arranged in a certain position on the board. If the geese were white, the old fox was red. The object of the game is for the old fox to catch all the geese without getting penned. He does this by jumping, in a straight line over one or more geese to a vacant space. He continues jumping over one or more geese in a straight line to a vacant spot until no such jump is available. All geese jumped are immediately removed from the board. Then one goose anywhere on the board can be moved one space. The idea is to get the geese arranged in such a position that the fox can neither jump or move from space to space. When he is thus penned, the geese win. The fox wins by jumping and removing all geese from the board.

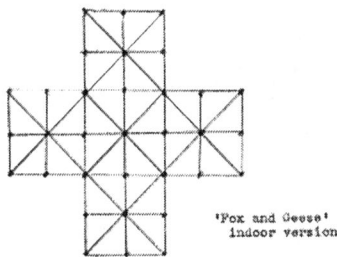

'Fox and Geese'
indoor version

Fox and Geese, Indoor Version

I may not have the board drawn correctly nor do I have all the rules, but you can see this is a game requiring skill and attention to detail. It is a game that any and all can play and neither age nor size has any particular advantage. The 7 or 8 year old may beat the oldest or biggest pupil or even beat the teacher. This was a good game for bad weather. No games were permitted during school hours although an unfinished game might be left in position in the desk to be finished at the next play period. Corn falling on the floor during school time frequently happened, to the embarrassment of the unlucky person who had stored it so carelessly.

"Some other indoor games were dominoes, checkers, blind man's buff, drop the mitten, and tic-tac-toe but I think you know how to play most of these."

"Grandpa, when did you have time to play all those games?"

Time was scarce. Sometimes we played a little before school which began at 9:00. From 10:30 – 10:45 we had a 15 minute recess. Noon hour was 12:00 – 1:00 and in the afternoon from 2:30 – 2:45 was another recess.

Everyone brought his own lunch in a bucket which had been prepared at home, ready to eat at school. (There were no hot lunches then!) All were required to eat their lunches while sitting in their seats with little walking about the room. This took about 15 minutes before all could finish and be ready to play.

In those years that teachers did not take part in play, cliques developed, quarrelling and arguing prevailed and some fights took place. Some controlling authority was necessary to guide play activities so all can have fun and enjoyment. No play was allowed after school hours, 4:00, or on the way home from school.

The law in West Virginia when we went to school was that children were under their parents' control until they got to school in the morning. After arriving at school, they were under the control of the teacher during school hours from nine to four. After school was dismissed, the children continued under control of the teacher until they arrived at their respective homes. Thus you see the reason for no play or loitering on the way home.

The entire community was included in many activities that took place in the schoolhouse. Some of these were spelling bees, ciphering matches, last-day-of-school dinners, picnics, last-night-of-school exhibitions, literary society meetings and debates.

Spelling bees and ciphering matches were frequently combined, one following the other with the same group or team. Teams were chosen by the captains in the usual manner. One of two methods was used at a time, or sometimes both during the same contest. In the first method, each team lined up in the order of choice on opposite sides of the schoolroom, facing each other.

52

Words were pronounced by the teacher from two or three books such as primer, primary, intermediate and advanced spelling books. Each was given a word suitable to his spelling experience for awhile. Those missing words took their seats. Gradually harder and harder words were used until advanced spelling book words were used exclusively and one team was spelled down.

The other method used was to have team members stand on the floor two at a time and spell until one was spelled down and took his seat and was replaced by the next in order on his team. Spelling continued in this manner until one team ran out of spellers and lost. The contest usually started with the ones last chosen which included primary pupils and poorest spellers. This type spelldown usually took longer and sometimes left several on the winning team who never got a chance to spell at all. Also since only two were spelling at a time, it left too many with nothing at all to do except watch the spellers or get into mischief. The first method permitted all to have some part in winning or losing and was more popular.

Interesting and exciting situations often developed using either method. One time a primary speller was competing against a much bigger and more advanced boy. The big boy was given the word 'dog' to spell. He confidently turned around and wrote the word on the blackboard,'d-o-g,' then, facing the teacher and the whole school, spelled 'g-o-d.' Everyone roared with laughter and he sheepishly sat down.

Sometimes people from three different schools in our area would meet for these contests. One young man, Erlo Nicholson, from the Pike Run area, developed such a spelling reputation that the team he was on almost always won, even when teachers and other good spellers were included. He was the main attraction at a community-wide spelling bee held at our school one Friday night. Many people came, some of them to take part and others to observe. Ma and Uncle Warren, who were then in their early 40's, were among the older people who were taking part in the event. Spelling proceeded as usual until Erlo was the only one standing on his team and Ma and Uncle Warren were the only two on the opposing side. All were intently listening in silence as the spelling continued until Erlo missed a word and Ma spelled it correctly, before the pronouncer could say 'next.' This was permitted by the rules. Our team cheered, of course, and it was quite a set-back for

Erlo, but a great honor for Ma and Uncle Warren. Both Ma and Uncle Warren had No. 1 Teachers Certificates and were good spellers.

Literary Society meetings usually occurred on Friday night. These meetings were attended by as many school children as could get there and all other people in the community who cared to attend, whether they took an active part or not. The program was usually varied and of interest to all. Children recited poetry, gave readings and engaged in debates. Generally, older people, whether good speakers or not, took part in debates, sometimes on serious subjects, sometimes humorous, but always as a means of general entertainment.

We have a secretary's book of minutes of The Lick Run Lyceum, which met at the Lick Run School from 1886 until 1890, in which Ma was secretary part of the time. Some of the topics they debated were:

Resolved: That the African has been more cruelly treated by the American people than the Indian.

Resolved: That there is more harm in playing cards than in playing ball.

Resolved: That a man will vencher (sic) farther for money than for woman.

Resolved: That electricity is more useful than a team.

Resolved: That the United States has reached the zenith of its greatness.

Resolved: That Chinese immigration to the United States should be stopped.

Resolved: That Mexico should be united with the United States.

Resolved: That capital punishment should be abolished.

Resolved: That more information can be obtained from reading than from traveling.

Resolved: That the chicken came before the egg.

Each of these subjects was fully debated with at least three people on each side. Then a winner was declared. A committee of three decided on the subjects to be debated. Attendance was from 30 to 50 people. The Lick Run Lyceum had a constitution but there is no record that any dues were charged.

54

THE LAST DAY OF SCHOOL

Preparations for the last day of school program might extend for two months for usually a play was presented that involved not only the school children but also older people in the community. There was much practice and study of parts and also preparation of the stage, curtains, costumes, furniture and other props. This preparation provided something for the young people to do and to be interested in. It was something for everyone to talk about and look forward to.

These exhibitions were usually held on the afternoon of the last day of school, if only the school children were involved. If older people helped, it was held at night sometime near the end of school.

A community picnic was also a feature of the all-day celebration of the end of the school year. The dinner, provided by the families in the community, was set out on a common table. Enough planning went into the event to insure a variety and enough food for all. Some poor people may not have been able to bring much, but all, including visitors, were welcome and urged to eat all they wanted. Very little urging was necessary.

Before noon, the men and young people engaged in various games such as high-jumping, broad-jumping, hop-skip-and jump, or handsprings while others were watching and talking. The women were busy with the dinner, assisted by some of the big girls, and everyone was being brought up to date on the neighborhood gossip and news. Men helped arrange the tables and available benches.

At dinner, all helped themselves and no lack of appetite could be seen anywhere. Afterward each family readied their left-overs to take home.

In the afternoon, several young men and women usually got a Squirrelly game started. In this game, the players joined hands and formed a circle big enough to include all who wanted to play. One or two were outside the circle and went around and tagged one in the circle who then chased him until caught, when both kissed each other. This kissing game was not a school game and was frowned on by most of the older people. The school children formed an interested audience to see who kissed whom and how often.

During the afternoon program, 'head-mark' winners were revealed and other honors given. No report cards were given until about the time I finished my one room schooling. Sometimes a spelling or ciphering match was held for all who wanted to take part. The crowd broke up before 4:00 and all were on their way home,

- - - - - - - - - - -

"That last day of school really sounds like fun, Grandpa. Did you play that kissing game too?"

"That's one of the places where my memory fails me! But these stories give you some idea of how it was to go to a one room school in the years between 1906 and 1915. There's another kind of school that I haven't mentioned. It was called a 'Select School.'"

"Did you have to be selected to go there, Grandpa?"

- - - - - - - - - - -

THE SELECT SCHOOL

The 'Select School' was not part of the free school system and was designed to give more advanced study and instruction in the same subjects that were taught in the one room school. If 20 or 25 people could be found in the community who were interested in attending such a school for six weeks or two months, the school was organized and the classes were held at the schoolhouse. The teacher of a Select School was paid a fee by each student. These schools were taught after the regular school term was out and were used more in the period before the regular school term was extended from 6 to 9 months.

"As you can see, such schools were special and not held at every schoolhouse. I never attended such a school but your Grandma says she has.

"Grandpa, how was it that you could be a teacher before you went to college? All our teachers have already been to college."

"There was a State Teachers' Uniform Examination that you could take and then you were licensed to teach. Let me tell you more about it."

- - - - - - - - - - - - - - -

THE TEACHERS EXAMINATION

At the time I finished grade school, there was not a high school in Gilmer County and there was none for several years after that. West Virginia had six Normal Schools for training teachers. One of them was located at Glenville, our county seat. It also gave a college preparatory course equivalent to a high school four-year course. Since these six Normal schools could not train enough teachers for all the schools, the state conducted examinations to secure qualified teachers.

There were no school attendance requirements for taking these tests. Questions were prepared under the direction of the State School Board, for each of the subjects in which an applicant was required to be tested. The questions were kept sealed until opened when the applicants were assembled, ready to take the test. State Teachers' Uniform Examinations were held at the same date and hour all over the state, with an hourly schedule for each subject so as to guard against anyone getting questions in advance. No one was permitted to teach, who was not eighteen by the time the school term started, or at least early in that term.

I decided to try to pass the examination for a teacher's certificate in the spring of 1915 when I would be 18 years old. Beginning in the spring of 1914, I started an intensive review of my school books, in addition to my regular farm and school work. It became apparent that I should learn definite answers to a lot of questions in all subjects. I got extensive lists of questions that had been used in previous examinations and diligently learned answers to these questions. I studied a book or two on methods of teaching. In warm weather, morning found me reading and studying until breakfast, before the regular day's work began.

The afternoon of the day before the examination was to start, I walked 12 miles to Glenville where the tests were to be held the next two days. Three examinations were given. One was about April 1st, the second was in early May while the last was in June. The names of all taking the examinations appeared in the county paper and a list of those passing, together with the certificate earned by each. My name appeared after the first test for a Third Grade Certificate. After the second test, my average was not quite high enough for a Second Grade Certificate. I came back in June for the third test and did raise my average enough to get a Second Grade Certificate, above the 80% average that was required. With a Second Grade Certificate, the teacher earned $40.00 a month; with a First Grade Certificate, one was paid $50.00.

I clearly remember two things concerning this third test. Winfield Burton and Linn Brannon, from about six miles farther up on Cove Creek had sent word that they would ride down to my home and we would all walk the 12 miles to Glenville together. We started walking at noon, on a cloudy day. We were about half-way, when a big thunderstorm came up and we had to run to make it to an old vacant house for shelter. When the storm was over, we went back to the road to continue. The road was soaked with mud and water all along. We had our best shoes on and they would be ruined if we walked in them the remaining six miles. Since we had no other shoes with us, we just sat down on the bank and took off our shoes and socks, rolled up our pants legs and proceeded on or way. When we were within 1/4th mile of Bailey's boarding house, we left the road and went down to the Little Kanawha River bank, washed our feet, put our shoes on, rolled down our breeches and walked into town where we got a room at Bailey's. Our shoes looked OK and no one could guess that we had just walked six miles over a wet muddy road!

The second important incident happened after supper at the boarding house when we were talking with some of the regular boarders who were going to school in Glenville. I spied a young good-looking girl whose name had appeared on the list of those taking the second examination and who had earned a First Grade Certificate. She was standing on the walk, sort of by herself, when I walked near and said to her that I had seen her name on the list of those making a First Grade Certificate. I may have asked if she was there to try to raise her grade. She was taking the spring term of school in Glenville. That good-looking girl was Miss Opal A. Morrison. We were married 7 years later. She doesn't remember meeting me until after I had come back from the Marines.

- - - - - - - - - - - -

"That conversation must not have been too impressive because your Grandma says she can't remember a thing about meeting me then!"

"Grandpa, how come Grandma made a Number One Certificate and you only got a Number Two? Was Grandma smarter than you?"

"It looks that way, doesn't it? But you wouldn't expect me to admit it, would you? Maybe we are just smart in different ways. I think that is something for you to consider."

"I read your stories about the marines and when you were in the First World War. Sometime will you tell us about when you were in the Navy in World War II?"

"We'll get around to that one of these days, but first I think you'd like to hear more about those Good Old Days we've been talking about."

- - - - - - - - - - - - -

59

OUR LIFE AT HOME

"Your school days sounded like fun. Did you have fun at home too, or did you have to work all the time?"

"When I recall my childhood, and the growing-up years at home and in the neighborhood, many things and happenings flit through my memory, one after another, in rapid succession, giving me a happy pleasant feeling right now. But when I try to reach out and take hold of one to tell you about, it seems to pass through my fingers, like trying to take a handful of fog or smoke. I'll see if I can capture a few of these memories as they go past, and hold them up so you can take a peek at them. Then you can decide if we were happy!"

"Grandpa, that would be like us trying to tell everything in a history lesson, after reading it over only once!"

"Yes, that's a good way to put it. These events I'll be telling you about took place between the years 1900 to 1915."

"We'll try to see your memory pictures as you describe them for us. We'll just close our eyes and pretend it's TV."

- - - - - - - - - - - -

THE PEDDLERS

You must remember that by the time I was 14 years old in 1911, there were 8 of us children ranging in age from the baby, Perry, to me and with Pa and Ma, that made 10 in the family. There were always enough people to play many different games. Getting lonesome was hard to do with that many at home.

One of the first signs of spring was the coming of Assyrian, Russian and Armenian peddlers. One came on foot, just about as soon as the cold winter weather was over and sunny spring days started. He carried a large pack and always came into the house and opened it. He talked so funny, and he did a lot of it, in showing his goods and telling us how fine they were and what beautiful colors he had. He laid his wares out on chairs for all to see, talking all the time. What a beautiful sight for us children! We might get too close or attempt to touch something and suddenly he became like an old hen guarding her chickens. On one occasion, he gave some of us children little trinkets that we thought nice and that pleased us. I can remember the pleased feeling, but not the trinkets. Can you imagine that?

A few times Pa or Ma bought something some of us needed but more often they did not buy. On one of these trips he was having such poor selling luck that he got mad and threw his stuff into his pack quickly, mumbling all the time as he rushed out the door and took off in a huff. We stood in awe, hoping he would miss something in his hurry. He did not miss anything but we had fun imitating him as we played peddler frequently after that.

When the roads dried up in the spring, another old peddler came around in a heavy buggy, hauling more and different articles. On one occasion, he wanted to buy some corn to take with him to feed his horses. We must have been getting scarce of corn because Pa did not want to sell. I remember the peddler's conclusive argument was, "Oh! A bushel of yearlings would not break you up!" He got the bushel of ears of corn.

Junk men were about the same as peddlers except they wanted to buy worn-out things. One such junk man wanted rubber junk. We got a few things together, including a pair of what we thought were worn-out rubber boots. I think he gave us 10 or 15 cents for the whole lot. I know Pa thought the boots were not entirely worn out and we should not have sold them. We had to be careful after that, to let Pa and Ma make sure we did not get something valuable mixed in with the junk. I am sure we never got rich in the junk business.

PLOWING – INDOOR STYLE

The early spring work of grown-up people suggested ways of entertainment to us children. One of these was spring plowing which we imitated in the house, long before we were big enough to actually help in the fields. We started our plowing early, before the weather was fit to be outside much.

We had a set of sturdy homemade split bottom chairs, which were ideal for our use. We turned them over so the two front posts of the seat and the two bottom ends of the back posts stuck up in the air, making the plow handles. We took hold of these up-turned plow handles and pushed the chairs backward and forward around the floor in the living room. More and more chair plows were brought into use as more of us took part. Any rugs on the floor were rolled up and pushed to the back of the room out of the way. Not having any horse to pull the plow did not keep us from controlling the imaginary horse with 'Gitty Up,' 'Gee!' 'Haw!' and 'Whoa!' The plows made a noisy plowing job.

By raising the chair back from the floor and using it to pull by, the chair became a sled on which one would ride and another became the horse pulling the sled, subject to all the horse-driving language, including the plow lines. Even an ox team driver's language was used, including the oxen's names and the Cracker Whip.

Pa's big rocking chair with arms was used for the big two-horse, sod-turning plow. Ma's small rocking chair, the one she used to rock the babies, had no arms and was suitable for use as the smaller, one-horse plow like the one Pa used when plowing with the old mare. Neither of these chairs could be used as a sled since the rockers got in the way. The rockers made excellent plow handles, however.

I am sure this play was more real than we thought since I have heard Pa say to Ma,

'They sound like a team of horses or a drove of cattle!' I can recognize these chairs anywhere now, by the sloping chair posts and backs where they were worn off plowing over the floor.

- - - - - - - - - - -

"Grandpa, is that big homemade rocker on Aunt Miriam's front porch the same one you used as the two-horse plow?"

"Yes, that's it and if you look at the chair posts, you can easily see how the tops are worn off from all that plowing. George and I had our pictures taken, sitting in that chair. I'll hunt it up and show it to you."

"Grandpa, I have the little rocker your Ma used to rock her babies. Grandma gave it to me."

"Yes, Jane, she told me she gave it to you. Ma was a small woman, about 5'2" and that chair fit her perfectly. Since you're so much taller, it probably won't fit you as well. Several of the straight chairs are still in the family, all showing signs of all that plowing!"

- - - - - - - - - - -

One fine sunny day when we were about 7 or 8, George and I were playing along the run, which was a small stream of water that ran down from the hill behind our house and across the bottom just outside the yard fence on its way to Big Cove Creek. We were building dams and floating little sticks in the run pretending they were saw logs. They would form log jams and we would break them up, having a good time out of doors. George left this game and went to the other side of the run to the old hog wallow which was probably 10 feet by 4 or 5 feet wide, and about a foot to 18 inches deep. He was probing in the water with a dry stick to see how deep the water was, trying to make the stick stand up in the water. He put a little too much pressure on the stick, it broke and he went head-long into the hog wallow. He did not go completely under but by the time he got out, he was wet and muddy all over, even though I helped pull him out. The whole family knew about it in less time than it takes to tell about it. He had to strip completely, take a bath to get rid of the mud and put on clean clothes. What an ending to an otherwise beautiful day's play!

- - - - - - - - - - -

I remember well the period of getting big enough for our teeth to get loose and hurt when we tried to eat, before they came out. We all dreaded this more than we dreaded going to the dentist after we grew up. Ma and Pa did the pulling of these baby teeth. Sometimes a quick pull or push with their fingers would do the job, when they were just seeing if the tooth was loose enough. We soon got on to that move. We had to keep working the tooth to get it out easily. If that did not work soon so we could eat without pain, Ma would tie a strong thread around the tooth and get a secure hold on both ends of the string and give a quick, strong jerk. This did the job so quickly that it was over before it hardly had time to hurt. Of course, crying was always in order. If the string slipped off or broke, the crying was for real. Such occasions called for a piece of candy, a little sugar or a spoonful of jelly. We were assured that if we did not stick our tongue into the place the tooth came out, the new tooth would come in gold. None of us ever got that gold tooth! Sometimes we put the tooth under our pillow to get a piece of money. Believe it or not, a few pieces of money have appeared under pillows from time to time over the years.

One morning Eunice came running in from the orchard, squalling and bawling. Ma thought she had been bitten by a snake and met her at the gate with,

'Did a snake bite you?'

"Nnoooo?' She was still crying loudly.

'Then what's the matter?'

'I I I LLLost my . . .'

'Lost your what?' Ma was doing her best to find out.

'Myyy tooth! Waaa!'

'Well is that all? Does it hurt very much?'

'Nooo'

'What are you bawling about then?' Ma asked reasonable.

'I don't know!' and by this time she was half laughing herself. We all had a good laugh but I am not sure whether any candy or sugar was won on this occasion. The worst part was that she didn't have a tooth to put under her pillow!

"That's the same thing we do with our teeth, Grandpa. And none of my teeth has ever come in gold, either."

"Yes, Joe, that's one of the things that has stayed the same. Probably the fairy leaves a little more money now."

"Grandpa, we've always heard about kids going barefoot all summer. Whenever I do, I always step on bottle caps and broken glass. And those little sharp tabs from cans."

"We really looked forward to the time we could 'turn out barefooted.' Sometimes people said, 'turn off barefoot' or just 'go barefoot.' Different people had various systems of deciding when the right time came. Sometimes May first was the day, but in our family, this is how it was. . . ."

When we heard the first Whip-poor-will, it was time to go barefoot even though there would still be cold days and evenings when shoes were needed. Our shoes were nearly always well worn by this time, with the soles thin or in holes. When the holes appeared, we lined them with cardboard for a little extra wear. Toes began to peep out, uppers were worn through, and heels run over. Sometimes there was scarcely enough shoe left to hang on a child's foot.

Barefoot time was not for just a few days in the spring; it lasted till late in the fall and greeted the return of frost. I can remember going with George after the cows near daylight on cold mornings when the dewy grass was laced with frost. We would find the old cows still lying in their beds and scare them so they would get up and we could stand where they had been lying, to warm our feet. This was almost as good as holding our feet out to the fire. Frequently, on foggy mornings, we found the cow's bed before we could see the cow, when they had already shuffled off, eating. When the beds were still warm, we knew the cows would not be far away. After warming our feet, we would hurry the cows to the milking place and close them inside. Then we went to the house for further warming before returning to help with the milking. Many farm boys and girls easily recall early fall mornings such as these.

I well remember one spring when I had just turned off barefoot. My feet felt so light! It was like flying when I ran! I thought,

'I am seven years old! How fast I can run!' These thoughts went through my mind as Pa and I prepared to go up on the hill behind the house to get a load of hay with the mare and sled. I could hardly wait until he got the shafts tied up to the hames. (The shafts were small hickory poles used to hold the sled from running against the mare when coming down steep banks. One was fastened to each side of the front of the sled and then tied to the hames which were part of the harness fastened to the collar, around the horse's neck and shoulder.)

Finally old Molly was hitched up and we started out. Part of the hill was so steep that I could not ride so I walked with Pa beside the sled. Pa held the lines and did most of the driving, although he let me hold the lines part of the time. I was almost a man now, in my thoughts. We got to the top of the hill and pulled the sled close to the stack of hay which we were going to haul down to the stable mow. This was what was left from feeding the cattle until grass came and they would no longer eat, or need, this hay.

Pa began piling the hay on the sled and I climbed on the hay to tramp it down. That was a man's work! I scarcely got started when I stepped on a briar mixed in the hay. I wasn't a man any more! Pa helped me get the briar out and we agreed that he could throw the hay on the sled without my help.

There were four standards, one at each corner of the sled, to hold the hay on the sled. Once in a while, Pa tramped the hay down with his heavy boots. It made a big load but when the boom pole was tightly tied down, it did not look so big and couldn't slide off.

We hauled the load out of the flat, and turned down the hill. At this point we stopped the horse. Pa helped me up on the top of the hay and handed me the lines to hold while he got up too. Then he took the lines to drive down to the stable which was about one-half mile away. We could not see it from that point but would see it from time to time on our way down the hill.

From our position on top our load of hay, we could see for miles around in all directions except to the west of us which was hidden by the knob of the hill we were on.

To our right in a southeast direction we could look down on Tom Scott's house and barn lot on the same side of Cove Creek as we lived. Farther on, Pa pointed out a hill, beyond which, he said, was the town of Troy where he went to the mill, store and to get the newspaper. Directly to the east, in front of us, we could see the long ridge which separated Little Cove from Big Cove. Beyond that we could see another, higher ridge rising to the horizon, beyond which, Pa said, Fink Creek ran. A part of the ridge beyond Little Cove, topped out in a pyramid-like hill with a cleared cornfield covering the whole hilltop. Pa said that hill belonged to Burkhammers. Looking to our left toward the north, almost directly below us, a little over 1/4th of a mile, we could look right down on Grant Scott's place which was also on our side of Big Cove. We could even hear their geese in the barn lot and geese always made a lot of noise. Both these Scott families were related to us since both Pa's mother and his grandmother were Scotts.

Farther to the north on the opposite of the creek about a mile and a half away, we could see another white building which Pa said was the schoolhouse. Just to the left of the schoolhouse, Pa pointed out a valley, running out of sight to the north, which he said was Crane Run. Then he pointed to some hills about as far as we could see and told me Grandpa Lewis lived behind those hills, just out of sight, about 4 miles away.

Now, of course, I don't expect you to believe that I remember all of this description from hearing it that time when I was seven years old, sitting with Pa on that load of hay. I was up that hill many times after that until I was 20 years old. It is sometimes hard to tell what is play and what is work. I am sure bringing down that load of hay was work for Pa and play for me, but I am equally sure that it was fun for both of us.

I will make a map of our neighborhood so you can understand how everyone was located. You can find our house, the school and Grandpa Lewis' farm.

MAP OF BIG COVE CREEK AREA – TROY WV

FARM MAP LOCATIONS

1. House, Corn crib and Stable

2. Orchard, 6 acres, set out in 1858

3. School we attended

4. Peach Orchard

5. Play Cornfield, also Big Slip

6. Jackson Rocks

7. Big tree where two soldiers fired muskets, Civil War

8. Battle of Pine Knob

9. Where I got my pike and took it up the hollow the back way home.

10. Little Orchard

11. Grandpa Lewis' home, 2 miles farther North on Crane Run

12. Troy, 1 mile farther South on Leading Creek

13. Ridge, ½ mi. West, at head of Left Fork of Crane Run, Buckhorn-Wolf Pen- Bloody Run- Big Run. Where the Staunton-Parkersburg Pike crossed the ridge.

14. Where George and I did our first ½ day grubbing.

15. The 'Load of Hay' talk location, also 'Bird Musings'

16. Where our first Christmas Tree was cut. Also a lot of tall white pine trees grew along the bluff.

17. Wooded ridge between Little Cove and Fink Creek

18. Perry's farm, where panther scratched log house, 1821

19. Some time after 1821, Alexander McQuain moved from Little Cove to here

20. Tom Scott oil/gas well

- - - - - - - Fences

/////////// Woods, showing slope of ground

Once in the early spring, I was with Pa and Uncle Zan who were shooting fish in the creek in front of our house. They waded into the shallow water to get the fish. I went in and got some fish and brought them out to the bank. Some of them were slippery to pick up and would slide out of my hands. I would have to pick them up again and again before getting them to the bank. I had more trouble with one which kept gradually getting into deeper and deeper water. I rolled my pants legs well up above my knees and ventured into the deeper water, up to my knees, then above my knees. It felt even colder when it got above where my pants had covered my legs. I began catching my breath as the water got deeper. It scared me and I did not want to go farther. I called loudly,

'It's too deep! I'm afraid!'

'Well, you come on out, we will get the fish out some way,' Pa answered. Uncle Zan said,

'That was getting deep out there.'

They could see that I was scared. So Pa took his shoes off, rolled his breeches above his knees and got the fish. He said the water felt cold to his legs too.

I was bothered with the earache quite often until I was 8 or 10 year old. That night I had the earache. Ma blew tobacco smoke from a pipe into my ear, then put a little sweet oil into it and plugged it with cotton. This was the usual treatment and it worked this time. Ma told Pa that I never should have been allowed to wade in the cold water so much. They both agreed that it was the wrong thing to do when the water was so cold.

Wading after fish may or may not have had anything to do with my earache but I can assure you that going barefoot had its drawbacks as well as its advantages. The briars in the load of hay and in the grass, stubbed toes, cracks under toes that required a wool string tied around the toe with salve for awhile, stone bruises, stings, splinters and hen pecks: these were a few of the disadvantages of going barefoot.

"Would you like to hear some more fish stories? We always liked to hear the ones Pa would tell."

"I bet they told stories about 'The Big One That Got Away' even then. Remember that last big one I almost caught at Indian Lake?"

"And you told us it was thaaaat big? Yes, we can remember that one!"

FISH STORIES

Spring of the year is always a good time of year for fish stories, if a good time of year is needed for such stories. Pa frequently told us children about the time a big pike got hit by the water wheel when he was sawing on the old mill. He happened to see it float away from the wheel. He stopped the saw and ran around down to the water, waded in waist deep, caught the pike in his arms and carried it out on the bank. It was unusually large, nearly 4 ft. long. This was before he and Ma were married in 1896.

Early one morning when I was about 10 years old, Pa called all of us to the back porch to see what he had. At first we saw nothing as he opened the door. Then the fish gave a big flop against the wall where he had hung it up by the gills on a 4 prong hay fork. This, too, was a big pike, about 38 inches long. He had seen it flipping over a shallow riffle. He then ran to the stable for the pitch fork. When he came back, there were two of them, going over the next riffle. He waded in and got one of them with the fork and carried it out on the bank. When he came back, the other fish had just disappeared into a deep hole of water. He waited for awhile but decided the pike might not go on through the hole of water for some time. Pike travel in pairs up-stream in the early spring to spawn. We had fried fish for several days. Ma covered part of it with salt to keep it from spoiling until we could get it all eaten.

73

Pa took the pike's head and spread its mouth wide open, then put a corncob in the mouth to keep it open. Then he set the head over a paling in the yard fence where it dried out and remained all summer. Pa proudly showed this head to visitors who were impressed by its size, especially the size of the mouth which looked big enough to swallow a cat.

Just a few days after Pa caught his pike, Ben Frymier who lived just across the creek from the lower end of the meadow, got one also. He was working in his clearing by the side of Big Cove, about a half mile farther down the creek from where he lived. He saw the pike on the riffle. With the double-bitted ax he had been using, he ran into the water and struck at the pike, cutting its head off. His fish was smaller than the one Pa caught but that did not necessarily keep Ben's fish story smaller. People always watched for pike coming up the creek every year in the spring.

Several years later, when I was cleaning trash off the meadow across the creek from the house, I duplicated Pa's experience, even to one getting away into deep water. There was one difference; it was against the law to spear pike when I got mine. This law was little enforced and people everywhere were getting pike but were less open about it. I was no exception. I spent little time looking for the second pike because I was afraid someone might come along the road at the upper side of the meadow and see my pike flopping on the bank in plain view. I threw my coat over it and thought about how I could get it home without going through the meadow which could be seen from the road.

I took a roundabout way, staying in the woods and completely out of sight all the way. We had pike to eat for a few days. My fish was about three feet long, lacking two inches of being as big as Pa's. I did not put its head on the paling fence as Pa had done nor did I talk of my pike so proudly to strangers, for obvious reasons. I was about 15 when these events happened.

- - - - - - - - - - - -

"Grandpa, we didn't know you caught fish that big. The biggest one I ever caught at Indian Lake was 24 inches. Mostly we catch bullheads."

"Well, we caught smaller fish too, which we enjoyed eating just as much."

"Did you use a hook and line too? All you've told us about were using guns, pitch forks and axes. What kind of bait did you like best?"

- - - - - - - - - - - - - -

MORE FISH STORIES

We were using a hook and line in just about the same way when I started fishing over seventy years ago, that you do now. We had reed and wood poles with line, hook, sinker and bottle cork bobbers almost exactly like the ones I now set along our dock at the lake. The nice rod and reel sets and artificial lures came along later, at least to our part of the country. The angleworms and night-crawlers we used were exactly like the ones we use now. They were just as slick, slimy, wriggly and difficult to put on a hook. Many youngsters and older people were squeamish about baiting their own hooks and much preferred that someone else do it for them. The minnows are the same too and were the preferred bait for some kinds of fish.

Ma went with us the first times we fished in the creek in front of our house. She helped with baiting our hooks and getting the fish off the hook. We caught a few fish almost every time we went. Some of the kinds were sunfish, black sunfish, bluegills, perch and silversides.

Pa nearly always went to the mill and the store at Troy every Saturday afternoon. This was our regular fishing time, if Pa left no jobs of work for us to do while he was gone.

George and I found that if we got out of sight right after noon until Pa started to Troy, we were less likely to have a job left for us. We hid behind the garden fence or some other place within easy hearing distance, should we be called for any reason. I am sure Pa knew what we were doing.

As soon as Pa got out of sight, we dug our worms and with as many of our sisters as wanted to go, were on our way. We were 11 or 12 years old and big enough to look after ourselves and the younger ones who accompanied us. There was good fishing on both sides of the creek within sight of our house. Later we extended our efforts farther up and down the creek. Our catch varied from many to few, from large to small. Such is still the fisherman's luck.

We also went gigging at night which was done extensively then, but has since been outlawed. The gig had three, four or five prongs on a convenient length handle, 8 or 10 feet long. The light was made by burning a ball of rags that had been soaked in kerosene and fastened on the end of a green stick. Sometimes the light was carried on the end of a stick, in a basket. Pitch pine knots, split to convenient size, were burned in the wire basket and made good light. Split pine wood tied together in a faggot or bundle was another way to make a gigging light.

One or two men carried lights, one carried a bag for fish and another carried more oil-soaked balls or pine knots to replenish the light. All carried gigs with which to spear the fish. Clear water was necessary and, of course, fish. At spawning time many types were usually plentiful. People started gigging trips in the evening just after dark.

From the time I was two or three years old, this type fishing has been intriguing. Pa generally knew all who waded in our part of the creek. He frequently took his gig and fish poke and waded along with them for a short distance. He used their lights which they carried and no one seemed to care. I heard him tell Ma one time that he thought some of them were a little jealous because he got about as many fish as they did in the short distance he was with them. Pa was a good gigger.

Gigging continued an interesting and exciting experience for fun and food as we first walked along the road, just watching, and as we got big enough later to go with pa and the neighbors. We gradually increased the distance we fished to about two miles and at the last were taking a horse and sled to carry the extra supply of pitch pine-knot fuel for our lights.

Fish got scarcer and at last, this type of fishing was made illegal. Two other types of fishing, seining and dynamiting or blasting, have been illegal as long as I can remember. We never used these methods but a few people did.

76

"Those were very good fish stories, Grandpa. Do you think the fish in the stories have grown any since they were caught?"

"Now Joe, if you won't cast doubt on any of my fish stories, I will listen to yours and not measure your fish too carefully. Is that a deal?"

"It's a deal. If I could just have landed that last big one, I could have written a story about him."

"He's still out there, growing bigger and waiting for you. Did you ever think of it that way?"

"Would you like to know how to make a whistle? We used chestnut wood, but you could use willow or birch."

CHESTNUT WHISTLES

When the sap began to rise in the chestnut tree in the spring, we had a limitless source of material for making whistles, using the small sprouts and branches of that tree.
The period of time when conditions were right for making whistles lasted from a month to six weeks.

Take a smooth section of the tree limb ½ to 1 inch in diameter and 6 to 10 inches in length. Make a slanting cut on the end to put in the mouth. About one inch from that tip, on the long side of the tip, cut a slanting notch, with the square side of this notch toward the slanting tip end.

Next, about 3 inches farther from the mouth end, cut through the bark by drawing the knife blade completely around the section at that point. Now tap the bark gently with the knife handle, from the circular cut to the mouth end. Take hold, with one hand holding the un-pounded section and the other holding the mouth end. The bark on the pounded section should come off in one whole unbroken section when twisted gently but firmly. Lay this bark gently to one side.

Where the bark has been removed, cut the inch-long end completely through, by extending the straight edge of the notch through the wood. On the longest side of the mouthpiece, whittle to flatten the wood slightly. Then lay this piece beside the whole section of bark.

Now measure 1 inch from the unpeeled section and cut through the peeled end at this point. Discard the small piece. Replace the bark on the partly peeled section, insert the mouthpiece and blow! You should hear a clear-toned whistle. The tone and volume will depend on the size of the limb used, the length of the hollow part, the size of the notched hole in the bark and the flattened side of the mouthpiece. You can vary any of these for different musical results. Whistles made in this manner and carefully dried will last a long time.

Unfortunately chestnut trees have disappeared but other types of wood will serve the purpose, mainly birch, willow, soft maple and hickory. Here are some drawings that may help to explain these instructions.

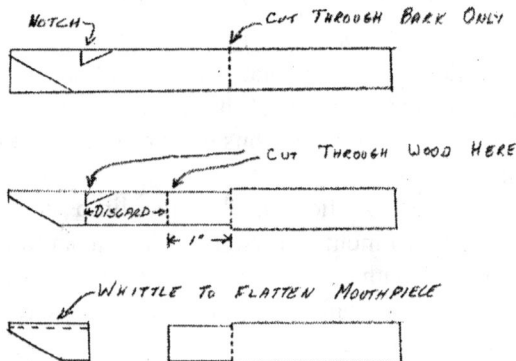

Chestnut Whistle

"I wonder if buckeye would work, Grandpa?"

"You could try it. Another that might be good for making whistles would be the horse chestnut. As soon as it gets warmer outside, we'll try some different kinds of wood."

- - - - - - - - - - - - - -

THE HUCKSTERS

"Remember the early spring peddlers I was telling you about the other day?"

"Yes, the one who left in such a hurry when you didn't buy anything."

"There was one who came who sold us many things and who bought our extra eggs and butter. That's where we got our red axes, but let me tell you more about it. . . ."

- - - - - - - - - - -

In early spring when the roads began to dry up so people could get over them with horses and wagons, we children, together with Pa and Ma would look forward to the time the huckster would start his weekly rounds once more. He used a canvas-covered, two-horse heavy spring wagon. He was sent out by one of the stores at Conings, a little town about 4 miles up the creek from home. His day's route began at Conings, went up Big Cove a little way, then crossed over the ridge to the head of Little Cove creek, down Little Cove to where it emptied into Big Cove, almost in sight of our house. After he stopped at our house, he went on up Big Cove back to Conings. The store had other routes for other days of the week.

The huckster wagon was loaded with a lot of store goods that they knew people along the route would buy. It had chicken crates, egg crates and butter barrels in which to haul these items that people might have to sell or exchange for store goods. If the huckster did not have with him everything people wanted, he would take orders and bring it with him the next trip. It was very convenient for the people along the route, as well as good business for the huckster and his store. It was like having the store come to your house every week.

In the course of the huckstering purchases, we got a sturdy red metal wagon which all of us children used. It was big enough for two to sit in comfortably and be pulled around by others. It was the source of a lot of fun and pleasure and, of course, arguments and disputes also. All were part of growing up.

After the Copley oilfield started up, some 7 or 8 miles away, the huckster said he could sell anything to eat there that he could get hold of. We had a row of big stalk rhubarb extending half-way across the garden which he was sure he could sell. He was making a special trip to buy such things to take directly to Copeley and we should have what we could spare ready for him early in the morning. The rhubarb stalks were 18 or 20 inches long. I can still remember the big bundles Pa and Ma had ready when he came. The price must have been all right since he made many of these buying trips that year. In the fall, we sold him several baskets of peaches.

On one trip, we had some fun about the pricing of sugar. It was 8 cts. a pound or three pounds for 25 cts. Ma asked him about this, thinking it should have been less in the larger package. It was a new man on the wagon and he would not change the price so Ma got her sugar at the special price of 3 pounds for 25 cts.

One day it was raining so much we were afraid the huckster would not get along before the creek got too deep for him to cross. He was a little late and when he came in sight at the lower end of the meadow, he had the canvas curtains pulled down all around his wagon except where he looked out to drive his horses. We put on our coats and went down to the road with Ma while she sold her eggs and bought coffee and sugar. What I remember most vividly was the wind and the rising water in the creek. Jerry Flesher was driving the wagon this time and said the water was almost into the wagon when he crossed at the mouth of Little Cove, just below our house. He had to ford the creek five more times to get back to Conings and knew he could not make it. Pa came down to the wagon at this time and he said the creek was 'out of ride' (too deep to cross) now and would be dangerous to try to ford with the wagon. Of course, we children were drinking in all this talk as we watched the deep muddy creek.

Jerry wanted to stay all night and it was decided that he could. He backed his wagon a little way so he could pull it into the barn lot. We had heard Pa tell of the creek getting over the whole bottom, even up into the yard in the big 'July Flood.' It did not get that high this time and next morning it was down enough that crossing was possible. Jerry hitched his horses to the wagon and drove out of the barn lot, onto the slick, muddy road on his way up Cove.

You can see that the huckster performed an interesting, useful and necessary service in our community that was not easily forgotten. On one trip he had an ax in his wagon which he kept for his own use. He could not sell it to us but said he had some just like it at the store and could bring them with him the next week. We persuaded Ma to order two, one for me and one for George. We said we could cut wood better with these axes than with the old hatchets we were using. And we needed two, one for each of us. We could scarcely wait till the axes would come.

After what seemed an interminable amount of waiting, the huckster and his wagon came again and with him, the two red-handled axes. Those axes were just the right size for us to do a lot of useful work with but many times, we couldn't tell the difference between fun and work. In fact, a lot of useful work was hard to separate from fun a great deal of the time!

- - - - - - - - - - - -

"Grandpa, how old were you when your folks got you the red axes?"

"I was about 8 years old and George was 7. That's why it was such a big thing in our lives, to have our own axes."

"The only time I ever used an ax was at Scout camp once. Our fireplace wood is always the right size. And Mom's afraid I'll cut off my toe!"

"Yes, we really used our axes. We couldn't wait to get started . . ."

- - - - - - - - - - - -

81

TWO RED AXES

What axes they were! We took them to the house with us after the huckster had gone on his way. Quickly we went around to the wood pile for something to chop. We chopped what was at hand, but how much fun it would be to chop down real trees, like Ben Frymier and the other lumbermen did. We had watched them cut trees and thought we knew all about how it was done.

We went out on the hillside in the pasture field in view of the house and picked out two we thought we would like to cut. Mine was a wild cherry tree, about 8 or 10 inches in diameter which was already leaning. George's was a smaller withy-top pignut hickory. We knew not to start cutting until we got permission. We asked Ma about the trees that afternoon but she said we had better talk to Pa about it when he came in from work that evening. I remember he said,

'You don't mean that big wide-topped cherry?'

'No, the one I want to cut is the smaller one you can see on the other side of the big one.'

'Can you cut it without any danger of it falling on you?'

'Yes, it already leans downhill.'

'All right. First cut a deep notch on the lower side. Then finish chopping from the back side. When it starts to fall, step back and away from it. Now, George, what about the one you want to cut?'

'It's that pignut hickory up the hill a little farther. We can push it down-hill.'

'You can try. If you need some help, wait until I come in and I'll help you.'

That's the way the conversation went, but the main thing was that we had his permission to cut the trees.

Our new axes were fine but we had found they were dull so we decided to sharpen them before beginning on the trees. We had turned the grindstone for Pa to sharpen his ax and we had watched how he held the ax on the stone. Ben and his son, Ray, had come over several times to sharpen their axes and we had watched them. We had heard him say his ax had to be sharp to cut timber. We were going to cut timber. The cutting edge of the ax was bright for about an inch. As we started grinding, we found the

82

stone changed the brightness where it touched the ax, just as it had for Pa and Ben. It took more time than we had expected to get the axes until they felt sharp.

We went out to our trees and decided how high to cut the stump and where to start out notches. We scarcely got started before Ma called to us from the house that dinner was ready and to come and eat. We had not been thinking of the time but realized when we heard her call that we were hungry, even though we hated to take the time to eat. I'm sure we took our axes to dinner with us.

We did not waste any time getting back to our timber-cutting after dinner. Our notches did not look as even as we had seen Pa and Ben cut theirs, neither did ours grow as fast as theirs. After chopping awhile, we paused to rest and compare notches every little while. Mine grew a little faster than George's and looked more like the ones Pa and Ben made. I tried to show George how but I did not have much better luck. He did not want me to work on his tree so I did not insist on helping. Along in the afternoon, we decided my notch was deep enough for me to start cutting on the back side. It was easier to cut on the upper side because the ground was not as steep. After awhile, we decided my tree ought to fall pretty soon. George watched while I chopped, to tell me when the tree started to fall. Even this took longer than we thought it should but soon he said it was shaking. Soon after that it went down with a crash. That was not as big a crash as when Pa and Ben cut trees but mine was not as big a tree.

George still did not want me to cut on his tree. We decided his hickory was harder to cut than my cherry and that it would be all right for him to cut all around the trunk, wherever it seemed easier. We got a pole to push his when it got ready to fall. I started trimming the limbs off my tree and threw them over the fence into the meadow so we could drag them into the woodlot to cut up for stove wood.

We worked all afternoon until we thought it was time for supper and besides we were tired enough to stop for the day. George had cut all around his tree and we could not even shake it when we pushed against it with the pole. We decided it would not fall on the cows if they came around. We would just leave it until tomorrow.

When Pa came in from work and found out how we had gotten along, he decided he would go out with us after supper and help get George's tree down. He said we had got along fine and agreed that the hickory was harder to cut than the cherry. It did not look hard as we watched him finish chopping while we pushed against it with the pole. George did not object to Pa helping fall his tree.

We continued chopping on our trees until we cut the trees into stove-length blocks and hauled them to the woodlot in the tin wagon and in wood wagons we had made. Splitting into stove-wood and all took us about a week. We could see from the house, the chips lying on the hillside where we had chopped our trees. These chips looked to us like regular timber men's chips and we felt important when some of the neighbors asked who had been doing all the chopping out there against the hill. I would not be surprised if cutting all that stove wood might not really be considered work, but we had a lot of fun doing it.

We did a lot of chopping, over the years, with those two red axes until they were supplanted with two brand new double-bit axes when we were 15 or 16 and started chopping the trees off a 6 acre clearing in Coon Holler.

- - - - - - - - - - - -

"What happened to your axes, Grandpa?"

"We sort of lost track of them for awhile. Mine had been used to mash coal before I decided to take care of it. It's out in the trunk of the car and is still usable. I'll give you some lessons on it tomorrow!"

"I wonder if Grandma would care if we chopped down her weeping willow. We'd better ask first."

- - - - - - - - - - - - - -

84

JACKSON ROCK PICNIC

"We had a favorite picnic place on the hill behind our house. 'Jackson Rocks' was about ☐ mile away."

"Why was it called 'Jackson Rock?' Who named it that?"

"We named it 'Jackson Rocks' because of an old family story about some of Stonewall Jackson's relatives. I'll tell you that story later but just now, I want you to hear about some things we did on picnics."

- - - - - - - - - - - - - - - - -

For several years we made a regular spring picnic trip to Jackson Rocks. These rocks consisted of a bold 15 or 20 foot high cliff about 100 feet long with 3 or 4 house-size boulders lying a little way below the main solid cliff. From the level wooded area above the cliff we could walk around either end to go down below where we could see the big boulders and look up at the cliff.

We usually laid our picnic dinner out on the gently sloping area above the cliff and well away from the edge. We were allowed to go and peep over the cliff only when Pa or Ma was with us. There was always a lot to do. There were small saplings to climb. Sometimes we could find a wild grapevine securely fastened to a limb or treetop in such a way that we could cut it loose at the ground and use it for a swing. Such a swing was not easy fun, since one had to hold on to the vine with his hands while swinging. This made it a restful wait while others took their turns. We made 'ridy horses' by bending a small sapling over and riding it, using the spring in the bent-over trunk to bounce up and down, giving a gentle push each time one came to the ground.

The 'ridy horses' really came to life quite by accident when Helen suddenly began screaming for help as she slid down to the ground from her 'horse' which reared on its hind leg for no apparent reason. She had given too hard a push which sent it straight into the air.

'That was fun,' she cried. 'My horse bucked and threw me off. Aunt Clemmie's colt bucked the other day and tried to throw her off but couldn't.'

The rest of us immediately started breaking wild colts just like we had seen them start breaking Aunt Clemmie's colt. Two had held it for the rider to get on. He had a hard time staying on at first. One or two of us held the small sapling down while the rider got on. Then we let loose and the horse reared into the air while the rider held on tightly. Sometimes we caught the horse and pulled him down so the rider could rearrange his seat, or re-mount if he had been thrown clear from his saddle.

By moving closer to the top, the tree-horse would not spring so far into the air. Sitting nearer the root caused him to rear the highest. With this control at the rider's command, interesting riding situations could be developed at will. These situations could just as quickly and unexpectedly get out of hand too. 'Ridy horses' provided almost endless opportunities and made a very interesting picnic pastime.

When we got through riding them, we took the bridles off our horses by pushing the bushes up as straight as we could, so they could eat grass and rest up and be ready for more fun the next time we came back.

Another activity not to be forgotten was gathering and chewing the young ground ivy (wintergreen) shoots which grew plentifully in the area. We always took a good supply home with us for future use.

Next it was time for us to search for the old silver-melting pot and silver which was said to have been hidden among these big rocks by Cummins Jackson on his way out of this part of the country. He was fleeing from Jackson's Mill, where the law had gotten after him for counterfeiting money, so the story goes. That was the reason we had named them Jackson Rocks.

We all went below the cliff to look up at it and to look back under the many overhanging portions. On our first such trip, Pa slipped away and climbed up behind a big rock that had fallen out three or four feet from the face of the cliff. Suddenly, he yelled.

'Boo!' Then each of us had to be assisted up to that spot which was also a good place to look for the silver-melting pot and treasure. We looked in several likely places that trip and on many more trips that followed but we never found anything. It was always an intriguing treasure hunt.

On one trip, we got caught in a quick thunderstorm and had to take shelter under the edge of one of the big rocks that extended

86

out far enough for all of us to get under. We had plenty of room to stand and sit in comfort. It was a pleasant view to watch the rain from our dry, comfortable viewpoint.

These picnics were always something to look forward to but it was a relaxing comforting feeling to get back in sight of home on our way back in the evening.

- - - - - - - - - - - - - - -

"Grandpa, you never told us about any counterfeiters. We'd like to hear about them."

"That's a long story which I would rather put off until some other time."

"And if you never found the treasure, then it must still be there. Do you suppose we could go and look for it some time?"

"We'd have to ask permission because someone else owns that farm now. I'd like to tell you about all the different kinds of berries we used to pick in the spring. And about strawberry shortcakes. . . . "

- - - - - - - - - - - - - - -

BERRY PICKING

It was always a springtime mouth-watering activity, looking for ripening berries of both wild and tame varieties. The serviceberries on the bushes across the creek along the bluff were among the earliest to ripen. These red berries helped satisfy a ready appetite as they were picked from the limbs. Sometimes an extra supply could be accumulated in a cup or bucket to take home to other members of the family for their enjoyment. I don't recall that these berries were ever considered of much value for table use.

We had both red and white wild strawberries that some years were too plentiful for all to be eaten while picking them and were available for table use.

Our tame red strawberries were quite a different matter. Ma made strawberry cobblers big enough for a whole meal for our family. When served with cream and sugar, these cobblers were hard to beat. Strawberry shortcake was freely used as a dessert and was never refused by anyone. Many of the strawberries were made into preserves or canned for later use. Again, the care and picking of strawberries was really work, yet it was also a home pastime that contributed fun and enjoyment also.

In my haste to satisfy my appetite and enjoy the early spring berries, I nearly forgot to tell you of the numerous sprinkling throughout the forest of beautiful dogwood and redbud trees. Their beauty, when in full bloom, apparently had no other use than to announce the arrival of spring. Other equally beautiful spring blossoms crowding upon us in profusion, simultaneously and in quick succession, were the 'sarvice' (serviceberry,) wild crabapple, wild plum, pear, peach and the other orchard trees, not to forget the white bloom of the chestnut tree. All these vied with one another for prominent places in the spring blossom festival that burst upon us as they reminded us of the wonderful things there would be for us to eat later in the year.

We cooked green apples so soon after the blossoms fell off in the spring that we called them our cooked 'apple blossoms.' Although they were small and green, they had a refreshing taste. By that time of year, the apples we had buried in the ground to use all winter, always had an earthy taste. New apples were welcome.

This spring blossom festival gave us a preview of what to expect during the summer and where to look for each variety. You can be sure we kept close watch on the development of the fruit during the summer and took advantage of each variety as it became available.   Of all the varieties, probably blackberry picking is the best remembered.

Blackberry picking came with the hot part of the summer when the extra clothing worn by many pickers made it even hotter. As protection against briars, clothing was worn that covered all the body except the hands and face. Younger children, 3 or 9 years old were often allowed to pick and eat in open areas where the berries were easy to pick and where there was little danger of snakes. As a protection against snakes, all, boys and girls alike, wore long pants tied around the shoe tops so as to flare out just above where tied. This loose clothing helped keep the snake from getting to the legs which were the most exposed part.

The clothing was some protection from the briars. We soon found that we could easily push into the briars but when we tried to back off, the briars hooked into the clothing and held fast, then pulled through the clothing and into our skin. The more we tried to back out, the deeper the briars sank in. We had to get help to get loose the first time but we soon learned how to keep from getting stuck so tightly thereafter. Some used leather half-handers or old stockings with the toes cut out which they pulled over hands and arms for added protection.

The chigger, or 'jigger,' and the common wood tick are no respecters of extra clothing but usually had to be given extra attention after getting back from picking. For chiggers, we washed with strong yellow soap and rinsed with soda water, then put on clean clothes. We just pulled the wood ticks off until we found that the head occasionally pulled off and was left sticking in the skin, causing inflammation and infection. By applying a little turpentine to the tick before trying to remove it, we found it would let loose easily and avoid any later trouble from infection.

Wild raspberries were set out and cultivated by themselves or along with the tame ones. Grown either way, they were abundant producers of delicious berries for table use and for canning, preserving and making jelly.

We depended entirely for blackberries on uncultivated types that were left in the wild state in patches throughout the pasture fields. Berries had to be picked every day or two during the ripening period which lasted for 2 or 3 weeks. Picking was usually done before noon by the whole family, the ones who were big enough and could be spared from the housework. The canning and working up the berries occupied the afternoon. Sometimes, the men picked in the afternoon, if they were not needed in the canning or preserving.

- - - - - - - - - - - - -

"Berry picking sounds like fun except for the part about snakes. How many could you pick in one day? And what did you do with so many berries?"

"The amount we could pick depended on how many of us helped and how big we were. There was one year we picked 40 gallons in a day. Let me tell you about it."

- - - - - - - - - - - - -

89

It was an extra good year for berries. Pa came home from Troy telling us about hearing Bill Carr brag about his family's berry picking. There were 10 or 12 almost- grown people in his family and Bill said,

'We went out Monday, picked 40 gallons and canned them. Again on Wednesday we picked 40 gallon and canned them too!'

We all agreed that he must have been blowing. And yet berries were well developed and plentiful that year. We wondered how many we could pick on Monday which would be our best picking day. About 6 of us started early and by noon we had nearly 30 gallon. George and I decided we could easily pick enough to finish out 40 gallon that afternoon and still get back in time to help with the cleaning and canning. We did not get them all canned that day, as Bill Carr's family had, but we got many of them canned and the rest cooked so none would spoil before we could finish them the next day. It was really too much for one day. We excused our family by saying that Carrs had more and bigger people than we had or perhaps he was bragging, as we had thought in the first place.

Berries shrink about half, or more, in canning from the amount measured as picked. People in our neighborhood depended on home-grown and home-canned or dried fruits to last them through the year. In seasons when the crop was good, we canned extra amounts so some would be left in case the next year did not have such a good year. As you can readily see, it took a lot of everything to last a big family a whole year without getting anything from the store.

- - - - - - - - - - - - - - - -

"I guess that's another time where fun and work got all mixed up, picking those blackberries, wasn't it?"

"Yes. We used our old mare, Molly, for much hard work. But sometimes we had fun with her too. . . ."

- - - - - - - - - - - - - - -

THE RIDE TO GRANDPA'S HOUSE

After we got big enough to ride old Molly safely, it was decided by Ma and Pa that we four oldest children might ride up to Grandpa Lewis' farm at the head of Crane Run, a distance of 7 miles. Not all of us at one time, of course, but two at a time. George and Eunice rode up and back one Sunday without any trouble. A week or two later, Lois and I took our turn.

It was the last of June or the early part of July and the weather was hot for the time of year. We started early one Sunday morning and were to come home well before dark. It was a pleasant morning and the shade along the road made the ride more enjoyable. We stopped to watch the martins at Burtons while Molly got her breath. Their martin house had 12 or 14 spaces and martins were going in and out of all of them. We thought it was beautiful to hear the twittering of the birds and to see the ever coming and going of the old birds as they fed their young.

After a few minutes we hastened on since we wanted to have as much time as possible at Grandpa's. We got to the first gate across the road at Keisters and were able to open it, go through and close it after us, without either of us having to get off. The road was open and fenced on both sides up to this first gate but from there on, the roadway was definitely laid out through the farms. It had been graded enough for a wagon or buggy to get over it but the farmers were not required to fence it to keep their stock in. The gate in each line fence kept the stock on each farm without fencing the road. At one of the next two gates, we had to get off and at the last one, Aunt Edna met us and opened the gate for us. From there, it was only about a hundred feet to Grandpa's house. They thought we were lucky to open and close two of the gates without getting off. We took the saddle off Molly and let her loose in the barn lot to eat grass and rest in the shade.

There were many interesting things to see and do, as always, on our visits to their house. Aunt Clemmie and Aunt Edna had a good dinner, as usual. They fried chicken, but what I always remember are the biscuits and chicken gravy.

The time passed all too rapidly. About the middle of the afternoon, we saw a thin light-looking cloud extending across the north-western horizon as far as we could see in both directions, but we could hear no thunder. Grandpa said that kind of a cloud was sure to bring a big rain, since it was so hot and still. We thought we should start home at once and get there before the storm arrived and before there was any danger of Big Cove Creek rising so we could not cross it safely. Grandpa thought we would have plenty of time since the storm was a long way off and that kind of storm usually came up slowly.

We saddled Molly and started at once, with Aunt Edna opening the first gate. At the other gates I jumped off and opened and closed them while Lois rode Molly through. It was much faster that way. We were about a mile on our way when we went through the last gate. The cloud was a little higher in the northwest, but the sun was still shining brightly. We rode on, knowing there was no danger of rain as long as the sun was shining, when the storm was coming from that direction. The temptation was great to hurry Molly along but we knew it was too hot for that, so we let her take her own time. Whether she knew she was going home or sensed the coming storm, in any event, we were pleased that she was stepping along at a pretty good pace.

As we passed Burton's martin box, they appeared even more active than that morning, if that were possible. This time we did not stop to watch them. The sun was still hot and bright but the cloud was higher. When we crossed Big Cove the first time we were a little over half-way home. By the time we got to our schoolhouse, the cloud appeared much higher and began to appear darker down near the horizon. It was now only 1 ½ miles home. Even if we got wet before getting home, we now felt sure we would get there before Big Cove started rising and got too deep to cross. It always rose rapidly after a heavy rain. As we crossed the creek the second time at John Flesher's, small clouds began drifting across the sun which eased the heat a little. Molly was beginning to dampen with sweat, even when she was taking her own time.

As we crossed Big Cove the third time at the mouth of Big Run, the sun was completely hid behind the clouds. As we continued along above the meadow toward our fourth and final crossing at the upper end of our meadow in sight of home, we could see a little clear sky in that direction.

We came to the upper end of a huge logjam which had been left in the creek by a former rise. This jam extended for 300 or 400 yards along Cove Creek. The timbermen had used a team of five yoke of oxen to haul the logs out of the ford so people could cross with wagons. They had also hauled out some of the key logs which had caused the jam so that the logs could be floated when the next rise came. They were sure they would have a lot of work to do to get the whole jam broken loose and floating again. There were probably as many as a thousand or more logs in the jam. It was the biggest one I ever saw in Big Cove Creek.

The logjam did not bother us. We just rode across in the space where they had cleared of logs and were almost in sight of home, at the other end of the meadow. In the meantime, we looked back at the ever-darkening cloud and the bright lightning area, now accompanied by the increasing rumble of thunder. We watched the clear sky gradually disappear in front of us as the dark wind clouds blew across overhead. Behind us, beyond the wind clouds, we could see the front line of the smooth lighter cloud where the rain was following us. It was going to be a close race. Molly was wet with sweat when we rode into the barn lot, just as the big drops began to fall. I took Molly into the barn, took off her saddle and bridle, and left her loose inside the barn so she would not get chilled in the rain while she was wet with sweat.

I ran to the house soon after Lois got there and none too soon, as the big drops were followed with a downpour accompanied by bright lightning and sharp rolling thunder. All were glad and relieved that we had beaten the storm. It continued unabated for an hour, and then was followed by another and another, one after the other, with little distinguishable difference in severity until long after dark.

- - - - - - - - - - - -

"But Grandpa, what happened to the logjam? All that rain must have been just what the loggers were waiting for."

"Any rain made Big Cove rise rapidly, as the water came down off the hills. And yes, this one was just what the loggers wanted."

- - - - - - - - - - - -

93

THE LOG JAM

The creek began rising rapidly by dark and soon after, we could hear logs bumping one another. We knew the logs that had been hauled from the jam had started to float past. The water was not yet deep enough to start the main jam moving. The water kept rising and it kept raining hard but not quite as fast as at the beginning of the storm. There were scarcely breaks enough to get out to the barn lot to look at the rising creek by the light of the flashes of lightning. Everyone was excited about the storm and stayed awake late.

Just before midnight, we heard logs bumping against each other, getting louder and louder, merging into a constant bumping roar all along in front of our house. We knew the logjam had broken loose by itself from the sheer force and height of the water. By the time the heavy log bumping had passed and only occasional bumping logs were floating by, the water was up across the road and running into the barn lot. Molly had dried off by this time and we turned her loose in the pasture well away from the high water. We did not know how high it might get. It was not rising as fast by that time. We could scarcely wait until daybreak to see what all had happened.

At daybreak, we saw two men carrying cant hooks, go around the flat above the house and continue out of sight up Cove. They were going up to the tramway log dump opposite the schoolhouse to help get the remainder of the logs rolled into the creek. The logging companies paid 25 cents an hour for drifters who had to work at unusual hours when the water was high enough to float the logs. A lot of wading was also necessary.

The creek had run down out of the stable lot and down out of the road. It was still out of its banks and several logs were still floating past. This indicated that more logs were being rolled into the creek and others loosened up so they would float away. George and I put on our long rubber coats and went along up the creek inside the meadow to see what had happened to the big logjam. It had been washed away completely, as we expected. The large sycamore trees, 12 to 18 inches in diameter which had been holding the big jam, were turned out by the roots and ridden down by the logs as the jam broke loose in the high water which carried everything before it. What a sight that must have been!

Even though the creek was lower than it had been, more logs were going past, showing that the drifters were still busy rolling more logs into the creek upstream. We started slowly back toward the house inside the fence, when suddenly one of the logs hit a tree in the edge of the water. Other logs bumped into it, driving one end farther up the bank behind the tree. The other end hit the bottom and caused a new logjam. The on-coming logs began piling up behind the crosswise logs and the jam kept growing as more and more piled up against it. George and I stopped to watch. We couldn't miss seeing this!

These were not ordinary logs. They had been cut from a virgin forest of some 12,000 to 15,000 acres and ranged in diameter up to 4 or 5 feet. The biggest tree was a poplar slightly over 6 feet in diameter. The bark had been peeled, or rossed, off all these logs at the time they were felled in the forest to make them smooth to handle from there on. Each log consisted of the usable part of each tree as cut in the forest. Thus the logs were of all lengths up to 60 and 70 feet, all of which made logjams frequent.

We watched the logjam grow. But it was not long before some drifters came and began rolling logs off the front of the jam, trying to loosen it so it would float out. It moved forward a little, but tightened up without moving much. While 5 or 6 men were trying to roll a long log, one man slipped and fell through a hole between the logs. The water pulled him out of sight under the jam. We wondered if he would get caught between the logs or would be pulled between the logs, through the jam and come up down-stream. This was his only chance. We thought he was under too long and noticed his brother's face was pale. Just then the man bobbed up, 25 or 40 yards down stream from the jam. A gasp of relief went up from all, as he began swimming toward the bank. Two or three rushed down and caught his hand, pulling him free of the water.

When everyone was sure the man had not been hurt, and was in no danger, they further examined the jam. They did no more rolling logs but began cutting the end off the first log that had been forced behind the tree. This seemed to be the key to loosening the jam. Everyone wanted to take a turn at chopping in the beginning but as the final cutting came, no one was rushing in to finish. Cautiously the final strokes were made. The logs let loose, and the man who finished the cut had to jump from log to log to get safely to the bank. With very little additional work, the entire logjam floated down the creek, out of sight, bumping and grinding all the way.

Two large logs were rolled off the creek bank and two men got on each log to ride down the creek to look for more jams farther on. They gouged the points of their cant hooks into the logs to keep them from rolling and then stood, riding out of sight. The other men said they would rather walk along the bank than try to ride logs.

This sort of periodic work and excitement continued for several years while the timber lasted and provided all of us with interesting topics for conversation.

- - - - - - - - - - -

"I don't think I'd want to try riding logs, Grandpa. Your creek must have been big enough for boats, wasn't it? Boats are fun!"

"Yes, most of the time the creek was big enough for boats. I think you'd like to hear about the boat that George and I made. We'd been watching the lumbermen and their boat. We wondered if we could make one by ourselves . . . . . "

- - - - - - - - - - -

BOATING ON BIG COVE

Not too long after the logjam I told you about the other day, the timber company decided to clean up the channel of Cove Creek from the tramway unloading area opposite our schoolhouse to the mouth of Big Cove where it empties into Leading Creek, because they were having so much trouble with logjams in floating their big long logs to market. They expected their logging job to last two years. They talked to Pa about cutting the trees that lined the creek along our place and also got whatever additional permits they needed farther down the creek.

They began at the tramway and worked down stream. We children did whatever farm work and chores we had to do and then

96

watched with interest, the tree chopping as they worked along the creek past our farm. About ten men were working in this operation but the thing that became of major interest to us was a beautifully-built, painted boat they were using. It had two oars with oar locks and a paddle to steer and row when the oars could not be used. By using the boat, they could trim and cut up trees that fell into water that was too deep to wade with their rubber boots. This kept them from having to pay wading wages, 25 cents an hour. The boat handled so easily and glided here and there so effortlessly as we watched them using it. When they finished using it in deep water, they took it a little way below where they were working and tied it to a stump.

Since it was far enough from where they were working for us to be in no danger from any falling trees, we went out to the creek bank to look at the boat more closely. That wasn't close enough. We wanted to get in it. We asked the man who seemed to be the boss and he said we could. He wanted to know if we could handle or row it. We told him we did not have a boat and had never tried but we would leave it tied so it would not get away. He said for us to be careful and not fall out.

George and I tied the rope securely to the stump before getting into the boat. It tipped from side to side easily and was more difficult to stand in than it had appeared to us, when the men were in it. It did not go where we wanted it to go without considerable work. When we used both oars and one guided, this was not easy either, when it had appeared so easy as we watched. We pushed and paddled for some time until it became easier to move in the direction we wanted to go. It was well the rope had been tied to the stump or we would have drifted down stream and perhaps had trouble getting back. The rope was long enough to give us all the room we needed to practice in. An idea struck us!

'Would you sell us this boat?' we asked.

'Oh no, we can't get along without it,' the boss replied.

This was a disappointment but perhaps was a good thing for we were not sure how we would be able to pay for it anyway. And maybe we couldn't have talked Pa and Ma into buying it. It was a good idea even though it did not get anywhere. The boss said they would have to leave the boat tied overnight since they had no way to take it home with them that night. He said it would be all right for us to get in it and row it around that evening as we had been doing. They left the boat and went home.

After supper we came back together with 2 or 3 of our sisters and all of us got into the boat. It could easily carry all of us. The men had tied the boat to a tree with a chain and padlock so it could not be untied. The chain was not nearly as long as the rope had been, although it gave us enough room to push and paddle around rather freely. We had a lot of fun with the boat but by dark, we were all tired enough to go to the house and get in bed without much urging.

The men came back the next day and moved the boat on down stream as they continued their work. In addition to cutting the trees along the creek, they blasted out 3 or 4 big rocks that had been causing logjams on small floating tides. This creek work did cut down the number of log jams however there were always enough to be interesting and enough to provide work for a lot of men. It was the best paying work to be had even though it was dangerous and involved a lot of physical exposure to all weather conditions.

One of our neighbors had a roughly-built johnboat made of rough-sawn lumber. He used it for crossing the creek when the water was high. It worked all right but it was not as large nor was it as beautiful as the boat we had just fallen in love with and which had just as quickly passed from our lives. Why couldn't we build a boat at least as good as our neighbor had? We needed a boat to get across the creek to school. There was plenty of water in which to use one and it would be fun too. We had more than enough reasons for having a boat but how could we get it?

What about a canoe? Pa had told us many times about an old canoe that his dad had made for use around the dam and sawmill they operated for a long time just across the creek about a hundred yards below where we lived. This had been no ordinary canoe as the ones you see around Indian Lake now.

They started with a huge poplar log about 16 feet long. After deciding what position they wanted the log to sit as a finished canoe, they flattened the bottom and shaped it to suit them. Their ax and broad-ax were the tools used to cut and hew it properly. Next, the log was turned over on the bottom so they could chop enough off the top to give the canoe the proper width. They then shaped the prow (front end) and bow (rear end) to suit their liking.

Next, the inside of the log was hollowed out to the desired depth, length and width, considering the size of the log they were using. Pa said the old canoe would carry a pretty big load but was wobbly and hard to stand up in. It was quite a game to see who could tip the other into the water when one stood on one end and another on the opposite end. Since nearly everyone got dunked in this game, it was usually a warm weather game.

Pa said that one spring they were about out of feed in the barn and the creek was up too much to haul oats from across the creek. They took the canoe up near the oats stack and carried and loaded it full of sheaf oats. There was room to stand on either end. Pa was standing on the front end to help guide the canoe while the others were on the oats and on the back end. They started down toward home. The weight of the load and the current soon got them going pretty fast. Where the ford crossed the creek, stakes had been driven on each side so people could see where to ride across in shallow water. When they came to the ford, Pa looked down directly in front of the canoe and saw one of those stakes just tipping the surface of the water. There was no time to guide the canoe to one side, no time to balance against the bump and nothing to catch hold of. The stake shoved the canoe quickly to one side and Pa was thrown into the water. He grabbed the edge of the canoe as he went overboard and was carried forward a good way before he could get back on. He said he never felt water colder, probably because he had just gotten over the fever.

Instead of going directly to the house and putting on dry clothes, he helped unload the oats first. He began chilling that night and took a relapse on the pneumonia fever. This was always a dangerous disease since it could change for the worse so quickly. This was over 100 years ago and modern treatment was unknown.

Pa was out of his head part of the time. His Pa and Ma began applying home remedies immediately which probably kept him from getting as bad as he might have if the treatments had not been started at once. Pa says that the treatment he remembered most vividly and that marked the turning point, was when his mother gave him a dose of hot pennyroyal tea with a little sugar in it. His ma said,

'Now Tom, take this and go to sleep! It'll help you.'

'Sometime that night,' Pa told us, 'I waked up feeling so good. I noticed the light from the fire flickering in the dark. I 'm not dreaming, I thought, this is real! I'm not sure if I called to Mother at once or if I just lay there feeling good until she came in to see about me. She was pleased that I was feeling better. The fever had broken and I continued feeling better and was soon up and around again. I shall never forget that dose of hot pennyroyal tea that my mother gave me that evening and how good it made me feel.'

- - - - - - - - - - - - - -

"But, Grandpa, why didn't they get a doctor for him?"

"This happened a long time ago, about 1870 when Pa was about 18 years old. Doctors were scarce and people depended almost entirely on their home remedies and home care to treat and cure illnesses."

"They wouldn't have had the miracle drugs then either. But you were telling us about the boat you and Great Uncle George built. Did you build a canoe like that big one your Pa fell out of?"

"We thought about it, but all we knew about how to build it is just what I've told you. . . ."

- - - - - - - - - - - - - -

THE JOHNBOAT

That type canoe would require a good big poplar log at least 16 feet long. We could not find, or think of, such a tree on our farm and surely none near the creek. The big timber had been sold off our farm several years before. Besides, if we could find such a tree and get it shaped and dug out, it would be heavy and wobbly. A canoe was out of the question.

A boat like the one the timbermen used would require more skill and better prepared lumber than we could muster for the job. So that was out.

But a johnboat similar to the one our neighbor had? That was possible! The construction was simple; at least we thought it was. We looked it over carefully in order to plan our boat. The stern

100

(back end) was turned up a little on the bottom and the gunwales (side boards,) besides being sloped up to form the bottom, were pulled in a little more at the stern than at the beam (middle) thus making the stern almost square. At the front end, the gunwales were sloped from a little farther back and a little higher at the extreme front end than at the stern. The two ends were pulled much nearer together than in the middle, thus giving the bow a better shape to go through the water. This type boat was not reversible and had to be propelled forward most of the time.

The beam board was cut at an angle on each end so as to give the gunwales an outward slope, wider at the top than at the bottom. The stern board was cut to fit the stern gunwales as bent into position. The bow board was also cut to fit the bow end of the gunwales when bent into position. When the bow and stern boards were securely fastened in place, the boat was ready to turn upside down and put the bottom on. With both gunwales evenly bent and secured, the edges were planed so that when the bottom was nailed on, it would fit closely over the entire edge.

Now that we had figured out what kind of boat to build, and how to do it, the next thing was to get the material with which to do the job.

Pa had a pile of oak and poplar lumber in a shed behind the barn which was our best place to look for lumber that was immediately available. We knew that the two hard pieces to find would be the two white oak boards to make the gunwales. We measured the width of the boards at the end of the pile and found two we thought would be about the right width, about 14 inches. Then we had to get them out of the pile and see if they were good the full length. Several boards had to be moved to get the two out. One was a fine board without a knot or crack. The other was a heart board with a crack from end to end. We saw 2 or 3 more boards the right width but deeper down in the pile. We wondered if we could get down to them without upsetting the pile. Since it did not look much like it would rain and wet the lumber we were moving out of the shed to get at the boards we wanted, we got to work. The first wide board was no better than the bad one we already had. In fact it was a perfect match, crack and all. What about the one deeper down? It was much better but not quite as good as the good one we had. We examined it closely and decided it would do. The defect was a tight twisty knot which we felt sure would not crack or split in bending or when put in the water.

We piled the boards back into the pile, putting the boards we wanted to use on top. I am sure we had asked Pa for permission to look for the boards and I am equally sure we had been told to pile the boards back as good as we had found them. I am just as sure that this must have been a Saturday afternoon when Pa went to the mill at Troy. At that time, we were 11 and 12 years old and almost able to do a man's work at hoeing corn and other farm work.

We got permission to use the lumber in trying to make a johnboat. Pa was a little skeptical about our ability to do the work but Ma was more encouraging. We probably were a little doubtful of our abilities ourselves, but not enough to dampen our eagerness to get started.

George and I started on our boat as soon as we were through whatever farm work was being done at that time. The regular farm tasks always took precedence over any other work that was not absolutely necessary. We planed the lumber by hand, taking off most of the sawmill marks so we could paint the boat when it was completed. We followed the general plan of our neighbor's boat. The bottom edges of the gunwales and edges of the bottom boards were painted, lined with strips of heavy burlap and lightly daubed with roofing tar as they were nailed in place. The bottom, of straight-grained poplar, was securely nailed to the white oak gunwales with care. We saw that each nail penetrated as near the center as possible and certainly with no nail splitting out on either side. Such a nail was pulled out, repositioned and driven correctly.

A coat or two of paint was applied before putting it into the water to make the boat look better, as well as to help it withstand the weather and the water.

We made oars from narrow boards and shaped them as nearly as possible the same as those we had used in the timbermen's boat. We fastened cleats on each gunwale, instead of regular oarlocks, in such a way that they took the place of oarlocks.

The launching day finally came. Would it float? It did, but we saw water seeping in through many cracks between the bottom boards. We expected this for awhile, until the boards swelled tightly together. The water could easily be kept dipped out with a dipping pan so we got in and began maneuvering the boat about in the water. It would easily carry 4 or 5 of us and was even more stable in the water than the timbermen's boat that we had liked so well. Our makeshift oarlocks worked all right and so did the oars and guiding paddle. Not perfectly, of course, but they worked. We untied the boat and ventured out into the water, confident of our ability to get back. After all, we could wade and pull, or push, it back if we needed to.

We had a boat! What a boat! Our sisters and Pa and Ma were as excited as George and I. All of them had to take a ride even though it was necessary to push it with the oars and a long stick at times to get it to go the way we wanted to go. This boat did not glide about under our unskilled hands any better than did the timbermen's boat. This awkward handling was improved by all of us, and in time, the girls and Ma could easily, safely and confidently cross the creek or go for a ride by themselves under ordinary water conditions. George and I developed our boatmanship until we felt safe to cross the creek, even in high water, when necessary. George, Pa and I have crossed in extremely high raises, when the midstream current was swift and developed swirling eddies and rolling, boiling waves. These currents were very dangerous. We avoided such water whenever possible as a matter of ordinary safety.

The backwater in big floods was safe enough, especially in the meadow where it was not very deep. We frequently rowed about in such water. The expanse of water was so big then that it gave us a feeling of helplessness which took away some of the desire for such backwater boating. Our boat enabled us to cross the creek safely and attend school regularly, which sometimes had been impossible.

George and I had a satisfied feeling of accomplishment in this boat-building venture which I am sure was shared by all the family, since all shared in its usefulness.

About 2 or 3 years later we decided to get out lumber for replacing this boat when it became necessary. We wanted thicker gunwales so there would be better nailing space on the bottom edge that would hold the bottom more securely. We also decided that wider and longer gunwales would be better. After some inquiries, we decided on a length of 16 feet, by at least 16 inches

103

in width, and at least 1 ¼ inches thick at the bottom edge and one inch at the top edge.

We would have no trouble getting good poplar lumber for the boat bottom since we were having lumber sawed for general use about the farm and much of it was poplar, oak and pine. But to find the big oak boards required for the gunwales presented a different problem. This required a white oak log 16 feet long and big enough to cut boards 16 inches wide. We found two trees big enough and long enough but this did not entirely solve the problem. The logs could be skidded downhill, to a haul-road that ran along the edge of the creek to the sawmill. We had two yoke of oxen we were using to haul the lighter logs to the mill but these were bigger and heavier logs. Could they pull these?

As it turned out, this was needless worry. Our two yoke of oxen performed beautifully. One wet rainy morning, they pulled the two big logs over the wet slippery log road with apparent ease. Without the wetness, I doubt if they could have done so.

When they sawed into the logs, one of them had wind shake cracks in it and was cut into other lumber. We got 4 or 5 good boards from the other log which would certainly furnish at least the two good ones we needed, after drying.

We built our new boat about two years later and followed the same general procedures as we did in building the first one, except that we built it reversible, so it could be propelled with either end forward. This made it a little easier to handle. It was not a true johnboat, since neither end was square. We discarded the old boat and used the new one for several years.

- - - - - - - - - - -

"I have a picture of your Grandma taken in this boat before we were married. I'll show it to you as soon as I get it located."

"We have never built a boat but Uncle David's family built a sailboat. Maybe they inherited their boat-building ability from you."

"When I looked at the picture of your Grandma in our second boat, it doesn't look nearly as impressive now as it did to us at the time we finished making it. And you are used to seeing much bigger boats at the lake. But to us, it was a wonderful boat!"

104

"Grandpa, you say you used two yoke of oxen to haul the logs to the sawmill. You haven't told us anything about them at all."

- - - - - - - - - - - - - -

THE OX TEAM

Oxen were used extensively in our part of West Virginia to do nearly all kinds of farm work such as plowing, mowing and hauling hay, fodder, corn, wheat, firewood, coal and oil-field supplies. In fact, they were used for anything that needed moving from one place to another. They were also used in all sorts of logging jobs, getting logs out of the woods to the sawmills and to the creeks for floating to market.

At the time, we were growing up, several big logging jobs were going on at various locations and it was common to see teams of oxen composed of one or more yoke, up to as many as 6 and 8 yoke in one team. The 6 and 8 yoke teams were the most exciting to watch, as well as to see the size of the logs and other loads such teams were able to pull. Even more exciting than the team itself, was the driver who controlled such a team and directed it where he wanted it to pull the load. The driver always used a heavy leather whip, which was a braided leather strap that tapered from an inch or inch and a half to the size of a lead pencil at the small end. At the tip there was a slit, or small loop, for attaching a twisted sea-grass cracker, which needed frequent replacement, since it was the point of most wear. These leather whips were from 8 to 12 feet in length. Each was secured at the big end, by a rawhide thong, to a tough hickory handle, 3 or 4 feet long, or of a length that best suited the driver.

A skillful driver could crack this whip, making a sharp noise like the firing of a twelve gauge shotgun. This was used to get the team's attention and to tell it to get to pulling or to pull harder. It was also a threat to a lagging steer to get to work, or he might get a sharp silent stroke from the whip. It got results. A good driver trained his team to do what he wanted with as little use of the whip on the animals as possible, although he did not hesitate to apply it as needed. However there was no limit to the shouting, bellering, whip-cracking, swinging, waving and threatening motions used to get the work done. This was prestige status, such as a race car and driver at the Indianapolis Five Hundred, or a speed car and driver at Daytona Beach. It was status standing similar to owning and driving a Lincoln, Cadillac, Rolls Royce or Mercedes.

This ox team driver could be heard for miles. When two or three teams were working in a neighborhood, there was little need for an alarm clock to tell when it was time to begin work, eat dinner or when it was quitting time.

With this sort of work going on in a big way, it was no wonder that the neighborhood boys got busy breaking steer calves to learn to wear yokes and pull loads so they could grow into bigger and more useful teams. It was like learning to drive a car or to water ski now days.

There were four or five families in our school district in which the boys were actively breaking calves for oxen. In one family the two boys, with their father's help, were breaking three yoke of calves. The father was planning for a sawmill set, in about four years, to have lumber sawed for a new house. He was sure the calves would make a good team by that time, with which to haul the logs to the mill. The boys in another family were breaking two yoke while, in the other family, the boy was trying to break one yoke. There was certainly something wrong with any boy not breaking calves!

We had no plans to cut lumber for a new house but we could see the immediate and continued use for oxen in our farm work, as a good reason for breaking calves. However the fun of the job would have been reason enough in itself. There were only two steer calves that year among our 8 or 9 calves. These two were enough for one yoke and that let us into the ox-breaking business.

- - - - - - - - - - - - - -

"I don't think I exactly know what a yoke of oxen is, Grandpa."

"I'm sorry, I guess I haven't been too clear about that, have I? A yoke of oxen is two steer cattle yoked together at their necks so they can be trained to do pulling or hauling work. Ox yokes are treated as antiques now."

"If it's big wooden thing, then I saw one in a restaurant the other day. We wondered what it was for."

"You can also see them where old furniture and farm equipment is on display. I have made a drawing of an ox yoke so you will understand it better. It works like this. . . . "

- - - - - - - - - - - - - -

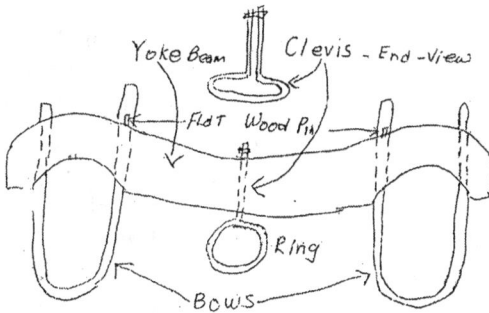

Ox Yoke

TRAINING OUR OX TEAM

The yoke is a heavy irregular piece of wood with a big iron ring hanging down in the middle and a large wooden bow stuck up through the piece of wood near each end. To put the yoke on the oxen, remove the wooden bow from one end of the yoke. This wooden piece has been shaped between the ends and smoothed off roundly with no sharp edges or corners, making it fit the top part of the ox's neck just in front of its shoulders.
Next put the open end of the bow under the ox's neck and bring it up around his neck through the two holes in the yoke, one to either side of his neck. Bring the bow up through the yoke far enough to put the notched flat wooden pin back through the hole in the bow from which you removed it, when taking the bow from the yoke. This ox is now yoked. You will see that the pin will not come out of the bow until the bow is lifted enough to clear the notch in the flat wooden pin. You will have to do this when you wish to take

107

the yoke off at quitting time. Now remove the bow from the other end of the yoke, bring the other ox under the yoke, place it on his neck and proceed the same as before.

Until steers are pretty well broken, it will take at least two people to yoke them. After the yoke is put on the first steer, one person would have to hold the other end of the yoke with the bow already out, while the other leads the second steer under the yoke where he is secured with the bow. Training cattle to lead and not be afraid of you is a big help in yoking them the first few times. It takes a lot of training and work to get cattle so well trained that you can take the yoke and walk up to the off-ox (one on the right side,) put the yoke on him and then remove the bow for the near-ox (one of the left side,) motion and call him to come under the yoke and have him come of his own accord, then put his head under the yoke for you to place the bow in place and complete the yoking process. We had two yoke of oxen which we kept until they were 4 or 5 years old. They were so well trained that all we had to do was pick up the yoke and the two would almost simultaneously move up and stick their necks under for yoking. Of course, there were times this did not happen and more effort was required.

We began training our two steer calves long before they were weaned. They were wild to start with and when we slipped a rope around the neck of either, it would jump and run making it difficult for us to hold. It was as hard on the one trying to hold the calf as it was on the calf. We had no advantage with the rope around the calf's neck, except that it would choke it down as the rope pulled tighter. This was not good enough, for the calf was stronger than either of us.

We made a halter by tying a loop in the end of the rope, the right size to go over the calf's nose and small enough to go only about half-way up to its eyes. Then we took the loose end up over his head, just back of his ears and down the other side, and then put the loose end under the loop around his nose. We pulled it through until it tightened around his head and tied it snugly in this position so it wouldn't slip off. With this halter, we could control the calf with greater ease for us and with more comfort for the calf. He soon became less afraid of us and learned to be led wherever we wished.

108

One day we had the calves in the barn lot leading them here and there. They were doing pretty well so George decided it was time to take a ride on a wood hand sled. He tied a rope around the calf's neck and to the sled and got on the sled, expecting to drive the calf with the halter rope. The calf got scared of the sled and started jumping stiff-legged across the lot, bawling every time his feet hit the ground. George was thrown off the sled about halfway across the lot. The calf continued to the other side where the sled caught on a corner of the fence and turned the calf completely around, facing the sled and pulling backward the full length of the rope which tightened around his neck and stopped his bawling. George was scared as much as the calf. When I found he wasn't hurt, I had to laugh. That jumping, bawling calf, going across the lot, was exciting to watch and, I am sure, was even more exciting to George. I doubt if he wanted an instant replay.

Our calves did not match in color. My calf, Buck, was light jersey-red, with two or three blotches of white over his body and a little white about his head. George's calf, Barry, was black all over with no markings. Both were muley (without horns) and about the same size. A small calf yoke had been in the barn loft ever since we could remember. It was none too big when we put it on Buck and Barry. They did not scare when yoked but the yoke was so short that, when they pulled away from each other, their feet got tangled together. This may have helped to get them stopped from pulling apart. It took quite a bit of driving around, pulling nothing, to get Buck and Barry used to going along evenly together.

Next we hooked a chain between them to the ring in the yoke and drove them around until they were used to the chain before we hitched anything else to it. We also kept a halter on each so we could control them better.

George finally decided it was safe enough to try for another ride on the sled. He held the end of his halter rope on Barry as he got on. I drove the team about the lot without incident and from that time on, we left the halter off Barry. One of us drove while the other rode the sled. This was fun. We tried to drive with a halter on each ox and both of us riding but that did not work as well. We taught them to stop at the command 'whoa' and to start at the command 'get up.' Of all commands 'whoa,' the command to stop and stand still, was the most important and the one to be taught as soon as possible. No matter what was happening, 'whoa' generally stopped it. When it was used, immediate obedience was necessary for the safety of all. It was like driving a car and not knowing how to stop it at once. Learning the other commands to drive a team, such as 'gee' (right) and 'haw' (left) and others could be taught and learned more leisurely.

It was necessary to observe safety precautions at all times in breaking oxen or calves, as in any other activity. To illustrate, I was once leaning over the yoke to adjust the chain in the yoke ring when Buck and Barry raised the yoke which hit me on the chin. A rough part of it cut my chin enough to bring the blood. I was careful not to do that again.

George and I helped Eunice, Lois and Edna halter and teach heifer calves to lead, one for each of them. We all worked about in the yard at this. One day, later on, I looked over and saw that Edna had tied the rope she was leading her calf with, around her own neck and was pretending she and the calf were yoked together. I was horrified! How could I get hold of that rope to untie it, without frightening the calf? What would happen if it got scared like the one that took George on the sled across the barn lot? I slowly eased over, got hold of the rope and untied it. It seemed to take an eternity. I sat down with a feeling of relief and exhaustion. I was so glad that no accident had happened that I could scarcely bring myself to scold her and tell her never, never to do that again. When she realized what might have happened, I am sure she was as frightened as I. When I think of it even now, it still frightens me. Maybe this, together with George's sled ride and my chin bump on the yoke, helped us to avoid any later serious accidents.

The second year we had two red steers with white faces to break, which made us a two-yoke ox team. These steers had horns and matched well in both color and size. We called mine 'Tob,' and George's 'Log.' Log worked on the near side, Tob on the off side. When we worked them separately, George generally drove Log and Tob, and I drove Buck and Barry. After Log's and Tob's horns got long, we fitted brass knobs on the ends which made them show up and look nice.

We helped our sisters break heifer calves to lead for at least two years. It was fun for all of us. George and I enjoyed talking with all the other boys in school about our various ox-breaking, driving and working experiences. Usually each boy in school could come up with a different and equally interesting tale. One of the boys said he had learned a new way to spell ox wagon. When he was asked how, he said 'oxygen' and that he had come across this word in his hygiene book. He got a laugh, but not quite what he had expected.

- - - - - - - - - - - - -

"Did you have your own whip, too, Grandpa?"
"Yes, we learned to make our own but one time Grandpa Lewis brought us a real one. I'll tell you about it. . . . "

- - - - - - - - - - - - -

BRAIDED OX-WHIPS

We learned to braid four strands together to make a round braid, the way ox whips were made. We braided round whips of hickory bark that we could crack like the ox-drivers did. The bark soon dried and got too stiff to do anything with. Then we tried tapering leather straps and braiding them into a whip. This worked much better. We could crack them and found that they lasted longer than the bark ones. The leather we could get was old and soon broke at the small end. We finished them out with sea-grass strings from untwisted cables. This worked better. We did not need to use the whip very much on our oxen but we liked to make it crack. Sometimes the leather we used came from old boot tops but these did not last very well for whip leather.

Grandpa Lewis had been at our house visiting many times and had watched us working our oxen which were about one and two years old by then. One time he came from Glenville and stopped to visit overnight. He gave George and me something tied in a round package and told us to open it. We did! We found a real leather ox whip about 7 or 8 feet long! What a beautiful whip! It had a hole at the big end and a leather thong through it to tie the whip to a handle. The small end had a small loop with a twisted sea-grass cracker fastened through it. It was a perfect whip, ready to be tied on a handle. We thanked Grandpa Lewis

111

but the joy we expressed without words as we unpacked the whip, was even more pleasing to him.

Grandpa Lewis did a lot of surveying all over Gilmer County and stayed quite a lot at Rod Lawrence's hotel when working near Glenville. Rod Lawrence operated the tan-yard also. Of course, Grandpa had been telling him about our oxen and Rod said he would make a nice whip for Grandpa to give us. I am not sure whether he charged anything for doing it or not, since he and Grandpa were very good friends. I talked to Mr. Lawrence several years afterward and he remembered very well having made our ox-whip.

George and I took the handle off the old whip we had and tied the new whip to it. Then we asked Grandpa to crack it for us.

He made it sound good!

We asked Pa to see what he could do. He, too, could make a loud sound with it. We were surprised and pleased that they did so well but could scarcely wait for our turns. Grandpa and Pa said we did well but that we would have to practice more, and eat more cornbread, before we could come up with them. We did not think there was that much difference but maybe there was.

- - - - - - - - - - - - -

"Oh, boy! I wish Joe and I had some calves to break!"

"Yes, John, I am sure you and Joe could have a lot of fun breaking calves but that would be about all you could do with them. People don't use oxen in this part of the country any more. It would also be hard to find a calf yoke or chain now."

"We could probably learn to braid a whip, but I don't think we'd better cut up boots to get leather. Perhaps those long leather shoestrings would work."

"Yes, you could do that. Almost everyone knows how to braid with three strands but using four, so the whip will be round, is a little different."

"Grandpa, I like the real life stories you tell about people who were our relatives way back then. It makes them seem like real people to us, not just names on the family tree. How was it that the Lewis family is related?"

"Well, Jane, it's like this. Ma was a Lewis and Grandpa Lewis' name was Oliver Hazard Perry Lewis."

"So that's where Uncle Perry got his name! What's your next story going to be about?"

"I remember an exciting event that took place in 1910. It was called Halley's Comet. . . . . . "

- - - - - - - - - - - - - -

HALLEY'S COMET
Or
MONEYPENNY'S COMET

Very few people will ever see Halley's Comet on more than one of its visits within sight of earth since it comes in sight only every 75 ½ years in its regular orbit. I saw it on its last visit in 1910 when I was 13 years old. Everyone was eagerly looking forward to its coming, some with fear, some with dire predictions about the end of time, or other disaster. It was expected to make a grand display of light in the sky. The visits of this comet have been traced back to about the second century and there seems to be every reason to believe it will be back again in 1985 with about the same brilliancy as in 1910 and former visits.

People were anxiously waiting and watching for the appearance of Halley's Comet but began looking too early that spring and could not see anything. One day, Pa came back from Troy with a story of how the people of Troy had seen the comet. It went something like this.

One rainy evening, just after dark, someone came running into each of the two stores saying he had just seen Halley's Comet going along the hilltop on the opposite side of Leading Creek. Everyone ran out to see. Sure enough, a bright light was going along the ridge near the horizon, disappearing behind high ground, and reappearing again, until it passed behind a much larger mass of high ground and never reappeared. The town was filled with descriptions of how the comet looked, its size, brilliance and final

113

disappearance. The stories varied so much that it was hard to believe they had seen the same phenomenon.

The next evening was clear and all expected to get a much better view. It was long past the time it had appeared the evening before, yet no comet was in sight. The expectant watchers finally gave up and returned to their houses in disappointment. The word soon got out, from the ones who were in on it, that it was a joke. Tom Moneypenny and one or two others had taken a big torch, lit it and carried it along the top of the hill, to see if they could fool the people. It was a complete success, however, the ones who had given such glowing accounts of the evening before, were hard to find after the joke had been revealed. No one had given a thought to being able to see the comet when it was too cloudy to see the stars, as it had been the night before.

Later that summer, comparisons of Halley's Comet with Moneypenny's comet brought forth sheepish looks from many who had given it the glowing descriptions.

The comet became visible, on bright, clear nights, near the horizon and gradually was visible higher and higher until it reached its maximum height, about 1/3 way from horizon to horizon. As I recall, we also had some northern lights which sent streamers far up overhead which, by themselves, would have been marvelous manifestations, but combined with the comet light which extended much farther across the sky, was magnificent to behold.

- - - - - - - - - - - - - - -

" I feel sure you can look forward to seeing Halley's Comet in 1985 without being disappointed."

"We looked for that new comet, Kohoutek but weren't able to see it. Once we thought we did but it may have been a plane making a vapor trail in the sunset."

"Yes, your Grandma and I went out in the yard and looked for it too, several times but couldn't see it. Kohoutek was a new comet that had no record of being seen before. The newspapers and TV had given much publicity to it. That's how it was in 1910, too, with everyone out looking for the comet."

"Grandpa, Moneypenny's Comet was a good joke on the people, wasn't it? Now all I would need to pull that again in 1985, is a big hill and - - "

"Maybe you could even get TV coverage! There was another sport that provided a lot of entertainment. Would you like to hear about a fox chase?"

"I've read about them and seen pictures of riders dressed in fancy clothes on beautiful horses."

"Our fox chases weren't quite like that. . ."

- - - - - - - - - - - - - -

FOX CHASING

Fox chasing, as a sport, needs no definition in West Virginia, and probably none in all of the Appalachian Mountains. In this rough area, no attempt was made to follow the hounds and the fox on horseback as was done in England, in Virginia and in other more level parts of this country. Horses were used by chasers to ride, leading their hounds, to the area where they expected to listen to the chase. Sometimes this included riding the horse and leading hounds to the top of the highest knob. The horses were hitched nearby while the men listened to the chase, and then rode them back home. Sometimes they led the hounds home and at other times the hounds made their own way home. Sometimes they rode only part way, leaving the horse in a neighbor's barn and the two walked to the listening point together, but nearly always leading the hounds so they didn't take off in some other direction than in the area they wish to let them loose.

Some chasers had buggies or light wagons for hauling their hounds to the hunting area so they would be fresh and ready for a good chase. Lots of times the listening point was in easy walking distance of their homes and they simply gathered at the point by the most direct route from their homes.

Fox chasers do not chase the fox to catch it but to hear their hounds run, barking, after it. Neither do they like for fur hunters to catch and kill them for fur.

Farmers with wheat, rye or oats that had started making straw stalks, were always in fear of fox chasers running their hounds through such fields and trailing the straw down, making it hard to harvest. Some chasers did just that but since many were farmers and had such fields of their own; they usually refrained from chasing foxes at that time of year in such areas.

In extra dry weather, it was difficult for hounds to follow the fox trail since little scent was left for them to follow. Rough frozen ground, ice and sleety times were hard on the hounds' feet which were easily cut if permitted to run under those conditions. Hounds would be laid up for several days or weeks until their feet were healed sufficiently to run again under good conditions. Chasers tried to avoid such conditions; however, hounds would sometimes get loose and run on their own. For a fox chaser not to have a hound ready for a chase was like a musician with no instrument; the music and entertainment stopped.

In fishing, the success of the trip depended on the number and size of the catch, together with the stories about the big ones that got away. Not so in fox chasing; no catch was wanted and no big one got away. However, the length and duration of the chase, how well it circled and remained within hearing, how much barking was done by whose dogs and whose contributed most to the success at the time it was actually in progress were important factors to its immediate success and enjoyment. These same factors became the basis for future stories and arguments about the chase, which were limited only by the imaginations and story telling abilities of the ones engaged in later discussions. They are comparable to fish stories and both were sources of much harmless entertainment.

Since we had no dogs, Pa, George and I made arrangements to go with some of our neighbors to hear their hounds on the case, which usually lasted until long after midnight. We took a good midnight lunch with us and so did all the others. The place selected from which to listen to this particular chase was a high knob on the ridge where Buckhorn, Left Fork of Crane Run, Big Run and Bloody Run all headed up toward each other. We spread out from this place so that it was easier to hear the hounds, no matter which direction the chase took or how wide a circle might be involved. Foxes frequently ran away from their den area and took a big circle and came back from another direction.

All the men who were expected, together with their hounds, soon arrived. They let two or three of their best hounds loose to pick up the trail. None of the first hounds would run rabbits, so they said. It was not long until they picked up a hot trail and began barking and running it. The other hounds were let loose at once and they took off after the first ones, all of them barking. We could tell where and in what direction the chase was going from the barking of the hounds. What we did not know was whose hound was barking where and which one was leading the chase. The 'we' I am talking about refers to Pa, George and me. The others knew!

We soon found there were considerable differences of opinions among them as to the accuracy of part of what various ones knew, or thought they knew. To us, it was a barking, yelping and howling lot of hounds with variations of volume to listen to. As the chasers conversation and differences developed with the chase, it all became the more interesting and amusing to us. It went like this,

'Listen! That's old Lead picking up that trail! He's hard to beat at that!'

"Bowser is right in there with him! He's in front of Lead now!'

'Listen to old Blaze come! She never stays back long! Just listen! Isn't she tongueing now?'

'Just listen to Towser!'

'What do you mean, "Listen to Towser?" He's the tail end of this chase!'

'But, did you ever hear such music?'

'Music, my eye! A bullfrog would sound better!'

'Yes, but what a frog it would take!'

'Bowser's ahead now. No denying that! Just hear him!'

'He'll not be there long! You mark my word on that!'

'Old Tyler is starting to close in!'

'Tip is right there with him. You're right! They're going to change this chase'

'That's right, go to it, Tyler!'

'What's that? Where's Lead and Bowser? Can't hear them!'

'They've lost him!'

'He's been an old gray fox and gone to hole.'

'That's right! They never run long.'

'I knew they were hot on his heels from their barking! It never fails.'

'They are all running about yelping now and looking for his trail. He's gone to hole. That settles this chase. I'm going to eat something while they are getting another one going. The rest of you can do what you want.'

Eating was popular now for awhile even though the quality of the chase and performance of various hounds continued the most pressing subjects of the lively conversations.

All of us had been so busy with the chase that no attention had been drawn to the beautiful display of light by Halley's Comet, then far overhead and stretching far across the night sky, lighting the cool, clear night with the brilliance of a full moon. As the discussion of the chase subsided, this became the topic on conversation, along with the bogus Moneypenny Comet that had fooled so many Troy people earlier that spring. Many of the stories about that comet were retold with no loss of vividness or detail. No doubt new stories were added. Neighborhood news, incidents and gossip were all cumulatively developed and discussed around fires during fox chases.

The hounds had continued wandering about the area emitting lonely barks here and there in the process. A rabbit hurried past us on his way. The barking picked up and someone said,

'You don't suppose those hounds are on the trail of that rabbit, do you?'

'That first one might but not old Lead. He's picked it up now!'

'More of them are on the trail. It must be another gray fox!'

'They're coming this way!'

'You're right!'

Scarcely had this conversation taken place when a silent lead hound trotted past us along the rabbit trail, followed closely by a whole noisy pack of hounds. The chasers created more noise than the hounds, trying to break up this chase and get their dogs under leash. This was a disaster, that so many fox-hounds were caught actually running rabbits.

The two or three chasers whose hounds had not gotten into the chase, chastised the guilty owners unmercifully, right there on the spot. They would never be able to brag about this chase.

'That finishes it for this place! Let's take out to that knob over there and let them loose again. They haven't been over that way this evening.'

'We'll have to do something to change our luck.'

'We can't make it any worse! That's for sure!'

All agreed and took off in the direction of the knob about a quarter mile away. This was getting nearer our home and we went along willingly.

The hounds soon picked up a new trail which developed into a longer and better chase than the first one. This gave the rabbit-chasing hounds a chance to wipe out some of their disgrace and thus allow their owners to talk with pride of the great improvement of their hounds. This second chase was accompanied by even more interest and enthusiastic discussion than accompanied the first chase. Descriptions of fox chases, like the chases themselves, are all similar but no two are exactly alike, so don't be surprised if my description is unlike any you have heard before.

- - - - - - - - - - -

"So that's my only fox chasing story. I've been on a few other chases, some better, some worse, but all similar."

"But Grandpa, the hounds do all the work, don't they? The hunters just stand and listen. We should make a tape of the hounds if we could be near another chase."

"I have stood out in the yard at our home on Big Cove many, many times and listened to the distant barking of hounds on the chase, with much better appreciation, than if Pa had never taken us on that chase."

"Uncle Perry took our cousins, Bruce and Kevin, on a coon-hunt on his farm one night. Joe and I were too little to go. We could hear the dogs barking then. They really did catch some coons that night."

119

"I'll have some more hunting stories later. Bring me that bowl of walnuts and I'll crack some for you. We used to hunt for many kinds of nuts in the fall. . . ."

- - - - - - - - - - - -

NUT GATHERING

Of all the fall activities, probably the one most eagerly awaited by the children was gathering nuts. These, named in the order of size beginning with the largest were black walnuts, butternuts (also known as white walnuts and long walnuts,) hickory nuts, chestnuts and hazelnuts. All these nuts can still be gathered in the fall except the chestnuts which died out from the chestnut blight 45 or 50 years ago.

We had black walnut trees scattered plentifully around our farm and near the house. I can't remember ever being without black walnuts in the fall for eating purposes. As we got older, we hulled and cracked them to sell.

Our butternut trees were not nearly as plentiful or as large as the black walnut trees. Butternuts had a thin outer hull that would dry on the nut and required no hulling. These nuts were easy to crack and the kernels came out, nearly all the time, in halves. They were delicious for general home use, but very seldom was there enough extra to sell.

The paper-thin shellbark hickory nuts were scarce on our farm, only 1 or 2 trees; however, there were more of the ordinary shellbark hickory trees. Squirrels always ran a good race for their share of these nuts but there were usually enough for all. The shellbark nuts, like the butternuts, cracked easily and came out in bigger pieces. The mockernut hickory and other thick-shell hickory nuts were hard to crack and the kernels broke and came out in small pieces. Some of these tasted better than the thin-shell nuts, but not enough better to select them, except when there were no others.

Hazelnuts were of no consequence on our farm or in our neighborhood. We had only a few bushes from which a few nuts were gathered, more for the fun of finding and sampling them than for any other reason.

120

The chestnut tree was one of the most valuable and widely distributed of all the nut trees. When they grew out in the open, they developed sturdy trunks with wide-spreading tops which bore abundant crops of nuts. The trees that grew in the forests attained great heights and developed high slender trunks with few limbs, even to their tops, which would be the general height of the forest. These smaller tops produced nuts in abundance; however these trunks were more valuable for posts and lumber because of the freedom from knots. The long slim trunks were a source of practically all the poles then used to support the telephone, telegraph and power lines. These poles and posts lasted well, untreated, and were also easily treated with preservatives that greatly extended their usefulness. The wood was easily split into posts, fence-rails, pickets, clapboards and shingles or for any use where a neat, straight stake or piece of wood was needed. Chestnut wood was sawed into lumber used for many purposes. The grain of the wood showed up well for interior varnished trim finish. In addition to making children's whistles, the bark was also valuable in tanning hides.

Now we will get back to the nut of the chestnut which I started to tell you about. These grew inside green clusters of burrs, the size of a large un-hulled black walnut. Sometimes they grew to the size of a regular baseball. The outside surface of the burr was a thick bristly surface, like that of a hairbrush, with bristles about $3/8^{th}$ inch deep. These did not feel sharp or stiff when green, but as they grew and developed, became stiffer and sharper until by the time the nuts were fully ripe in the fall, merely touching the burrs with the hand would cause pain. Some spines might remain stuck in the hand and have to be removed one by one. Stepping on the brown burrs with the bare feet was very painful and always resulted in a large number of the spines remaining embedded in the foot, the removal of which was a painful procedure. Needless to say, this made it necessary to wear shoes when picking up chestnuts.

When chestnuts got ripe in the fall, the burrs would split open and many of the nuts would fall out before the burrs fell from the tree. Any still in the burr were jarred out when it fell to the ground, thus nearly all were out of the burr when it fell to the ground, ready to be picked up. Those remaining stuck in the burrs were not worth fooling with. It generally took 1 or 3 weeks for all

121

to fall from the trees but we began gathering them as soon as they started to fall.

One year there was an unusually bountiful crop. We did not realize they were getting ripe until one evening Pa came in with his pockets full of nuts that he had picked up as he came 2 or 3 big trees on his way home from work. He said there were a lot on the ground and we should get out the next day and pick up some of them. He had enough to roast and boil, and also to eat raw that evening so we would all have a desire for more. These chestnuts were similar to the ones you sometimes see in the stores now.

The chestnuts were easily opened with a knife and were delicious to eat raw at the time they were gathered and were even more desirable after drying. They would keep all winter and could be roasted or boiled any time, if desired. They would roast on the stove-top better after drying, if they were soaked in a little water first.

Roasting brought out more delicate flavors that made this a favorite way to eat chestnuts. Boiling, likewise, further developed the flavor and made the nut softer and easy to chew. It is no wonder the Pilgrims and Indians used them to eat and to season their Thanksgiving dinners.

The next day after Pa brought home his picket-full of chestnuts, was Saturday, and no school, so we got out early gathering chestnuts. By noon we had more than we had ever before gathered in that length of time. We went to different trees that afternoon and got so many that we decided to take some to the store to sell. Pa took about 2 bushels to the store the first of the next week and got what he thought was a good price for them. I don't remember the price per pound but we sold enough chestnuts that fall to get a new pair of boots or shoes for each of us who were going to school that year. We still had plenty remaining for our own fall and winter use. We may have sold enough to buy other things but the shoes stand out most vividly. No doubt you think that was a lot of nuts and you are right. We had many big chestnut trees, 50 or more standing out in the pasture fields and meadows which made it easier to gather their nuts than had all been in the woods.

Now, don't get the idea that all chestnuts were free of worms. They were not. That year we gathered so many that they were relatively free of worms. This varied from year to year. The chestnut worm looked like the hickory nut worm and may have been the same kind. Chestnuts would lie on the ground through the winter into early spring. Many remained good to eat. I have often eaten them as picked up in winter or early spring and many had even a better flavor than in the fall.

'Hull-Gull' is a game we played around the fire of evenings using chestnuts. Two at a time played this game. One would hide one or more, or none, nuts in his hand and hold it out, saying, 'Hull-Gull.' The other would reply 'Hand-full.' The first one with the hand-full of nuts would ask 'How Many?" The other would guess. If the guess was the correct number, he got the nuts. If it was wrong, he had to give the other player the difference. The game finished when one ran out of nuts. Sometimes the nuts were divided evenly and the game played over again. Sometimes the loser was required to go to our storage place after more nuts for everyone.

- - - - - - - - - - - - -

"Grandpa, we could play 'Hull-Gull' with marbles, or some other kind of nuts, now that we don't have chestnuts anymore."

"Buckeyes would work just fine. But don't try to eat them!"

"I saw a little table you made out of chestnut wood, Grandpa. I thought it looked something like oak."

"Yes, Jane, although the wood has even more contrast in the grain than oak. I made that small table for your mother while she and Miriam were little girls. They had many tea-parties at that table. We also had a dining room table in Glenville that I made. We used it all the time your mother and her brothers and sister were growing up, both for meals and for homework."

"You told us about the blackberries you picked. How many other kinds of fruit did you have on your farm?"

"Have you heard of the ground cherry, or the paw-paw? The persimmon? huckleberries and mulberries. . . ."

- - - - - - - - - - - - - - -

FRUIT AND MORE FRUIT

An interesting pastime in the early fall was looking for early ripening wild fruits, not so much because of their value for food purposes but just for something different to do and new flavors to enjoy.

One of the most useless of these was the ground cherry found in the cornfields and garden areas. It would grow up after cultivation had been finished and produced small, round fruit in a paper-thin, loose-fitting, inflated bladder-like husk, both of which were yellow when ripe. It was fun to pop the husks open to get at the berry which was full of small seeds, surrounded by pulp, and was about the size of the tip of ones little finger. The flavor was quite pleasing. Some people used them for sauce, preserves and pies but we never had them in such quantities for that.

We had several small paw-paw trees (we called them 'pop-paw') scattered about our farm and such trees were also widely scattered in our part of the state. The fruit grew 3 or 4 inches long with a thick skin resembling a banana, inside of which were large round, flat seeds, surrounded with banana-like edible pulp. Some people were delighted with its flavor and praised it highly but I was never carried away with it. Our use of the paw-paw extended no further than in-season eating pleasure.

Wild grapes abounded in the wooded areas and were fairly regular each fall. A small black grape grew near water and in swampy areas which we called 'water grapes.' These were very sour and of little use for eating purposes. The squirrels and birds ate them when other food was scarce. Another variety, found on higher ground and among the hills, which we designated as 'hill grapes,' were larger and less sour, about the size of large huckleberries. They were good, sour eating. The black grapes were more sour than the slightly larger blue variety which were more desirable to eat directly from the vine by both man and squirrel. When other berries and fruits were scarce, these grapes were canned whole or made into very good jams and jellies as a welcome addition to the food supply. This blue grape would cling to the vine well into the winter and, after drying out some, tasted more like sour raisins. They were really fairly good to eat. I have seen as many as 6 or 8 squirrels feeding at one time on vines full of these grapes around Christmas. Various of these wild grapes began ripening about the time of the first frost but improved in edibility after a few more good frosts.

Wild plums were distributed widely in our part of West Virginia and our farm had its share of them. Frost sometimes killed them when in bloom, but usually some in sheltered places escaped, making a complete crop failure very seldom. Ripening began in August and lasted as late as October. Size, quality and flavor varied widely among our trees. Ma liked the fruit from 3 or 4 special trees, to use in canning and in making plum butter. Plums and apples cooked together made an excellent sauce for any occasion. Wild plums also formed a variation in the diet of squirrels and birds.

Wild crabapples were abundant but of little use to eat directly from the trees. When they were made into preserves and jelly, which required a lot of sugar, they were hard to beat.

We had several clumps of blue and black haw trees or bushes, about 20 feet high, which were usually covered with fruit that began to get good to eat about the coming of frost. This fruit would stick on the bushes well into winter. The berry-like fruit grew on sprangly bunches bound together at the base, similar to pine needles. Some trees bore more delicious fruit than others and were eaten as picked from the trees, mainly as a novelty for the change of flavor. We would take a mouth-full of haws, separate the pulp from the flat seed in each haw and spit out as many seeds as haws at the end. That was the best way we knew to eat them. I know of no other use except that the birds would finally strip the trees as winter wore on.

We had 25 or 30 large persimmon trees about 7 to 10 inches in diameter at the butt and 25 feet or more in height. These were scattered around the pasture just behind the house. These trees were loaded with persimmons nearly every year. They began losing their puckery taste as they started to ripen, about the time of the first frost in the fall. Some trees ripened more quickly than others but all were soon good to eat just as they fell from the tree, which was the most popular way to eat them. We ate some with cream and sugar and they were delicious. Some people used them to make puddings and other delicacies. I am surprised that more ways of using persimmons had not been developed in our neighborhood. It could be that a scarcity of the fruit may have been the reason since I have never seen more than 3 or 4 trees together at other places, other than on our farm. We would have as many as 20 to 40 bushel every year. Practically all of them went to waste. They would hang on trees until midwinter and longer. Cattle ate them as they fell to the ground. Skunks, raccoons and opossums were frequently caught by fur-hunters in the vicinity of our persimmon trees. Possums have been caught up in the trees, eating persimmons, when they could not find the fruit on the ground.

We hauled fodder and stacked it in a fenced area around a persimmon tree from which we fed our cattle twice a day for several years. Several other trees were nearby and the cattle kept the fruit that fell to the ground, cleaned up so that it was hard to find any. I could always find persimmons on the ground under that tree inside the fodder pen and could club more off other trees. As freezing weather came on, the persimmons dried out with a natural sugary taste very similar to dried dates, and nearly as good. I remember looking forward to this evening and morning feast, as I went after the cows. I often took some home for other members of our family to enjoy.

Many birds were in the trees at this time of year, pecking at the persimmons and knocking them to the ground. Late in winter, because of food scarcity or migratory birds, the trees would be completely stripped of fruit, in only a few days. I never liked to see this happen; it was like losing a good friend or eating the last piece of cake or pie.

Fifteen or more large, wild, black mulberry trees grew in the pasture fields near our house. These mulberries, when ripe, were as much as half-inch in thickness and up to 2 inches in length. They were sweet and good to eat as picked from the tree. They made excellent pies. They were used to make jelly but apple juice, or something to make them jell, had to be added. I have seen many squirrels and birds eating the fruit on these trees.

- - - - - - - - - - -

"Those black mulberries we had were much bigger than the red ones I have seen growing here in Ohio."

126

"Grandpa, how did it happen there were so many different kinds of wild fruit and nut trees growing on your farm so handy to your house?"

"I am not surprised that you ask this question. I, too, have asked Pa how that happened and the answer he gave me will probably answer your question as well as it did the one I asked."

"Pa told me, 'These fruits and nuts grew wild about over the farm and we enjoyed their many uses so when we helped our father clear this land, we left a lot of bearing trees and sprouts for later use. You will notice that many of those are on rough ground, not suitable for growing corn and wheat. Others are on good ground because we liked their fruit and nuts so well that they more than made up for damage to growing crops. There was a big family of us and we liked all these extras.' That was the answer Pa gave me to your question, when I was about your age."

"How many were in your Pa's family, Grandpa?"

"Eight. Five boys and three girls. Ten, including their father and mother. I will tell you more about Pa's family later."

"And that was the same number that were in your family. Only you had five 5 girls and 3 boys!"

"Let me tell you about more simple ways to find enjoyment without TV. . . . ."

- - - - - - - - - - - -

SIMPLE PLEASURES

What are simple pleasures? I wonder. Is it watching little lambs on a warm spring evening as they gambol and play about their mothers, running and jumping hither and yon. They suddenly dart off, all together, to mount a big rock and look away, wisely, toward the distance, each in his own direction with a careless air of importance. Maybe this is a simple pleasure for both the lambs and the watchers.

I sometimes think simple pleasure comes without special or particular planning, but as a side benefit as one goes about his regular work, perhaps from doing nothing very special.

I have a relatively clear picture in mind of such an evening after a late afternoon thunderstorm. The rain had ceased and the sun lit up the tops of the hills and the western faces of the massive, cumulative thunderhead clouds. The lightning flashed under, over, around, between and among the various cloud formations, continuing an ever-changing picture of natural beauty, emphasized by the peeling, rolling thunder accompanying each change and the whole spectacle slowly dying away in the distance. All of this was emphasized more and more as darkness settled over the display.

We children vied with one another to find clear pictures, faces, cloud shapes and fancied formations to trace and describe to one another in this ever-changing evening display. It became so real at times as to cause arguments about which cloud picture each could use. It wasn't fair for two of us to describe the same formation. These descriptions and discussions helped us develop clearer, plainer observations than would have otherwise been the case.

While taking a leisurely, aimless Sunday afternoon walk on the hill behind our house, I came to a thick, cool shade near the hilltop which had a pleasant gentle breeze. We had enjoyed this shady space many times when working in the area but the rests

129

had always seemed so short and incomplete as we again resumed our work. This time I lay down, thinking of fully enjoying this place on this warm late summer afternoon. High overhead, 2 or 3 buzzards soared aimlessly here and there. They appeared to be floating in midair as they drifted higher and farther toward the southwest, gradually getting smaller and smaller, until they disappeared from view.

A large hawk, uttering his familiar call, sailed into view and began his soaring circle, soon followed by his mate who followed in the circle. They appeared to meet on opposite sides of their spiral ascent until reaching enormous height when they appeared to become tired. They faced about in the wind and rested motionless, in one position, with no motion in any direction. Having rested, if that was why they stayed motionless so long, they began drifting off toward the east until they disappeared from view.

In the meantime, night-hawks, emitting their plaintive cry, had begun to gather for their evening exercises. Their one white mark on each wing and tail was easily seen since many of them flew almost level with where I sat near the top of this high hill. Others flew lower down, out farther over the valley and the tops of their wings, together with the white markings were constantly in view. Those flying lower down between the hills were still above our house in the narrow valley below. These night-hawks assembled and flew as if catching insects, for several weeks in late summer and early fall, to strengthen their flying muscles before leaving for winter living-quarters farther south. We used to think they were whip-poor-wills getting ready to go south and looked forward to their early fall flying exhibition.

Besides the flying entertainment in the air, all the features of the valley were visible in the surrounding countryside. So the rest of that pause in the shady place was spent in day dreams.

- - - - - - - - - - - -

"Grandpa, we still look at clouds and see things there. Once I saw a white horse on his hind legs. He was just perfect!"

"Yes, and you watch the martins as they come and go. Do you spend time lying in the grass just day-dreaming?"

"Sure, and sometimes it's fun to watch ants."

"Tell us more about your yard. Did your Ma grow flowers the way Grandma does?"

"And tell about the big pine tree. I don't think you've even mentioned it yet."

"I'll get around to all that. We also had a hammock made out of barrel staves. . ."

- - - - - - - - - - - - -

OUR YARD

In our yard were several groupings of perennial flowers and bushes that came up every year and required little attention, yet afforded a lot of pleasure to the whole family. A clump of Sweetshrub bushes about 8 feet in diameter and 6 to 8 feet tall, grew at one end of the garden. The dark red blooms, each about the size of a hickory nut, gave a pleasant fragrance what pervaded the whole area. These blossoms, which were quite popular to wear in a lapel, gave a beautiful fragrance wherever the wearer went.

Three or four bunches of red and white peonies were later divided and extended along the fence across the front yard. Two white snow-ball bushes, one at each end of the front yard also contributed their share of beauty. Several white lilies and tiger lilies were scattered here and there near the house foundation and yard fence for good measure. There were 2 clumps of purple asters, about 3 feet in diameter, at the south end of the house. These were especially favored by the bees, in their eagerness to collect the nectar from the flowers. Several roses grew about the yard including a few on trellises. These bloomed once a year, at different times, white, pink and red.

There were two large Concord grape vines that had been set out by Grandpa and Grandma McQuain about the time they moved there in 1848 or 49. The one in the front northeast corner of the yard covered a trellis on posts 20 by 10 feet with the vines extending along the fence also extending along the fence 10 feet or more in both directions. The vine in the back yard was on an equally extensive trellis. Its vines were also tied up along the eaves of the smokehouse on the side next to the trellis and across each end to the far side. The smokehouse was about 20 by 10 feet. That was the size as I first remember them, when the vines were about 50 years old. The extent and size did not vary much during the next 25 or 30 years. Each vine afforded thick pleasant shade under the trellis during hot weather while the growing grapes were pleasant to look at during the growing season and even more beautiful as they ripened into delicious fruit. The flavor and taste of the grapes from these two vines was slightly different with the one near the smokehouse being the favorite to eat as picked from the vine.

Ma always planted a few flowers in beds in various places around the yard which were sort of protected from the play activities of us children. Such protected beds were dug against the paling fence. They were about 12 inches wide, with a 3 inch lath set on edge along the outer edge to hold the loose dirt in place. For some flowers, no lath was needed. We children were interested in having beds of our own to grow and care for. I am sure now that Ma encouraged this, not only to have more flowers, but also to get help in weeding and caring for the flowers. We were also more careful in play to protect the beds. Each one was assigned a specific panel or two of fence along which his bed of flowers could extend. The flowers I remember best were 'Purty-by-nights' (Four O'Clocks,) Touch-me-nots (Balsam) and Zinnias. It was fun to pinch the Touch-me-not seed pods when ripe enough, and watch them snap apart and scatter their seeds. To save seeds for planting the following year, we let them burst inside our hands to prevent them from flying into the grass and getting lost. We planted one or two bean vines each to train on the fence. Tomato vines were set out and trained on the fence to see who could get the biggest vine with the most and biggest tomatoes. George had his tomato vine just below the garden gate where dishwater was frequently emptied, which must have been good for it! It grew to the top of the fence. He tied it to the branches of a plum tree until it got so high that I had to help him use a ladder to keep it tied as it grew higher into the tree. It branched out and grew higher than we could reach, producing a lot of average size tomatoes. This made him the champion in number of tomatoes and size of the vine. Others grew larger tomatoes. There was some argument as to whose vines would get the dishwater that was thrown out in later years.

George set out a cedar sprout in the yard to the south of the walk leading from the kitchen to the back gate. I set out a small white pine between the walks leading to the back gate from the new kitchen and the old log kitchen. We set them out about the right time of year and kept them well watered. Both grew for many years. We took considerable pride in watching them develop.

In front of our house was a large, wide-spreading white pine which was much higher than the house. About 12 feet north of the pine was a large red cedar tree about half the height of the pine. An 8 or 10 inch in diameter pussy willow grew in the yard along the fence but was not very outstanding except when full of fragrant bloom each spring. The pine and cedar provided thick cool shade through which a gentle breeze from the south or north was generally in motion. There was no hill for more than 1,000 yards up and down the bottom on either side of the house to interfere with such breezes. This pine tree had been set out by Uncle Zan when he was small and was about 40 years old when I can first remember, and was 18 to 20 inches in diameter two feet above the ground. This tree was cut down in 1970 and was just about 100 years old.

Another bigger pine had stood just outside the yard fence to the north which my Grandmother had set out about the same time the grape vines were planted. This tree had died and been cut down several years before. All I can remember is the stump and part of the knotty rotten top part of the log. We split pieces of both the log and stump for firewood since I can first remember. After several years we were able to get out the last pitchy parts of the roots which burned well and made a good fire.

The shade and breezes under the old pine and cedar tree were enjoyed for many years during the hot summers. Great quantities of pine needles were cast from the tree each year. We would rake these into huge piles and had great fun romping in these piles. We would scatter them on a steep part of the yard and slide down the bank on them like in snow. After this sort of play got old, we hauled them out to the wash place where they could be burned safely while heating the wash water or boiling the clothes. This was really work but by using the red metal wagon or one of our homemade wood wagons, it was more like play for us.

When the weather began warming up one spring, Ma and Pa made a barrel stave hammock. We all tried to help but I'm sure they did most of the work. It took all the staves from a wood oil barrel to make our hammock. Holes about ¾ inch in diameter were drilled about 2 inches from each end of each stave, and a third hole through the middle. With the staves laid out evenly, two fencing wires were woven up and down through the holes and back up between the staves, until all were pulled evenly and snugly together, leaving wires extending out at each end about two feet. These wires were brought together and securely fastened to a ring at each end. We drove a hook into the old pine tree at the right height to fasten the hammock at one end. A rope was secured in the ring at the other end, tied around the cedar tree, and tightened sufficiently to raise the middle off the ground when loaded. This rope had to be adjusted occasionally to take care of the stretch of the wires until they got set. This hammock was left up night and day throughout the summer until bad weather, when it was rolled up for storage.

We used quilts, blankets, cushions and pillows to make the hammock comfortable. It would hold 4 children if they would let their legs overlap and not try to kick about too much. We could not all get in at once, but had to take turns. Relatively little quarrelling or arguing was permitted. The ultimate rules were approved by Pa and Ma. If force was necessary to enforce those rules, they furnished that also.

I am not sure whether we got the hammock first and then got the whooping cough or whether it was the other way around, but in either case, the two were very much intermingled that summer, with the hammock contributing so much in the care and treatment of the cough patients. I have heard Ma say many times that the hammock was a great help in caring for all of us that summer.

Ben Frymier's family had the whooping cough first. They lived on the other side of Big Cove Creek about 1/4th mile away. Neither family visited or let the children get together because we did not want the disease. We became exposed to it by accident. Ben got bit by a snake while hoeing corn and came home to get turpentine to put on the bite. They had none. Mrs. Frymier rushed over to our place to get some. She stopped outside our front gate while Ma went inside the house and got the turpentine for her.

In the meantime, George and Eunice ran out near the inside of the gate while she waited on the outside. At the end of the right number of days, they both began hacking and coughing and developed the whooping cough. Then the rest of us kids took it from them. That was the nearest contact any of us had with the disease. I have heard Pa and Ma talking about it. They thought that perhaps Mrs. Frymier had just put down a coughing baby when she rushed over to our gate and the wind blew the germs from her clothing to us. At any rate, our cases lasted a long time that summer, by the time all 5 or 6 of us caught it and got over it.

I was 8 or 9 and was not nearly as sick as the others and can remember helping care for them. George and Eunice had it bad and so did the baby, who had to have the phlegm wiped from her mouth by Ma or Pa or whoever was watching or holding her at the time. Sometimes the baby would sleep in the hammock with us, or nearby in the cradle where she would be rocked by someone in the rocking chair. The cool breeze and the shade of the pine tree, together with the hammock, was our hospital by day during good weather. The rise of the hammock toward each end was about right to keep the patient from strangling when coughing.

I helped a lot, (at least I thought it was a lot,) in caring for the younger ones, especially while Ma prepared dinner and supper which were often served in picnic fashion under the pine tree. It was just like having meals in bed. It was extra work for Ma, but when we could take care of ourselves outside, it was a relief to her not to have us underfoot in the kitchen. I remember very clearly helping care for the children and rocking the baby, not only while Ma worked in the kitchen, but at other times. I was glad I had gotten over it and was able to help with the others. While I recall little about carrying the meals out or the dishes back to the kitchen, I am sure we older children had a part in that too, including helping wash the dishes. The best thing of all was that all of us finally recovered with no after effects.

- - - - - - - - - - - -

"We get shots for whooping cough now, Grandpa."

135

"Yes, they say there are doctors who haven't ever seen a case! But when I was young, it was a most dreaded illness."

Your yard sounds nice, but how did you mow the grass? There weren't power mowers."

- - - - - - - - - - - -

MOWING THE YARD

It was quite a chore trying to keep the grass cut in the yards. Pa would mow it with his scythe when it got 5 or 6 inches high. We did not have one of the early lawn mowers which were pushed by hand. George and I used our scythes on the yard but it was continually getting too tall. It took a sharp scythe to cut short grass and, besides that, it was hard work. As a consequence, our yard never looked like the short evenly clipped yards you see everywhere since the power mower came into general use. We did cut a lot of plantain in the yard but it seemed to thrive best where we children played most. It kept getting ahead of us more and more, as time went on. Later on, we did get a push type mower that helped us keep the grass short.

FUN WITH RATS AND MICE

Did you ever hear of having fun with rats and mice? They are never good to have around a farm but we children did have some exciting experiences with them. We had several rats and mice around the granary and corn cribs where there were several places they could safely hide from the dog and cats while they fed on the corn. Each spring, when we cleaned out the cribs and shelled the corn, shelled it and put it in barrels or covered boxes, we scared many from their hiding places. The dog and cats would chase them and catch several. It was exciting for us to watch.

The kitchen and porch floors were so close to the ground that our cats could not get under so there were always rats hiding under these floors. They could get plenty to eat around the corn cribs or out where the hogs were fed. We put out rat bait but still we had rats.

There were several cracks between the boards in the porch floor that were big enough for us to put bread crumbs through. When the rats came to feed on the crumbs, we shot them with metal pointed arrows or sharpened heavy wire arrows. These same sharpened arrows could be used as spears but it was hard to move quickly enough to get them before they jumped away. Using the drawn-bow to propel the arrow was quicker and if the point was held against one edge of the crack as a guide, was very effective, if the rat happened to come across the exact point we were aiming. Some of the floor boards were loose and we could turn them back to get the rat we had speared on the arrow. One day we were doing this rather successfully while Newt McQuain was interestedly watching. He told Pa that he had never seen rats caught that way so successfully before. He said he had not thought about being able to shoot an arrow hard enough to go through a rat, as he had just seen me doing.

Lest you think we were over-run with rats and mice, like some city slum areas are now, scratching and biting people in their beds, I hasten to say that such was not the case. We had them only in hard-to-get-at places I have described. There were none in the living areas of our house for long. We kept the doors and cracks tightly sealed so they could not enter. We had a dog and several cats that caught them, if they ventured into the open. We had a few house-broken cats which were allowed in the house at times but, for the most part, cats slept in the barn or other out-buildings. We cut special access holes for the cats to roam at will through the granary. These porch and kitchen floors were later remodeled so as to destroy these hiding areas. Due to these precautions, none of us was ever bitten. Many years later, I learned that pouring strong lye water in the rat holes and runs would get rid of such pests.

- - - - - - - - - - -

"Having a creek going through your farm must have been fun for you. The logjam, and your boat, those big fish."

"Yes, that's where we all learned to swim too. . ."

- - - - - - - - - - -

SWIMMING

Big Cove Creek was the source of many of our simple pleasures, especially swimming. No, we did not just go out and jump in and take off swimming. A lot of wading, splashing and getting wet preceded and accompanied learning to swim. We learned no fancy strokes or special breathing. We learned simple dog-paddling to keep our noses above water at first, followed by swimming on our backs, learning to tread water with our feet alone, to stay afloat. We also learned to hold our heads under water without strangling, followed with efforts at diving and swimming under water. This did not happen all at once either. We started wading and splashing in the creek when 3 to 6 years of age for us older kids. However, all that was necessary for the younger ones to go in with us, was that they are able to walk and at times that was not necessary. They played and dug in the sand and got wet in shallow warm water near the edge. Ma always went along when we were all small and when little ones went with us. She sat on the bank or on a chair nearby. Sometimes she dressed in old clothes or a pair of Pa's trousers and waded and splashed about in the creek with us. This was always extra fun and amusement for all. Pa took part in this less often, but the few times he did, we thought were great. We always put on old clothes or clothes that were ready to wash for these swimming efforts since the road ran along the edge of the creek.

The creek averaged a little more than knee deep except in a few deep places that were waist or shoulder deep. These made good places to test our abilities to swim across without touching bottom. These deep holes were well known and anyone trying a special feat always asked for and got everyone's attention, especially if it was among his first tries. The distances across these deep places varied from 5 or 6 feet to as much as 15 or 20 feet. There was plenty of room for all to splash about, with little danger to anyone. After some of us were able to swim a few strokes and all became less afraid of water, we went up the creek a little farther to a bigger and deeper place, about 300 by 45 feet. Here it was waist deep along the entire far side and across the upper end it was neck deep. For a short way it was over one's head, although it was over smaller kid's heads across the whole upper end. On the side next to our house was a small sandbar surrounded with shallow water for learners to wade and splash in. This was ideal and satisfied the most venturesome. Yet we knew exactly where the deep area was and could watch carefully any who were using that part of the pool. The water was pretty clear except after big rains when more care had to be observed, even when using the shallower water down in front of the house. The older children acted as life guards for the younger ones in assisting them when testing their abilities in deeper water swimming and diving efforts. The safety precautions given by Pa and Ma were learned and observed by all of us and were good reasons why we never had any serious accident in our swimming, diving and wading experiences.

One immediate advantage to the whole family of all these swimming and wading activities was that for their duration, a somewhat tedious, unenthusiastic, less-than-popular Saturday evening bath was forgotten!

We frequently used our johnboat in swimming and jumped or fell into the water. We have turned the boat upside down and dived under it, into the open space beneath and then talked from beneath, or pounded on the bottom, which sounded different. We took turns at this. It was a different type of fun and not very dangerous in shallow water.

When George and I were in our teens, we swam quite a bit at what we knew as the swimming hole below the mouth of Big Run, about half a mile up the creek from our house. The hole was about 200 by 50 feet with an area at one side about 20 by 30 feet that was over our heads. We fastened a springboard on the end of a sunken log that stuck out of the sand at the upper end of the hole, from which we could dive into water deep enough to keep from hitting bottom. Guy Scott and Earl Heckert, who lived nearby, often met us there to swim. Pa and Uncle Warren went swimming there with us on several occasions. The swimming there was of the skinny dipping, birthday suit variety. I remember some of us boys went skinny dipping a few times after attending Sunday School near the mouth of Crane Run.

A few times, timbermen have hauled logs into the swimming hole so they covered the whole area as they lay side by side. We have skipped over these logs which would roll over and tip up and down from our weight.

- - - - - - - - - - - - - -

"Wasn't that a dangerous thing to do? I bet our Mom wouldn't let us try that."

"We could have slipped between the logs, under the water and logs and not have been able to get out before drowning. Yes, it was dangerous and I doubt if Ma gave us permission to try it. When I think of our foolhardiness, I still get a few cold chills!"

"Then, in winter, creeks freeze and are good for skating. . . ."

- - - - - - - - - - -

WINTER SPORTS

Our summer swimming areas were still enough to freeze over quickly in cold winter weather forming safe skating ice. We had an old pair of wood skates with steel runners. A big screw in the heel of the skate was screwed into each shoe heel, together with two straps to hold the skates to the shoe for skating. We tried these skates both on creek ice and ice on the ground, but had trouble keeping them on. Later we got four pair of all-steel club skates, two pair for boys and two for girls. The boys' skates fastened with adjustable steel clamps at both heel and front part of the shoe sole. The heel of the girls' skates had a metal piece for the heel to fit into, secured with a strap around and over the instep. An adjustable steel clamp fit the sole of the shoes. Our shoe heels and soles were of heavy leather and these skate clamps held securely. Perhaps skates were made with the shoe attached but we had none of that kind.

When Lois was beginning to learn, her skates slipped backwards from under her and she bumped her forehead on the ice hard enough to give her a black forehead bump and one black eye. She continued and became a very good skater, by our standards, as did all the rest of us. To be able to skate with confidence always required considerable practice. Trying to stand without falling, or to hit the ice softly when we did fall; trying to get the right push on the skate to propel one where he wanted to go, always required time and practice. I never knew I had so many muscles until trying to get out of bed after having such practice gyrations in learning to skate. Sore muscles were everywhere.

We older children would pull the small ones, who had no skates, over the ice on sleds and in this way they entered into the skating experience. It was great fun to be pulled on the ice by a good skater. At other times, we would ride the sleds out onto the ice.

We learned to cut a figure 8 on the ice, the smaller and faster, the better. We also learned to lock arms and skate in unison, but in no way were we able to approach the fine and intricate skating we now see on television. Even though our skating was clumsy and our falls equally as awkward as the falls of present time experts, these did not keep us from having a lot of fun in our youthful skating experiences.

Just above the mouth of Big Run, on past our favorite swimming hole, is a stretch of quiet water about a quarter mile long and 50 to 70 feet in width which, when frozen over, was an excellent place for any kind of skating or ice games such as 'Shinny on The Ice.' After we children got older and became better skaters, we have gone up there where, together with some of the neighbors, we enjoyed the greater distance for skating and games not so readily played on less extensive ice. Greater skate speeds, together with greater skater-pulled sled speeds, were safely enjoyed on this larger expanse of ice.

These winter activities would be incomplete if I failed to tell you something of our downhill sled and bob-sled riding, together with our barrel-stave ski ventures. We had difficulty fastening the skis securely to our shoes, but when that had been overcome; we found still more difficulty with standing on the skis and guiding them the way we wanted them to go. In fact, we couldn't guide them at all and simply went downhill facing any direction except the way we were going, whether on the skis or rolling over and over or sliding on our backs feet first. Yes, it was excitement but the uncontrollable type. We decided the barrel staves were too crooked and rounded to guide well so we did not use them too often.

For sled riding, the meadow below the house and the one above, both had long smooth downhill slopes, steep enough for

141

rapid rides and bottoms wide enough to slow the sleds and prevent them running into the fence along the side next to the road. Our sleds were the homemade wood type. We had nailed steel tires from buggy wheels to the runners on two of them. This made these sleds run better and faster on certain types of snow. Each one who was big enough had a sled, however it was more fun to double up and ride, 2 or 3 at a time, on longer sleds. We had a wide light board which we used to connect two sleds, making a bobsled, with the front sled pivoted on a bolt so it could be guided by the front rider. Three or four could ride with little danger on this bobsled which added extra excitement to our downhill sledding. In deep snows we have flattened the snow in narrow tracks down the hill in which to guide the sleds. These kept them in line and they would run faster than in loose snow. Of course, in such deep snows, sleds would not run at all except in such paths. One disadvantage to this downhill riding was that one had to walk up-hill, carrying or pulling the sled to get to ride downhill again. Nevertheless, it was great winter fun.

- - - - - - - - - - - -

"Grandpa, you should have invented the ski lift! You were lucky to have so many good hills for your sleds."

"We would have needed to invent electricity too, for we didn't have that until 1940 on our farm."

"Grandpa, tell us what you did in the evenings at home. You didn't have TV to watch, or even a radio."

- - - - - - - - - - - -

BIRD WATCHING

One of the best things about long evenings during any period of the year is that they afforded time each day for rest from the work of the day, without having to feel guilty for using time in that way.

The up-coming long outdoor evenings were foretold by the pond frogs singing on early warm spring evenings. This singing was frequently stopped by icy windows over their watery retreats until spring had fully arrived. These evening frog recitals often began far away down the creek and gradually came nearer and nearer as each succeeding frog joined in, until in front of our house, all groups sang in unison. Then, seeming to tire, their calls gradually died away in the distance upstream. This constantly changing frog gossip was amusing to hear and comment about. The Cove Creek hounds often joined in the frog chorus, or set up one of their own to add variety. The lonely whip-poor-will and hungry hoot owls often added their plaintive cries to the evening entertainment. We children and sometimes older people too, tried to imitate the various calls and at times seemed to strike up conversations with some. The silent bat added his bit to the evening, not only by his crazy flying antics in catching his evening meal of insects, but also, by taking off wildly after a pebble was thrown near him. It was amusing on damp or rainy evenings to watch the robin hop haltingly about the yard, listening or looking, at each stop. Suddenly he would grab and back up, pulling a long night crawler on angleworm, from its underground runway. Sometimes he swallowed it on the spot but other times, the worm was carried immediately to a nearby nest to feed the wide-open hungry mouths of the young birds, as they stretched their heads above the edge of the nest, begging for food.

The gold finches, (we called them sunflower birds) were amusing to watch as they completed their supper of sunflower seeds picked from the ripening sunflowers. They began picking the seeds as soon as they started to get ripe, by hanging to the edge of the flower and picking far under, toward the center. They could get nearly all the seeds from the small, multi-headed type sunflower that way, but areas in the center of the large, single sunflowers were more difficult to get. The evening sun on their flitting bodies added shine to their bright colors.

We watched humming birds go from flower to flower, sticking long bills into each to get the nectar. This bird could stop dead-still in the air before a flower apparently to see if it were safe to go nearer, or to see whether it was worthwhile to stick its bill into the flower, It could back up and dart off so fast it was difficult to follow in flight. I understand it is the only bird able to fly backwards. Once we found a humming bird's next on the limb of a tree in the woods at the end of our cornfield in Coon Hollow.

This nest was about the size of half a hen's egg, set on top a limb, quite a distance away from the tree trunk, beyond where the limb turned sharply downward. Some said that snakes, climbing trees for food, would not go farther on a limb when it started to turn downward, but would go back toward the trunk and try another limb. If that is correct, the nest on the down slope would be safer. We have watched the birds in this nest many times when eating our dinners in the shade nearby. The nest was built of grass, sealed with mud and lined with a downy, soft material.

Some Baltimore Orioles swung their nests in the big walnut tree about 100 feet west of our house. One of these nests was in plain view against the evening sky near the end of a small limb. It was secured by a pencil-thick cord fastened securely to the limb and woven into the nest 12 or 15 inches below, in such a fashion as to form a stretched-out round nest with an entrance hole about mid-side. It was always interesting to see the birds hanging to the nest as it moved in the wind while they were building it and later while feeding their hungry young birds. The wind blew the nest in such a way that it appeared to dodge their every approach.

We got books about wild birds from the Audubon Bird Society that described many of their habits, activities and benefits, and included identifying pictures. Ma and Pa knew many birds and encouraged us to learn more about them and to protect the many useful varieties.

Pa came in one evening from work and told us of a neighbor coming by with a gun. He was very proud of this gun. His guns were always the best and most accurate, to hear him tell it.

'Tommy, just watch me pick off that bird in that brush heap!'

'Don't shoot my Joe-wink!' Pa protested.

The neighbor shot, but missed. The Joe-wink (that is what we called them. Towhee is the correct name,) continued leisurely hopping from brush pile to brush pile looking for food, all the while calling, 'Joe-wink' either announcing his own arrival or calling to his mate.

The neighbor made all sorts of excuses for missing such a good shot. He later said that he found that the sights were set for greater distance shooting. It may have been a simple case of 'buck ague' (nervous, excited shaking.) In any event, Pa's Joe-wink was safe.

144

The evening quiet was frequently broken by a hawk diving among the chickens in the lots outside the yard to get his evening meal. By the time we could make a noise or create a diversion, we would see him sailing away, either empty-handed, or laboriously flying with a chick in his claws. The small hawks were the most dangerous to small chickens; occasionally the large hawks would carry off a full-grown hen for a real meal. I have seen them drop hens when half-way across the meadow toward the woods. These few lucky hens made their way back to the chicken lot, little the worse for their hawk ride. Several chickens were lost to hawks every year.

Tall white pine trees composed about half the forest extending a quarter of a mile along the steep bluff across the creek, overlooking our house and the bottom land on both sides. The tops of many tall pines had died and now made high perches for hawks to look over the entire area. We could easily see them as they sat on these lofty trees, uttering their threatening cries. Pa kept a loaded mountain rifle lying on top the cupboard in readiness for shooting at these marauders. Ma knew how to shoot too.

One evening a large hawk sat on top one of these dead pines looking for his evening meal. Ma got the rifle, rested it on the well curb, sighted and fired. The hawk flew as if hit. We all thought Ma had hit it. Pa and a hired hand were coming down the road to supper when they heard the shot and saw the hawk fly. They, too, thought it had been hit. When they got to the house, they asked who had shot at the hawk. On learning that Ma had done the shooting, we could see they hated to admit that they thought it had been hit. Whether it was hurt badly or not, we all felt that it had had a good scare. That was part of the reason for shoot, to keep them from feeling too safe while looking for chickens from these high vantage points. Ma was almost as pleased that Pa and the hired man thought she had hit the hawk as if it had actually fallen and we could have gone and brought it home.

Crows that had nests in the woods would frequently drive hawks away from their nesting area by flying above them and diving to pick or claw their backs. It was pleasing to us to see the kingbirds (we called them bee-birds,) flying even higher than the crows and diving alternately at both crows and the hawk. The crows usually were the first to pull out of such flights and leave

145

the kingbirds a free hand to drive the hawks out of the vicinity. The kingbird cleared both from their nesting area at any time of day that either came near.

The barn swallows and chimney swifts vied with each other, gathering their evening insect meal, each appearing to show off his swift, easy, effortless flight as if he knew we were watching his antics.

- - - - - - - - - - - -

"Grandpa, you really had a lot of things to watch during those long evenings. Did you play games too?"

"Yes, we played games in the yard and some of them are ones you've played too. We also had chores to do, so I shall tell about some of them. . . "

- - - - - - - - - - - -

EVENING GAMES and CHORES

We children played games in the yard and surrounding lots, such as Hide and Seek, I Spy, Croquet, Leapfrog. We also played with our wagons, and then watched clouds, and the stars come out.

There was a small run that found its way across both the chicken and hog lots, across the end of the meadow and road, and into Big Cove. It was dry at times, but by building small dams when it was low, we had great times floating small boats and using small sticks for saw logs and crossties. We pretended a lot of timber operations that we had seen take place in Big Cove Creek. Dams, mill wheels, canals and water-wheels were built and operated in abundance. Bridges got washed out and people had to go around steep hills to get to other bridges, or find safe fording places. The activities along this run were a source of much fun.

It must not be forgotten that the cows and calves had to be taken care of, and the milking done, each evening and morning, just as regularly as eating supper and breakfast. The hungry wood box had to be kept full, even if it did take part of our long evenings to keep that done. Good meals required good fire in the stove.

146

Feeding the chickens and slopping the hogs were among other things that had to be done at regular times. Such chores, including washing the dishes after every meal, were divided among all of us so that all shared fairly equally. When we were all small, I can remember very clearly that George and Eunice did the breakfast dishes, Lois and I did the dinner dishes. We took turns with Ma doing the supper dishes. We tested whether the dish was clean by rubbing our fingers over the wet dish before putting it into the rinse water. If our fingers made a squeaking noise, it went into the rinse. If not, it got more washing. It was often necessary to add more soap and hot water to the washing water to get the dishes to pass the test.

Late one Sunday afternoon, the preacher called at our place and was asked to stay for supper. When Ma went to the kitchen to prepare supper, she found the wood box empty. She told George and me to bring in some wood. We found no wood ready-cut in the wood yard. We began quietly trying to break wood into stove length, so the preacher wouldn't hear us working on Sunday. Then a piece flew up and hit me across the nose causing it to bleed freely. It was no use trying to be quiet about it. So George hunted what he thought would be easy pieces to cut, while I cut them. I am sure my ax never sounded louder than it did that quiet Sunday evening, while I was chopping wood to cook supper for the preacher. I hesitated to come to the table with the patch on my nose, but Ma said to come on and eat as if nothing had happened. I did. Of course the preacher said nothing to me, nor did he look at me critically, but I thought that part of his table blessing was directed toward me. Perhaps we were more careful after that to keep stove wood in the box. Many times afterward, when George and I were out working on the farm, that box would become empty and Ma and our sisters had to cut wood so they could cook the meals.

CHICKENS and PIGS

A part of our regular chores included feeding the young chickens, but Ma usually supervised this rather closely since special feed mixtures were necessary until the young chickens could eat wheat, corn and other rough feeds. They also required doctoring for gapes, limber-neck and other young troubles.

147

The older chickens' diet was principally corn which Pa scattered out for them at the time he slopped the hogs. Taking care of the pigs was Pa's special chore and he enjoyed watching them eat. He was very particular about the feed mixture for them. He kept a swill barrel (made by sawing a wood barrel in half,) full of a mixture of feed that was allowed to sour. It consisted of clabber milk, buttermilk, whey, sour milk, dishwater and food scraps from the table. Bran and middlings were added when needed, to enrich the swill and keep a big enough supply ahead so it maintained the proper sourness, suitable for feeding hogs. This swill was kept on a bench inside the yard and was covered to prevent chickens, dogs, and small children from toppling into it. I once heard about a child falling into such a mixture. She was instantly pulled out before any harm was done, except that it took a lot of combing and washing to get the slop out of her long hair.

Water was used when needed to keep the mixture at the right consistence. Hogs liked the slop and thrived on it.

I remember one time, some neighbor's dogs got to knocking the cover off the tubs and upsetting Pa's slop buckets. We told some of the neighbors that dogs were bothering us and that if their dogs were running around at night, to tie them up, because we were going to stop these dogs messing with the slop barrels. They said their dogs didn't run away from home, which relieved us, although we had an idea they might be mistaken. We tried to get a shot at the dog two or three times, but it got away too fast each time.

One evening, I had gone to bed upstairs and was sound asleep when Pa called to me from the foot of the stairs. About half-awake, I answered. He said,

'Bryan, that dog is out here again!'

I grabbed the twenty-two rifle and hurried downstairs and out onto the back porch just as the strange dog, followed by a small dog we had, ran toward the yard gate. It was dark and all I could see was the dark outline of the dog, as I fired at it. I knew it had been hit since it hit the gate as it went through and crashed through the bars at the far side of the hog lot. Our neighbor's dog was shot by a twenty-two that same night, although they thought it was at home, and never left home at night. Dogs didn't bother Pa's swill barrel any more.

Our chicken house was built pretty tight. Open areas were screened to keep out weasels, mink, hawks, owls and other chicken enemies. We tried to train all the chickens to roost inside at night so we could close the door after dark and they would be more secure. Some continued to roost on the fence or in low trees but, by far, the most that were roosting outside, flew up into a shellbark hickory tree whose limbs began about 8 or 10 feet from the ground,. They were fairly safe in this tree since it was too large to climb easily. When the leaves were on, the chickens were pretty well hidden from the view of owls or hawks.

It was interesting to watch them flying up in the tree about dark, each evening. After the leaves fell from the tree, the chickens lined up on the limbs in groups of twos, threes and fours, here and there, and were in full view against the evening sky. Of course, they did not show up quite as well from an owl's point of view, looking toward the ground. The thick tree limbs were some protection from flying enemies. I can't think of a colder roosting place than that hickory tree on cold winter nights.

Just before Christmas one year, a big hoot owl caught one of the chickens from the hickory tree roost and carried it over to a big walnut tree about 30 feet away. He ate part of it there before he was scared and dropped the rest to the ground and flew away. We knew he would be back the next night to complete his meal, so we staked the hen to the ground so he would have to eat it there. We set a steel trap beside the hen. It was late the next night when the dog began barking and waked us up to find the owl caught in the trap. We had to shoot him to get him loose. He flapped his wings at us and struck out with his huge, sharp claws. We did not take any chance of getting scratched with such claws. This would have been an excellent specimen for mounting.

Owls never bothered our chickens very much. I remember one other time, many years later, when your Grandma and I lived at Glenville. The chickens got to making a big noise just after dark. We went out. At first, we could not see anything and then one old hen came out making a great to-do, fluttering and flapping. I caught her and still could see nothing until I held her up by the tip of one wing. There, close under her wing, a little screech owl had fastened himself, and was clinging on tightly. I knocked him loose and the old hen quieted down and went back to roost, little the worse for the experience. The owl would have probably killed her if we had not come to her aid. Some time later, a little screech owl came down our chimney, into the fireplace when there was no fire. We had to open the fire screen to get him and put him outside the house. This could have been the same one that had been fastened to the old hen. We thought we were having an owly time of it.

- - - - - - - - - - - - -

"Your mother might have been old enough to remember that owl coming down the chimney."

"I'll ask her sometime. Owls eat lots of mice too, don't they?"

"Yes, they do. Far more mice than chickens. Have I told you about my Pa's pet guinea hen? Well, one evening Pa came in after feeding the chickens. . ."

- - - - - - - - - - - - -

PA'S GUINEA HEN

'You should have seen that old guinea this evening,' Pa said to us. 'I scattered the corn out for the chickens, ducks and guineas and all began picking it up rapidly. All of a sudden, that old guinea uttered a sharp cry, as he does when a hawk is near, and all rushed under the granary as they do whenever he gives that warning. This time he remained out busily picking up corn. I could see no hawk anywhere. I have noticed him doing that before but he generally ran toward shelter himself, then hurried back and began eating before the others got back. This time he made no effort to stop eating. I am sure he is doing that just so he can get more corn. You ought to see how slick he does it! He even sort of clucks after he has eaten awhile, as if to say, it is safe to come out now!'

Many of us have been out to watch Pa's educated guinea although sometimes he would disappoint us, as if to tell us he doesn't want to push a good thing too far, too fast.

Pa often told us about killing a hawk with a rock as he and his father came home from sawing on the old mill. As they came

150

through the barn lot toward the house, a small hawk flew across the garden and lit on a post on the lower side. Pa picked up a rock and threw it, saying,

'I'll kill that hawk.' The rock did hit the hawk, knocking it off the post, dead. Pa said his Dad was very surprised and that he himself was also surprised, since it was over 100 feet away. Pa said he and his brothers were good throwers and got a lot of practice at squirrels and other animals. He said they would stand in the front yard and hit trees in the woods along the bluff across the creek, a distance of 125 yards or more. He said a cousin of his was an extra good thrower and could hit a big chestnut tree standing 200 yards distant, in the field above the bluff. He thought his cousin would have been a good baseball pitcher if they had been playing ball then. I have hit trees in the woods, but never could throw a rock to that big chestnut tree in the field above.

- - - - - - - - - - - - -

"Maybe that's where I got my Little League pitching arm."

"Yes, Joe, you can practice throwing at trees for accuracy. Sometimes we threw rocks at cows to get them to come in at milking time. We weren't really trying to hit them. ."

- - - - - - - - - - - - -

MILKING COWS

Cows with young calves were usually sure to be at the milking lot each morning and evening to suckle their calves and be milked. After the calves were weaned, they did not come in of their own volition. Some people fed their cows a little, morning and evening, to get them to come in, but we had plenty of good grass out in the pasture throughout the growing season and depended on that for cow feed. Since evenings and mornings were the most pleasant grazing periods, it became a regular chore to go out into the pasture and drive the cows in at milking time.

151

Some farmers had their dogs trained to do this chore, which was fine when the dogs would do it in a quiet manner, which some dogs were good at. Others chased the cows off the hills which got the cows all excited so they wouldn't give their milk down, and fidgeted about while being milked. We tried our dogs a few times but the cows became scared and the dogs became fiercer, so we had to stop trying to train them and go after the cows ourselves.

This was one of my earliest chores. When I was small, some of our cows acted as if they wanted to butt me, so I was told always to carry a heavy hickory switch to strike at them to keep them away. We did not keep such cows more than one season. When two of us went together, each had a big switch or stick. We used them very little for protection but by waving the switch or hitting the ground, cows at some distance away would start off toward the house. We often threw rocks to get them going, which did the trick, whether the rocks hit them or not. Calling or hollering at the cows, from halfway up the hill, sometimes got them going toward the house, without having to climb to the top of the hill.

- - - - - - - - - - - - -

"You had lots of ways of getting the cows to come, didn't you?"

"Yes, we did. We played in the hay mow too. You've done that, haven't you? Perhaps at Uncle Perry's on a rainy day. One time Pa really scared us. . . ."

- - - - - - - - - - - - -

THE HAY MOW

We often played in the hay mow, sliding down the steep slopes or jumping from one loose pile to another loose pile of hay. Sometimes we would simply lie in the hay and listen to the patter of rain on the clapboard roof.

George and I were playing there one evening when we looked through a crack in the end of the mow and saw Pa riding up the road on his way home from the mill and store at Troy. We knew he would come up in the mow to throw down hay to Molly before going on to the house. By hiding on top of the hay and making some queer noises when he came up to feed Molly, we were sure we could scare him. We hid and waited. Sure enough, up the ladder he came. When he began forking the hay, we started our scary racket. At first he stepped about noisily and we were sure he was frightened. We could scarcely keep from laughing aloud. He mumbled something about getting it. Suddenly, the fun ceased! Something bumped against the hay and four prongs of a pitchfork appeared above the edge of the hay as if ready to be plunged at us. We crouched low in fright, both yelling,

'Stop! It's us! Don't gouge us!'

'You squalled just in time! I was just ready to throw the pitchfork. You might have been hurt!' Two scared, sheepish-looking boys climbed down off the hay, much relieved, and eager to help carry the groceries to the house. We were very scared by the four-prong fork, but I am sure Pa knew all the time what we were doing, and just turned the joke about on us.

- - - - - - - - - - - - - -

"Your Pa must have been good with jokes and stories. Tell us some more about him."

"Pa was 45 years old when he and Ma were married, so keeping up with us 8 kids must have kept him busy. He'd already been sheriff of Gilmer County, and had lots of stories to tell. I'll tell you more of them later. We especially liked his deer stories and the ones about when was young. . ."

- - - - - - - - - - - - -

PA'S BOYHOOD

Once, when Pa was a boy in his early teens, he came into the house and sat down before the fire to rest after a long day's work in the field. He sat there quietly, half dozing, until his mother thought maybe he was sick, and asked,

'What's the matter with you, Tom, that you are so quiet? Are you sick?'

'Oh, nothing much. I'm just resting,' he replied.

'That's not like you. What do you think would help you?'

'I don't hardly know.'

'Is there something I could get you?'

'I- I - - believe a bunch of dried grapes up there,' pointing to the dried grapes handing up next to the ceiling, 'might help!'

She got him the bunch of grapes, grinning as she handed them to him. Pa had such a pleased expression on his face each time he told us of that dried grape incident, that I am sure he was re-living the pleasant taste of the grapes, and his mother's care and interest in getting them down for him.

Pa told us how he and his brothers had made and played with bows and arrows when they were boys and the fun they had with them. George and I persuaded him to help us make each of us a bow and arrow, including one for him. This extended over several evenings and included getting the bow material of hickory and straight gum sprouts for arrows. We did not add points or feathers to the gum sprout arrows at that time. Pa made a larger bow for himself and helped us make two smaller ones. We spent many pleasant evenings practicing with our new bows and arrows.

Pa told us about an old Indian who was with a show, coming by many years earlier and wanting to buy a chicken. The Indian proposed that if he could hit one with an arrow, that it would be free. Such an agreement was made and he was to shoot the one of his choice. He aimed at a big hen, pulled his bow string back and let the arrow fly. He missed completely and was so disappointed that when he picked up his arrow and saw that it was crooked, he broke it into pieces. He paid for whichever chicken they were able to catch for him, perhaps not the same one he shot at.

This was encouraging to us, when an Indian, who is an expert with his bow, could not hit a hen; we didn't feel badly at miss the target occasionally. We never practiced on chickens and were cautioned not to shoot toward anyone.

One time, Guy Scott, George and I were out in the orchard shooting at birds. Guy shot near one which he said 'stunted' it. He meant 'stunned' it. We did kill a chipping sparrow and brought it in proudly to show our parents. Neither Guy's parents nor ours approved of this, or of shooting song birds. It was all right to shoot English Sparrows which made such a nuisance of themselves and seemed to drive away more desirable birds. With this restriction, our later practice was directed more on targets, rats (which I already told you about) and other destructive animals.

HOW TO MAKE OUR SPECIAL DART

We made a dart somewhat like this drawing. The wide end helped make it fly with the sharp end forward.

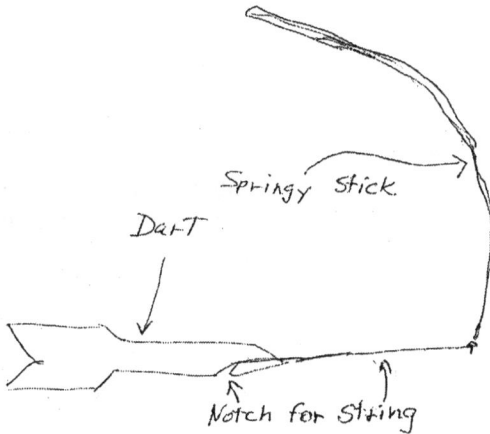

Our Dart

In order to make it fly, we used a springy stick, 2 or 3 feet long with a string about 2 feet long tied to the small end of the stick. There was a knot near the end to keep the string from pulling through the notch near the sharp end of the dart.

We took the large end of the springy stick in one hand, the wide end of the dart in the other, with the knotted end of the string in the dart notch. Then we pulled the dart back, which bent the stick (which acted as a bow.) When we let loose of the dart, it would fly quite a distance or high into the air. Both the arrows and darts were used over and over, if they could be recovered after each shot.

- - - - - - - - - - - - - - -

"That sounds like it would be fun to make. Can we try it tomorrow?"

"Yes, I'll help you. Right now, if you will set up the wickets, I'll beat you in a game of croquet. That's one thing that hasn't changed much although perhaps we played if oftener years ago. . ."

- - - - - - - - - - - - - -

CROQUET

Your Grandma has told me how her mother, when she was young, helped her sisters and brothers cut the four round balls off the tops of the posts of their four-poster bed to make croquet balls. They did this without asking their mother's permission. It was not mentioned what punishment they got for defacing the bed so I'll leave that to your imagination.

Another story she tells happened one evening on their croquet ground when several were playing and watching. Her youngest sister, Kathleen, had a kitten which was running and playing among the people on and near the croquet ground. Her brother, Page, who was then about 10 or 12 years old, said, in fun,

'What would happen if I hit that kitten?' as he motioned at it with his croquet mallet, attempting to stop the stroke before the mallet hit the kitten. He did not stop soon enough; it hit the kitten, killing it instantly. Page said he never intended to hit the kitten at all. Of course, Kathleen thought he had tried to hit it and cried until finally she was pacified by being promised another kitten. Page was given a good scolding for acting so carelessly.

- - - - - - - - - - - -

"You'll notice almost all these things we've been talking about are outdoor activities."

"I bet Uncle Page was more careful around kittens after that!"

"That's true. Did you know the teacher used to visit in the home of each student and sometimes stay overnight?"

- - - - - - - - - - - - - -

FIRESIDE GAMES

As the long daylight evenings shorten and dark evenings lengthen and get colder, evening entertainment activities change from outside to indoor fireside pastimes.

During the nice fall weather after school began, the teacher tried to visit the home of each of the pupils and sometimes stayed overnight. I remember some of these overnight teachers' visits to our house, including one overnight visit by the County Superintendent of Schools. These visits always included discussions with Pa and Ma about the progress of each of us children in school in a general way, since we usually had no particular problems that required special attention. Pa and Ma were usually praised for seeing that we kept our school work up when we missed school. During such visits, there was generally time for some games for all, such as dominoes, fox & geese, checkers, riddles, telling ghost stories, telling fortunes by reading palms or asking questions of the Ouija Board or the walking table.

An extra lunch was sent with us to school the next day so the teacher and we children could eat lunch together. This was always a high point of the visit, but I am sure the mothers were glad when such visits were over. Of course, it was an opportunity to show off their cooking abilities but perhaps this honor did not pay for the extra work involved.

When school was in session, the first thing for us children, was to do whatever school work that was required for the next day. Then we were free to do individual reading or other things of interest. One or two evenings each week were sort of reserved for family activities which included games, reading, talking and story-telling; this is where Pa's deer stories came in.

Ma was a good reader and sometimes read stories for the younger children while the older ones were preparing their school work. After the lessons were finished, or on reading and story-telling nights, Ma would read aloud from books in which all of us were interested. Sometimes some of us older children would take turns with the reading. We did quite a bit of the reading aloud because we usually had only one oil lamp sitting on the table before the fire and all of could not get sufficient light to read at the same time. A few of the books and stories we read in this way were <u>Robinson Crusoe</u>, <u>Leather Stocking Tales</u>, <u>20,000 Leagues Under The Sea</u>, <u>The Sky Pirate</u>, <u>Little Women</u>, <u>Get Rich Quick Wallingford</u>, <u>Cudjo's Cave</u>, <u>The Lost Cause</u>, <u>Davy Crocket</u>, <u>Lewis Wetzel</u>, <u>Daniel Boone</u>, <u>Kit Carson</u>, <u>Daring Deeds and Thrilling Adventures of Pioneers of the Ohio Valley</u>, <u>Black Beauty</u>, <u>Peck's Bad Boy</u>, <u>Tom Sawyer</u> and many more.

Before daily delivery of the mail, we subscribed to weekly papers that were picked up on Saturday evenings at the Post Office at Troy. Among such papers over the years were The Glenville Democrat (local county paper,) Toledo Blade, Cincinnati Enquirer, Atlanta Constitution, The Commoner, Farm Journal, Ladies' Home Journal, Clarksburg Exponent and others. Several of these papers had serial stories running from week to week. Some had funny pages, including such characters as Little Willie Winkie, Mutt & Jeff, Slimmy & Bicky and many others in the brightly colored comic pages. These were of great delight for us children and amusing for older people also. These papers furnished a wide variety of reading material for people of all ages and were eagerly looked forward to on Saturday evenings.

Every so often we would decide to have an evening for Pa to tell his deer hunting stories which he did in a manner that was very interesting for all of us. Sometimes he would ask what story to tell. We would tell him part of the one we wanted to hear first. In fact, we got to know many of them well enough to tell them ourselves but it was more interesting and fun for him to tell them. We liked to hear them over and over. We children knew where all the licks, runs, hills and places were located that Pa mentioned in his stories. We could follow them as if we were going along with him on their hunts. It was almost as exciting to us as being there.

- - - - - - - - - - - -

"Perhaps I can remember enough details to tell you 2 or 3 of Pa's stories, to give you an idea of what they were like."

"You can pretend you are your Pa, when you tell the story. . ."

- - - - - - - - - - - -

158

PA'S DEER STORIES

Since the leaves came out, we had not gone out to hunt with the hounds because it was hard to see the deer, with everything in full leaf. Since the weather became hot, deer would be going to the licks for water. In addition to the water, the deer needed the salt which is in the lick water. Salt is not found in all springs but we knew of 3 or 4 not far away so we decided to see if they were being used yet. We started out one afternoon. We went to a small lick on Board Cut first. There were no signs of deer coming into it to drink. We had left our hounds tied up so they would not run the deer out of the area, if they were using any of the licks. We had only two guns, a muzzle loading percussion cap rifle and an old musket. It, too, was muzzle loading and used percussion caps to explode the powder in the breech to shoot the bullet. One had to be sure there was powder in the tube when putting the cap on, to be sure the explosion of the cap on the tube, when hit by the hammer after the trigger was pulled, would explode the powder in the breech behind the bullet and shoot the gun. We carried the guns with the safety on, that is, with the hammer raised slightly off the cap, and tube not fully cocked. Oll was carrying the rifle while Zan started out carrying the musket. We expected to take turns carrying each. (Oll and Zan were Pa's brothers, Oliver Cromwell and Alexander McQuain.)

We followed the ridge to the Bear Wallow on the ridge at Queen's place where we dropped over on the Crane Run side and continued on toward the big lick near the head of the Left Fork of Crane Run. Here we found the deer were making paths into the lick to drink. We had never watched this lick. There was a big up-rooted tree hole near the lick that could be used as a makeshift blind, but had very little roof to protect from rain or to keep deer from seeing us as they came down the hill into the lick. We carried a few poles and loose bark from an old dead tree not far away. We improved the blind and roof so it would do to use if we decided to come back and watch this lick some time later.

159

We decided to cross over to the Big Lick near the head of Big Run. We were picking and eating huckleberries as we walked along the path, when suddenly, out ahead of us, we saw an old buck. I was in front and carrying the old musket which I took off my shoulder, cocked and began getting into position so I could see to shoot, when the buck winded us and took off down the hill. Oll did not get a chance to shoot either. We started ahead and I un-cocked the musket and started to let the hammer down on safety, when my sweaty thumb slipped off the hammer and the musket went off. The bullets went back above Oll and Zan. I had not lowered the musket to my shoulder before my thumb slipped, but when the musket went off, I did not know this and became more frightened as the seconds passed. We had loaded the gun with 2 or 3 rifle balls. We reloaded the musket and Zan said he would take a turn at carrying it. I felt relieved that he did.

In a little while, we came to the Big Lick. Deer had been using it more than the one we had just left on Crane Run. There was plenty of water in the main lick and in several places below, where they had been drinking. There was a fairly good blind here but we made a few repairs and added a few pieces of bark from an old log to the roof. We put more clay on the roof where pitch pine splinters and pieces of pine knots were used to make a little light to see by when waiting for deer to come into the lick. Deer were not afraid of fire since they often saw it burning in the forest. Some hunters thought it was better to have a small fire when watching a lick, since they thought deer were not so nervous and easily frightened where a small fire was burning. We did not expect to watch a lick that night, since we knew that in fixing up blinds and looking around the licks, we would leave so many tracks and signs that deer would shy away for awhile. We had things ready then, to slip back some night soon and try our luck. With this in mind, we returned home.

George Sandy, who lived on Big Run, came down about the middle of the week and wanted us to go with him and watch the Big Lick that evening. He said a lot of deer were using it. We told him we would be up before dark and go with him.

Oll and I went up and we all got to the lick before dark. It was hot, dry weather and the lick had been used much more than when we had been there before. We went into the blind from the east side, since the wind was blowing in that direction, away from the lick, and toward the blind. The wind usually blew from west to east. A supply of small pieces of pitch pine knots and splinters were placed in the blind to replenish the fire, on top the blind, which we lighted before dark. Soon after dark, we began to hear what seemed to be several animals shuffling along about 150 or 200 yards away. At first we thought it might be a drove of thirsty deer on its way to the lick. We listened quietly. A small tapping against the blind began near where George Sandy was sitting. No mistake, it was near him. I reached over and put my hand on his arm. He was trembling all over.

'What's the matter, George?' I asked.

'I can't hardly wait for the deer to get here!'

'Quiet down, George, I don't think the noise we are hearing is made by deer. It is staying too much in the same area. Did you hear that?'

'Yes, that sounded like a log rolling. Did you hear that grunt? That's an old bear and her cubs feeding on grubs and bugs among the rocks and around that rotten log. I've heard them before. Deer won't come near while they are feeding over there.'

George had stopped trembling now. This nervous anxious waiting among hunters was called 'buck ague' or 'buck ager.' We had been talking in low whispers so as not to frighten any deer that might be near us. Gradually the bear and cubs shuffled their way over the hill and out of hearing. Night quiet settled about us. Our quiet watch continued. Once I heard a twig snap. George said it was rabbits trotting around. He dozed off. I knew there were deer around because no rabbit would have snapped a twig in walking. Oll and I kept a sharp lookout. After awhile, we heard two coming in and could dimly see them nearing the lick. George began to stir. I was afraid he might make a noise so I touched him on the arm and whispered to him to be quiet, that one was coming. He rose up excitedly exclaiming,

'Where is he, Tommy?' at the same time knocking the rifle from Oll's hands. The deer trotted away.

'I was dreaming of eating venison,' George said.

We decided that dreaming was all we could do if our luck did not change. We had 'styled' (sighted) the musket near me, on the drinking place of the lick. We decided to sight the rifle Oll had, on another less used part close by. We added fuel to our light and sighted Oll's rifle the best we could. Both were cocked and all we had to do was pull the triggers when we could hear them drinking water. Oll was to pull the rifle trigger and I, the musket. The moon had gone down now and the only light was from the small blaze on top the blind. All quieted down and the watch continued. George began dozing and I was sure I would not again try to quiet him if deer should come back. Oll and I became sleepy and must have been half asleep when I looked up on the bank above the lick and could barely make out the forms of two deer. They were perfectly still, as if looking to see whether it was safe to go in to drink. I touched Oll and whispered to him what I thought I could see. He could see the same thing. They appeared to be going toward the two drinking spaces. We had to depend on the sound of them drinking the water to be sure they were where our guns were aimed. Oll was to push his finger against me lightly and both were to pull our triggers as nearly the same time as possible. At the gentle pressure, we both pulled our triggers. The guns banged almost at the same time, followed instantly by George, rising from his sleep, bumping into us and the two guns, exclaiming,

'What is it? Did you hit it?'

We all rushed out to the lick together. There was the big buck but nowhere did we see the smaller deer. We carried the buck a little distance from the lick to stick him so he would bleed freely. Then we gutted him and cut him into pieces so we could carry him. It was full daylight when we finished this work and were ready to start home with our prize. We went back to the lick to see if we could tell what had happened to the little deer. There lay a bunch of white belly hair, but no blood that we could see, any place around the lick. We decided the rifle bullet had passed close under its belly, cutting off the hair but missing the deer. They said the buck had bled profusely where he fell, but I could see no blood. I thought they were trying to fool me but when they pointed out a mass of blood to me, I knew it was blood but could not distinguish the color. This was the first I knew that I was blind to the color red. I have since tried to see blood when others were tracking a wounded deer by the blood left along the trail; I could not see it.

George Sandy wanted to take the hide home with him and tan it for moccasins. We let him do that. There was a pretty well defined rule among hunters that the first bullet hole took the hide but Oll and I were not particularly anxious for the tanning job and

162

were glad he wanted it. The venison was fat enough to cook unusually tender; George said it was the best he ever ate.

- - - - - - - - - - -

"That must have taken your Pa a long time to tell."

"Yes, and if he changed it in any way, we were sure to let him know about it. That was a summer deer hunting story, but he told about hunting at other seasons of the year too."

"After the leaves were down during the late fall and winter, they hunted pretty much as people hunt deer today. They stationed people at low gaps and places where deer would pass as they ran from one area into another. These hunting trips varied in details and results; some were successful but many were not, from the standpoint of getting a deer. The elements of excitement and expected success were always there."

"Here's one of Pa's winter hunts, again with Pa telling the story."

- - - - - - - - -

PA'S WINTER DEER HUNT

George Sandy had been wanting us to bring our deer hounds and go up by his place and go deer hunting. We said we would have our work caught up so we could get away by the last of the week and we'd be up then. He had seen deer on the head of Crane Run but could not get near enough to shoot.

By Thursday, we got our work finished so we could take time off to go hunting. It had been raining during the night but it looked as if it would be good hunting. Oll and Zan carried the guns and were to go up Big Run and get with George Sandy. They were to station themselves in low gaps at the head of the left fork of Crane Run, where the deer might cross over toward Big Run or Horn Creek. I led our two hounds and was to cross over from Board Cut to the lower part of Crane Run where the big woods began. I would let the hounds loose there and then meet the others at their stations.

163

At the mouth of Board Cut, I left Oll and Zan and started over the ridge to where I would let the hounds loose. They said they would be in position by the time I got there. As I went up Board Cut, I could see deer tracks here and there. It was all I could do to hold the hounds. I scolded them and we made considerable noise as we went along to frighten any deer, and, hopefully, cause them to run on ahead of us. I don't know how successful I was at keeping the deer ahead of me but I was certainly glad to let the hounds loose when I got there, because they were so hard to hold. They were pretty good at hunting along on both sides of the run as I walked up toward the head. I had about a mile and a half to go to the low gaps at the head of the run.

There had been deer here. The hounds kept trailing, first on one side of the run and then on the other. It was a cold trail. It began to warm up when we were about halfway, although they seemed to be on different trails. One was going toward Big Run, while the other was on a branch that went toward Horn Creek. I decided to go toward Big Run and then follow the ridge from there toward the low gaps farther on toward Horn Creek. I heard a shot toward the Big Run gap and hurried in that direction. George Sandy was at this station.

'Did you get him, George?'

'No, Tommy, he ran off toward Horn Creek.'

'Where was he when you shot?'

'He was up there, just in the open, coming straight at me!'

'Why didn't you wait until he got closer?'

'I thought I could get another shot when he got nearer if I missed the first one, but he turned off and went the other way. I see I made a mistake. I'll load up.'

'Do you want me to help you?' He had the 'buck ague' so bad by now that he could not pour powder into the charger from the powder horn. Just then we heard a shot in the low gap ahead and we hurried in that direction without reloading. When we got there, Oll said he had shot at one and was sure he had hit it. He had reloaded and when Zan came running to us, we all started after the wounded deer. They kept talking about seeing the blood as we hurried along. As I told you, I couldn't see any blood because of my color-blindness. I looked far ahead of us and saw a man on horseback with a deer across the saddle in front of him, about to round the turn out of sight.

'Doesn't that man have a deer?' I asked.

'He certainly does!' said Oll, 'I'll bet that's my deer.'

The hound had come back to us now. We hurried on and found the place where the deer had fallen. It looked as it someone had pulled the deer to the horse and then took off. We had no idea who the man might be, but we were sure now that it was our deer we saw on his saddle. If Oll had followed the deer at once, without first reloading, we might have had that deer we saw carried away on horseback.

'I'll reload now,' George Sandy said.

I watched him and saw that his 'buck ague' was gone. He now had no trouble pouring powder into the charger (a small hollow tube to measure the amount of powder for each shot.) He was a good shot when hunting rabbits, squirrels and other small game but got too excited when waiting for bigger game to come near enough to shoot.

'George, what are you doing now?' I asked him.

'Tommy, I've run out of bullet patching cotton. I'm cutting patches from the tail of my shirt that sticks down into my breeches. It isn't much good there. Anyway, I leave enough between patches to hold my shirt down.'

He finished pulling the tail of his shirt out and laid it across the muzzle of his rifle, pressed the bullet and shirt into the muzzle and then cut the tail off even with the muzzle, leaving a hole in his shirttail about an inch in diameter. He then pushed the bullet down with the ramrod and bounced it a few times on the bullet to pack the powder. At this rate, the holes would get above the top of his pants before winter ended. The tail of his shirt wouldn't hold hickory nuts now.

'George, you can have part of this worn-out shirt I'm using and save your good shirt.'

'I'm glad to get that, Tommy. I can't cut many more patches from this shirt before the holes get above my breeches and start letting the wind in.'

I tied my lead rope to the hound that had come back to us. That dog was about as disappointed at losing the deer as we were. The other hound had gone over toward the head of Big Run. Oll and the others were going on up the ridge to low gaps between Big Run, Bloody Run, Wolfpen and the head of Horn Creek. I would take my hound down the pike a little way and, after giving them

165

time to get in position, let him loose. This I did, and then followed up the Horn Creek branch toward Wolfpen, over a mile away. Deer had been active here and the hound finally picked up a hot trail going toward Wolfpen. I heard a shot in that direction and hurried toward it. When I got to the low gap, no one was in sight. I heard Zan call from farther out the ridge,

'I'm out here, Tom. I got one!' I hurried to him and saw that it was a nice four-prong buck.

'I shot him back where you were. He only made it this far.'

We gutted the buck and tied his legs together so two of us could carry him on a pole between us. Before we had this job completed, George and Oll came to us. We took turns carrying until we got to George Sandy's cabin where we skinned the deer and divided the venison, giving George over a third of it, together with the skin. Zan wanted the horns so we took them. Lib, George's wife, said they would have a lot of good messes (meals) of their share. They had no children and depended on hunting for most of their meat, finding it pretty scarce at times. We were all very well satisfied with that day's hunting, which might have been better, had our luck with the other deer been different. We have been on hunting trips when we never saw a deer, much less getting a shot at one.

Another time, George Sandy was out by himself and some hounds scared up a deer which trotted near George who quickly shot at it, breaking its neck close to its head, instantly killing it. I came by his place a few days afterward and he was showing me what a good shot he had made and I said,

'You almost hit it in the head!'

'Yes, that's where I aimed but he was running and that must have been the reason I hit a little behind where I was aiming.'

'That was certainly a good shot, George!'

I thought to myself that he probably would have missed completely if it had not been running. It happened so quickly that he did not have time to get his usual 'buck ague.' George wasn't a very good deer hunter, but neither were we. It was good to have an older person with us part of the time, since we were not fully grown.

166

- - - - - - - - - - - -

"This gives you an idea of what Pa's deer stories were like. He had about a dozen or more of such stories that we liked to hear him tell."

"Grandma said she has a deer story to tell us. Can she do that now?"

"I think her stories are more up-to-date than those of Pa's."

"It's your turn, Grandma. . . . "

- - - - - - - - - - - -

GRANDMA'S DEER STORY

A few years ago, Bryan and I were back visiting in West Virginia. We went over to my old home place on the head of Sinking Creek where we drove into the barn-lot next to the house, just as we had done so many times in visiting my mother and father when they were living there. No one lived in the house anymore and the place was going to pieces. Some of the windows and doors were gone. It made me sad to look around, for Mama and Dad always took such pride and enjoyment in keeping things up nice. It was a sad occasion, but brought to both of us many pleasant memories of the happy times we had enjoyed there. We had wandered about the place and then sat down on the steps to the front porch to rest and look around.

I was looking up at the meadow on top of the hill where we used to pick peaches from the trees that grew along the rail fence at the lower edge of the meadow, when I saw an animal coming across the meadow toward us. I said to Bryan,

'What is that?' and before he could answer, I saw that it was a big buck with many pronged antlers.

'That's a big buck!'

'I saw what it was as soon as I asked you.'

'There! Did you see how easily he jumped over that fence?'

We sat quietly as he came slowly down the hill toward us, nipping at vegetation as he came along. At the run, he veered up toward the Orpha house, easily loping over what fence was left around the turkey lot. He seemed in no hurry as he continued nipping and eating things as he continued up the hill. Bryan thought there might be dogs far behind, following him. As he passed over the top of the hill, out of view, we thought we could hear a hound, barking on beyond the meadow where the deer had come from. Soon two hounds came, slowly across the meadow, over the fence and down the hill, following the trail the deer had made. The hounds seemed tired; barking intermittently, as they slowly followed the trail. Half-heartedly, they continued the trail, over the hill, out of sight. We wondered how much farther they would continue and what the outcome would be.

Since we were there, someone has bought the old Morrison place and has built a new house. All the fields have grown up again and no one farms it any more, using it for a summer home. We told Perry about seeing the big buck, when we got over to his farm and he said,

'I've been seeing deer pasturing in the meadows in the bottom land of evenings. I've seen 4 or 5 there before dark. Sometimes they come in from Hudkins Hollow and sometimes they come down from the hills on either side, into the bottoms farther up Little Cove toward Berkley Barbarow's place.'

We kept looking from time to time, toward the areas he indicated. Once or twice that evening we thought we could see deer in the short brush outside the meadow, but none came out into the meadow to graze.

'We'll get in the truck and go over there after dark. Then we are pretty sure to see them, if you don't get to see any before dark,' Perry told us.

We kept looking but none came out before dark. Sometime after dark, we all three climbed into the truck cab and drove over in the meadow toward the Hudkin's Hollow. We saw 3 or 4 by the truck lights before we stopped and turned out the lights.

'It is dangerous to keep the lights on,' said Perry. 'Deer are sometimes blinded by the lights and jump right into a truck. Can you see their eyes out there in the dark?'

We looked and could see two eyes shining like cat's eyes as we caught the form of each deer. After we sat there a little while with the lights off, he turned them on again. The deer continued eating nervously, but soon trotted away and easily loped over the fence and gracefully disappeared into the woods beyond the brushy pasture. Perry says there are far more deer in the woods now than when Pa, Oll, Zan and George Sandy used to do their deer hunting.

- - - - - - - - - - -

"Our dad took us deer hunting at Uncle Perry's farm one year. I was glad we didn't kill one. I'd rather just watch them. Grandma, feeding us these cookies while you told your deer story, was a real good idea!"

"Yes, Joe, your grandma thought the cookies might make her story the most interesting of all. Our Pa had another kind of story he used to tell on those long winter evenings. They were Tall Tales, with heroes much larger than life. Paddy McCann was our favorite.

"You'll have to imagine that you're living in the Rich Mountain area of West Virginia, over a hundred years ago."

"Was Paddy McCann a Paul Bunyan type person, Grandpa?"

"You can decide that, when you hear about him, Joe. . ."

- - - - - - - - - - - - - -

PADDY Mc CANN

Paddy was an Irishman living in a log cabin with his wife and children near the foot of Rich Mountain, when this story took place.

'Here comes old Paddy now. I wonder what he has been doing since we saw him last.'

'He is sure to have something!'

'We'll soon find out.'

'Good evening, Paddy. It's been a coon's age since we have seen you. We thought something awful might have happened to you.'

'I am feeling good now, and the old woman and kids are fine too.'

'You talk as if things might have been bad lately.'

169

'Things have been terrible! I'm most a feared to go up in them mountains anymore.'

'Tell us about it.'

'You know how scarce grub gets this time of year. We had meal to make bread with but were just about out of meat, and grease to season our corn pone. So I went up on the mountain to see if I could get a deer. I left that pesky old dog at home. You know he runs so fast that he just runs the deer clean away. I can't get a chance to shoot at them when he's along. I saw several deer but you know how hard it is to get close enough to shoot, even when no dog is along to keep them scared and running all the time.

'I'd get about close enough when the deer would get wind of me and trot off. Another time I was getting so I could see him real good, when I stepped on a stick which broke and made a noise. Off went that one. This kept up all afternoon. I thought I would sure fail and we would have nothing to go with our corn pone. The kids do like something to eat along with it. I was just about ready to start home when I saw a nice deer standing between me and the sky, on a bald knob of the mountain. It was a long shot but I got me a rest, aimed careful. Pulled the trigger. I saw him fall, through the smoke of the gun.

'The kids would have meat to go with their pone this evening! I could taste it myself, even then. When I got to the deer, he was a big one. I always load my rifle before I gut a deer. You know there may be another one near by. I set my gun against a big rock and hung my shot pouch on a little hook sticking over the top of the rock.

'I proceeded to gut the deer and then tied its legs together so I could hang it over my shoulders to carry home. It took me a little longer than usual. You know how that is. I put the deer over my shoulder, picked up my gun and was ready to start home. My shot pouch was not hanging by the rock. I could not see the snag I had hung it on. I looked around on the ground. No shot pouch! I straightened up and there was my shot pouch hanging out there. I could not anyways near reach it.'

'What happened, Paddy?'

'I had hooked it on the corner of the new moon and the moon had moved on out of reach while I was working with the deer!'

'How did you get it back? Or did you?'

170

'I couldn't reach it. All my bullets were in the pouch and all the powder in the powder horn. I only had one shot in the gun. Good thing I had loaded the rifle first thing! It would soon be dark too. I knew I couldn't get it that evening but I happened to think that the moon would be back by there the next evening. That was what I would do. Be back tomorrow!'

'Did you come back?'

'Just don't rush me. I'll tell you about that. I got back home a little after dark. The old woman cooked some of that venison as soon as I got in the house. They had already eaten some corn pone before I got home but when that meat and broth got done, you should have seen them kids and their ma eat. It did me good to watch them, when I could get time between bites. You see I was hungry for something good too. We weren't long getting to bed afterward."

'Did you sleep well?'

'We must have. When the dog waked us up the next morning, scratching on the door, it was broad daylight and the sun was shining brightly. I'd have to hurry to get back up on that mountain to get my shot pouch.

'We had a late breakfast of venison and corn cakes. Good thing all my ammunition was not in the shot pouch. I put some extra bullets and patching in my pocket and another small horn of powder over my shoulder. Not safe in those woods without ammunition. Took the dog along this time, too! That dog was chasing everything that moved. You should have seen how quick the squirrels took to the trees when he got after them. The fastest dog I've ever seen!

'We went through a strange part of the woods. Could hear something making a queer noise ahead of us. The dog kept close to me for awhile. That wasn't like him. The racket got louder and louder as we came nearer. The dog ran up over a hog-back out of sight and soon let out a howl of pain. He ran back to me, licking his nose. I crept up to the top of the hog-back, until I could see over. Never saw anything like it in my life.
Couldn't believe my eyes! The dog kept close to me now.'

'What was it? What did you see?'

''Now, you won't believe this. It was a log rolling backward and forward in the hollow. First up one side, back down the up the other side, back down and up, endlessly, without stopping! I'll bet you never saw a thing like that, did you?'

'No, I never did. What kept it going?'

'I don't know. It was a puzzle. Unless. . .'

'Unless what?'

'The only thing I could see that could have caused it was. . .'

''Was what?'

'It was so crooked; it didn't have a side to lay on!'

'Is it still rolling?'

'No. I was back by there the other day and there were only a few sharp ended chunks lying in the hollow. The log had worn itself out, I guess. It beats me!'

'Did you get your shot pouch back?'

'I was just getting around to that. It was getting into the shank of the afternoon. The dog soon forgot about that log and went about chasing this and that as we went along. He caught a rabbit and two squirrels. I'd have a load if he kept this up. Here he came! Right toward me after another rabbit. The rabbit just missed a little sapling but the dog hit the sapling and split himself in half. It was lucky I was right there! I grabbed the two halves up and slapped them back together without that dog losing a drop of blood. The parts stuck together right now!'

'Did the dog live?'

'He sure did! Was a little wobbly at first, though. We had to hurry to the big rock where I had hung up my shot pouch. I climbed upon the big rock so I would be sure to be able to reach the shot pouch. It was a good thing I did. The dog was lying by the big rock resting. I sat down on top the rock to wait for my shot pouch. I must have dozed off. I was awakened by the bullets rattling in the shot pouch as the moon came along. I reached up and unhooked the shot pouch from the point of the moon as it went past. It was lucky I was on top the rock, as the moon passed by a little higher than it had the evening before. My bullets and powder were all there. I was afraid the lady in the moon might want to put some of my powder on her face or decorate her hair with my bullets.'

'Was the dog any good after his ordeal?'

'I forgot to tell you. I made one little mistake in putting him back together so quick. I got the legs on one side up and the other side down.'

172

'He was no good, then, was he?'

'Oh! Yes! He was as good as two dogs. He could run along on one side until he got tired and then just flip over on the other two legs, while the tired legs rested. The other day I saw him playing with the children and they would each grab a resting leg and all run along together, having fun. The little girl just learning to walk, would get hold of one of the legs and hold on, while the dog walked her around the house or yard.

'I tell you that rabbit and two squirrels made us a laropin mess that evening for supper!'

- - - - - - - - - - - - -

"Grandpa, do you suppose they got the idea of heart transplants from Paddy McCann?"

"Who knows what fires the imagination of people. Perhaps Paddy McCann helped people get to the moon."

"They probably didn't know it was possible until he hung his shot pouch there!"

"You heard all those stories about Pa's hunting. Tell us about the hunting you did."

"First I have a few stories about bears, wolves and a panther. . ."

- - - - - - - - - - - - -

BEAR STORIES

When we children were growing up in Gilmer County, no big game was left in that part of the country, such as bear, deer, panther and wolves. There was an occasional wild cat, so we had to depend on old hunters' stories for our knowledge of where such animals were still available to hunt.

One such story concerned some bear hunters whose dogs had surrounded a big bear in a big root hole where a large tree had uprooted. The dogs were running up and biting at the bear, which in turn was biting, striking with his paws and snapping at them each time they got near. When the bear was striking and snapping at one dog, another would bite at him from the other side. It was

173

an active whirling fight. All the time, the hunters kept trying to get a shot without hitting a dog. One hunter lost his footing and started slipping into the root hole toward the bear. He discarded his rifle and pulled his hunting ax from his belt as he slid nearer and nearer the bear. It was his only chance. As he came close the bear, he directed a heavy blow at the bear's head which knocked the bear out cold. The dogs grabbed the bear, but there was no fight since the blow from the hunter's ax had stopped his fighting. Hunters would rather lose the bear than take a chance on shooting a good bear dog.

On another occasion, a man was out hunting by himself and came to a large tree with a big hole in it, up a little way from the ground. Part of the bark had been clawed off and there were also claw marks on the tree where a bear had been climbing. The hunter pounded on the tree to try to get the bear to come out, if any was inside. Nothing stirred. He climbed up to see what sort of a den it might be. It was large. As he was trying to see into the dark area, he lost his balance and fell into the tree, sliding to the bottom, even though he tried to check his fall by pressing his hands and legs against the sides of the hollow tree as he fell. A bed of leaves in the bear nest at the bottom broke his fall. There was plenty of room at the bottom but how was he to get out? If he could get started up the smaller part of the hollow, leading to the hole at the top, he could make it. It was only about shoulder high, but try as he would, he couldn't get started on his climb. He tried to pile up pieces to get up higher but with no success.

He had time to remember stories of cutting hollow trees and finding human skeletons in them, and stories of hunters who never returned. These were no help to him in getting started at climbing. His despair was not lessened by a scratching sound outside the tree. The scratching continued higher and higher on the tree. The bear was coming back. What could he do? He had nothing but a small hunting knife against the claws and fangs of the bear. The bear darkened the opening and began sliding down backward toward him. A ray of hope hit him! He seized his hunting knife in one hand and waited, as the bear, clawing to check his descent, let himself down. Reaching high overhead, the hunter grabbed the bear's tail securely with one hand as he gave him a sharp stab with the knife. Then he held on with both hands as the bear desperately began climbing, pawing and scratching upward, pulling the hunter

174

behind him. At the top, the bear cleared the hole and quickly slid to the ground where he ran off as if he had seen a ghost! The hunter grabbed the edge of the hole in the tree and was left hanging there to watch the bear's escape. He climbed out of the hollow tree and let himself safely to the ground, feeling quite thankful to the bear for helping him out of the hollow. It was late in the afternoon when the hunter hurried home where he told of his narrow escape, else, how would we ever have known about it?

A WOLF STORY

The danger from hungry wolves was well known by early settlers in our area and many stories involving that danger were told. Packs of starving wolves were known to be able to wear down and overpower the strongest wild animals and had often attacked domestic animals.

One time a man and his dog wandered into the forest in search of deer. Wolves kept up their mournful howling in the distance. Before he realized it, he was far from where anyone lived. He turned to go back home a different way.

The dog was then attacked by 2 or 3 wolves and came running back to him. The wolves stopped when they came near the hunter but continued their howl, as they circled him and his dog. Other wolves answered their call and seemed to be coming nearer. The man climbed up into a tree which was about 12 inches in diameter and had limbs near enough the ground so he could jump up to get a good hold. He took his rifle with him and began shooting the wolves as fast as he could reload. He was trying to protect his dog from his own secure position in the tree.

His first shot killed a wolf but the second only infuriated the pack, by the howling cries of the wounded wolf. The second wounded wolf's cries further infuriated the growing pack. The dog seized this opportunity to leave and run toward home, without being followed by any of the wolves. The howling pack began trying to jump to the limbs and climb the tree, at the same time gnawing at the tree trunk in desperation. The hunter decided to stop this by shooting another wolf which seemed to make them try all the harder to climb and gnaw. These must have been starving wolves, as they seemed to be eating the two dead wolves. Where

175

were they all coming from? Would the dog get home? Would anyone know to come to his rescue?

Or would he end up like the hunter in a wolf story he had heard? In that story, the man, too, had climbed a tree to get away from the wolves but had run out of ammunition and the wolves finally gnawed down the tree. They later found his skeleton near the gnawed-down tree. His rifle lay near the tree. His powder horn contained powder but there were no bullets in his shot pouch. Skeletons of wolves lay near the tree, which indicated he killed some before running out of bullets. These were horrible thoughts running through his mind. He had plenty of ammunition, but did not want to waste any. He would have to shoot every little while, to attract the attention of any who might come looking for him. It seemed that wounding a wolf, slowed the gnawing at his tree as much, or more than, killing one. It was getting dark and it would be harder to hit the wolves at night. He made himself as comfortable as possible, wedging himself among the limbs.

What was that he heard after one of his shots? He reloaded as quickly as he could and fired again. Sure enough! A shot answered him in the distance. He reloaded and fired again, and this time the answering shot was closer to him. They were coming to rescue him! By the time he had reloaded, some dogs began barking savagely at the wolf pack. It was no use to waste more shots now. The dogs were joined by still more dogs. The savage barking of the dogs had never sounded so good to his ears before. The furious attack of the dogs broke up the wolf pack, which began retreating.

Where did all the dogs come from?

The men who had come to his rescue told him that when his dog came home by himself, bearing the marks of a wolf fight, his wife became scared and got word to their nearest neighbor. Thy immediately began rounding up men and dogs for the rescue. It was lucky he had told his wife the direction he was going to hunt that day. The deer were scarcer and the wolf threat, far greater, than he had realized when he started out alone that morning to hunt.

A PANTHER STORY

Another of the old time hunting stories involved a lone hunter who wandered far from home in quest of deer. Late in the evening his patience and persistence were rewarded by getting a fine young deer which he prepared for carrying home. Its legs were tied together in such a way that he could carry it slung over his shoulders like a shot pouch. In this way, he could easily shift the weight from one shoulder to the other.

Darkness came on as he started down a two-mile run toward his home. The light from the moon would help him follow his path down the bottoms and over the run crossings. He had left his dog at home to keep him from frightening deer, but now it would be nice to have his dog's company and protection.

Over to his left, against the hill, he became aware of footsteps going the same directions he was going. The sound faded out ahead of him. He had scarcely started feeling good, that whatever it was that was making the sound, had gone, when the same sound going in the opposite direction, came from his right. This sound, too, disappeared behind him and soon was heard again on his left, going in his direction. It was a night sound that travelers fear, a panther stalking his prey. Panthers seldom attacked humans except when very hungry, or starving. This was little comfort because he did not know how hungry or starving this panther might be. It might be the scent of the deer he was carrying.

The stalking circle was gradually getting nearer and nearer. He must do something! He did not want to lose his deer. A wide sand bar appeared ahead in the moonlight, beyond the run that he would have to cross. This was his chance. He took his hunting knife in his hand and when he was about midway across the sandbar, reached up and cut the thong holding the deer's feet together. The deer slipped from his shoulders to the sandbar behind him. He had gone scarcely 100 feet when the panther, uttering its fearful attack screams, pounced on the deer. Before the panther could start dragging the deer toward the forest cover, the hunter whirled and shot at the form of the panther in the moonlight. It shrieked with pain as it disappeared into the forest. That ended the panther's stalking for that night.

With a sigh of relief, the hunter returned to the sandbar where he got his deer, tied its legs together and again slung it over his

177

shoulder. He continued on his way home, but not without first reloading his rifle, as a matter of safety. I am sure he retold his experiences to his wife and neighbors while eating the many good messes of venison they enjoyed from the deer the panther had tried so hard to steal.

AND MORE PANTHERS

This is about one of Pa's cousins who lived on the Scott place and hunted cows up Cove past the old home place before Pa's Mother and Father were married and started living there. With the exception of a small cleared area around the old house, it was unbroken forest from below the mouth of Little Cove to near the mouth of Crane Run. He always took a dog with him after the cows for company and protection. After he was big enough to learn to shoot and handle a gun, his parents got him a new gun which he was allowed to take with him after the cows, or when he was on other errands about the neighborhood. As he became more confident in his marksmanship, he often left his dog at home and then tried to get near enough to shoot game that came along his path. He had brought home rabbits and squirrels to add variety to the family meals.

One evening, he traveled farther than usual up cove in search of his cows. He came to the mouth of Big Run and was admiring some fish in the water and trying to decide whether he should shoot some of them to take home for supper. A sound attracted his attention. There on the end of a log, extending out over a pile of drift on the other side of the creek stood the biggest panther he had ever seen. He thought it was ready to jump on him. He froze motionless in his tracks as the dangerous animal remained poised above him. It was too far away to jump on him, but he was so scared, he didn't realize that. The panther remained, looking about a little while, then turned slowly around, walked back down the log toward the bank and trotted away toward Big Run, disappearing into the forest. As the panther disappeared from view, the boy broke and ran down the bottom toward home. After passing our old house, he was nearly out of breath and had to stop running. He had never thought of his gun, still clutched in his hand. He had run over a half mile so scared he didn't think of shooting at the panther. As he drove his cows on home, he decided not to say anything about what had happened. A slip of his tongue at the supper table let it out and he reluctantly told the whole story. It has been told many times since, sometimes in his presence, but probably more often as a good, entertaining story.

- - - - - - - - - - - - -

"But Grandpa, you said you'd tell about the hunting you did."

"Yes, we're ready for that now. First it was rabbits and then a skunk. You know how skunks smell, don't you?"

"Yes, and it must be hard to wash enough to get it off. Sometimes cars hit them and they smell for a long time."

"The rabbit hunt comes first. . . . ."

- - - - - - - - - - - - -

HUNTING RABBITS

The first hunting we children had an opportunity to see was when several of the young men on Little Cove hunted rabbits in the high weeds and small brush in the pastures on the ridge across from our house. They carried shotguns and had a dog or two along nearly all the time, to scare out the rabbits. The men would form a line up over the ridge, 40 or 50 feet apart and slowly follow the dogs from the lower end of the ridge until they disappeared from our view farther up the ridge. If a rabbit started running, every one in the line who could see it took a shot. Once in a while, someone would hit a rabbit and then some friendly argument would follow as to who had been the lucky one. They seemed to have as much fun over a complete miss by all, as when a hit was scored.

One time it seemed that all the hunters in succession got a shot, beginning at the far end of the line, to the end nearest us. After the shooting ceased, we saw the lone rabbit running along a path around the end of the line, safely out of view of any of the hunters. He hopped leisurely out of sight, since no dog was following him. We saw this happen many times. Sometimes the rabbit would dodge into one of the many safe holes along these

179

paths, especially if a dog was following too closely. This sort of hunting was largely for fun, but they always took the rabbits home for table use. They were good eating. We enjoyed watching the hunting and shooting without the cost of providing the shells; neither did we have a chance to enjoy eating the rabbits.

One Saturday, our cousin, Guy Scott, George and I went rabbit hunting with Guy's ferret. The ferret was put into the holes to run the rabbits out to us, waiting at the mouth of the hole to catch them. The first rabbit went into a hole and Guy put his ferret in after it. We could hear the two making a racket, back in the hole. Suddenly, the rabbit gave a squeal and started toward the mouth of the hole in a hurry. Guy grabbed it as it came out, held it up by the hind feet and gave it a couple of rabbit chops with his hand, just behind the head and ears, which killed it almost painlessly. We soon caught another in the same manner.

Soon our dog holed another rabbit just a little way from us. This appeared to be a sinkhole with two or three openings. The rabbit ran in the opening farthest down the hill, so Guy went down there and put his ferret in after it. George took the second opening and I took the one farthest up the hill. We had no idea where the rabbit might come out. The first two holes were 15 or 20 feet apart. They could hear the rabbit scratching and kicking to get through the tight crooked places as it came nearer and nearer to George's opening. George grabbed it before it could get past and come on toward me. We all went to watch for the ferret to come out. It was in no hurry.

'Fanny! Fanny! Fanny! Guy began calling but no ferret came. He said a ferret's name should begin with 'F' such as Frankie, Francis and so on, since such names could be called distinctly and carried better underground. Be that as it may, we all took turns at calling Fanny. Still no Fanny came.

Guy began to get worried. He said once she stayed in the ground overnight. That time he had left his ferret poke lying inside the mouth of the hole and then stopped the hole up. They came back after dark, but the ferret had not come to the poke. When they came the next morning and opened the hole, there she was, comfortably curled up on the cloth bag. She seemed glad to see them. We did not know how far this sink hole extended or how many openings it might have. While we were discussing our situation, we saw Fanny coming toward us.

It was getting frosty and cold enough so that the storekeeper had started buying rabbits at 10 to 15 cents each, depending on the size. Guy said his Dad was going to the store that afternoon and he would have him take our rabbits and sell them for us. He would bring the money to school on Monday and we could divide it there. One of the rabbits was small and only brought 10 cents, but the next Monday, Guy brought 40 cents to divide. We took 10 cents each and decided Guy should have the other 10 cents for the use of his ferret and marketing our catch. The price soon fell to 10 cents or less, so we did not hunt together much more, although Guy and his brother-in-law Earl did quite a bit of hunting and canning rabbit meat for later table use.

Ferrets were used to chase rats from their dens so they could be caught. Some people thought rats would leave if they were chased out by ferrets frequently. It became illegal to keep ferrets and their use in hunting was not allowed.

- - - - - - - - - - - - -

"Are you ready for the polecat story? Perhaps you can smell it already."

"Yes, Grandpa, we're ready when you are. We have clothespins ready for our noses in case our imaginations turn into smell-o-vision!"

- - - - - - - - - - - - -

THE # 3 POLECAT

It was on a bright sunshiny Sunday afternoon early in September. Four or five of us older children had gone out on the point near Jackson's Rocks to get ground ivy and to look for hill grapes. Soon after we got there, Towser caught and killed a polecat with a large white 'V' shaped marking on its back, making it about a #3 grade for fur sale purposes, worth about a dollar. This was early in the season and the fur was not fully developed. We had heard a saying that fur was good if caught in any month

181

that had an 'R' in it. That made the fur good, but what an odor! Towser thought so too. He kept rubbing his nose in the grass and rolled over and over trying to get rid of the polecat smell. The smell seemed to die down after awhile or maybe we were beginning to get used to it.

George and I decided to skin the skunk. We thought we could be careful and wash our hands afterward and get rid of the smell. We proceeded with the skinning and the smell kept up with us. When we finished, we breathed a sigh of relief and took the pelt home. We stretched it over a board as we had seen other do it, and scraped off some of the fat. It looked pretty good. We hung the board up on a nail in the woodshed for the hide to cure. We were not entirely satisfied with our first skinning job but we were sure we could do better on the next one. We decided to ask some questions of people who knew how, the first chance we had.

Our sisters went on into the house. Pa and Ma wanted to know what they had been into. They had not helped in the skinning any more than just watching, but they had absorbed the odor and carried it into the house with them. George and I had rolled our sleeves up before starting to wash. Then we took some strong homemade soap and gave our hands and arms a good scrubbing at the run before going into the house. Of course it wasn't enough. We got hot water and more soap and gave our hands and arms another going over. Pa and Ma said we'd have to move out to the barn. We ate supper, but then they didn't make us sleep in the barn. Ma wondered what would happen at school the next day with all that smell.

We did not notice the smell the next day as we went to school but when we entered the schoolhouse, the odor was easily apparent. Other kids had been skinning and were far less successful in avoiding the odor than we were, so ours was scarcely noticed. The odor was replenished at school many times during the fur season.

It was pretty warm that fall and our pelt did not cure as well as it should have. A fur buyer from Troy came along later and looked at our fur. He said it hadn't cured properly and that we should have skinned it a little differently. It would have been a #3 if everything had been all right, but he could only pay us for a #4 or about 45 cents. We let him have it. He later told Pa he lost money on it. His buyer called it a scab and threw it over into the scab pile. He said he kicked it back into a better pile, but the buyer saw it and threw it back into the scab pile where he got 35 cents for it. Such was our first experience in the fur business.

- - - - - - - - - - - -

"Your grandma has a skunk story too. Here she comes to tell it to you."

"Oh Grandma, we really like your stories. Ummm, and ice cream to go with this one!"

- - - - - - - - - - - -

GRANDMA'S SKUNK STORY

When we lived on the head of Big Run near the top of the hill, the woods came almost to the edge of our back yard, making an excellent shade for us children to play in. One day, one of my younger brothers, then about 3 or 4 years old, came to where the rest of us were playing. He was proudly carrying a tiny black and white animal he had picked up where he had been playing. As he came near us, he was beaming with excitement and said,

'See what a pretty kitty-cat I found!'

We all backed away with equal excitement for he was carrying a small skunk that he thought was a kitten. We tried to get him to put it down, but he held on proudly, all the time fondly patting it. It had not yet sprayed him with its foul perfume but we didn't know how soon it might. All the time he continued caressing it, which may have been the reason it had not used its defensive scent, or it may have been too young.

My brother wanted to keep it as a pet and was not satisfied until Dad got a crate and put it under the granary for the skunk. Dad would feed it warm milk as he came in from milking, morning and evening. He probably fed it other things but I only remember the milk, and that Dad had to change the straw in the box often to keep it from getting smelly. We children would look at the skunk, but none of us handled or petted it. Dad seemed to enjoy feeding and looking after it more than any of the rest of us.

183

It grew and did well, but Dad took it out away from the house and let it go early that fall. It was almost like one of the family.

- - - - - - - - - - - -

"Well, I'm not sure which was better, the story or the ice cream. I'm glad you let the little skunk go."

"Your Grandma is a top-notch story teller, isn't she? We used to set traps in the winter to catch mink and muskrats for fur."

"Tell us about it, Grandpa. We know what minks look like. Remember the ones we saw along the dock at Indian Lake last summer?"

"Yes, we watched those often, last summer, but they moved away after the neighbors built their new cottage too near their home. We were never able to catch mink often. . . ."

- - - - - - - - - - - -

TRAPPING MUSKRATS

Catching fur-bearing animals and selling their pelts during the late fall and winter was one way people made a little extra money to use for getting the things they could not raise for themselves. Nearly every family engaged in trapping, with some far more active and successful than others. Some had miles of deadfall trap lines which they tended regularly, every 3 or 4 days, with good results. Others trapped mink and muskrat along the waterways less extensively, perhaps because the steel traps cost money and needed close attention.

We began trapping with 5 or 6 steel traps for mink and muskrats, which we set along the creek not far from our house. Carrots, parsnips or apples were good for muskrat bait. Muskrat holes in the creek bank usually opened under the water and then sloped upward above water level to their den or nest area, which was dry and warm, except when flooded by high water during rainy weather. Such den entrances were good places to set traps

184

under water with no bait. It was always necessary to fasten the trap so the animal could not get out on the creek bank where he was sure to gnaw his foot off and get away. A limb or bush extending out into the water was a good place to fasten the trap chain. Where none was available, the trap was fastened to the end of a short pole which was fastened in the bank, with the end extending out into the water, far enough to hold the muskrat from getting out of the water. If caught in a trap set in this way, the animal would usually drown.

Another method was to dig a level space in the bank below the water level on which to set the trap, and then put some bait on a stick, which was stuck into the bank so the bait would be 10 or 12 inches above the trap.

Mink and muskrat traveled mostly at night so we sometimes went to our traps in the evening to see that they were still under water and properly baited. We always visited them early each morning, before daylight if possible, to remove anything caught during the night. We have caught a few muskrats in this way, but since people living all along the creek kept traps set and all of them caught a few, it kept them from getting plentiful.

Mink were seldom caught in this manner. Traps had to be carefully covered and set in their run-ways or about sinkholes where they visited, in search of food or at play. I have heard of people catching one and throwing its carcass into a sinkhole with a trap set nearby. Then others were caught that were attracted to the area. We had very little luck catching mink. Their being hard to catch and the fur good, helped keep the price up to 10 or 15 dollars each. Muskrat ranged in price from 35 to as much as 75 cents, perhaps even a dollar for an extra good one. Prices varied during each season and from year to year.

- - - - - - - - - - - - - -

DEADFALL TRAPPING

We had a 4 or 5 acre new-ground cornfield over the hill in Polecat Hollow, just out of sight of our house. This hollow got its name from a polecat which had been caught in a deadfall trap. Someone had skinned it and put the carcass in the forks of a sapling just out of arm's reach of the ground. It was hanging there

185

in late winter. It dried out and continued hanging there late into the summer, so we designated this unnamed run 'Polecat Hollow.' This was about 1905 or 1906, and the name continues to this day.

This cornfield was surrounded by woods except for about 200 yards which joined a pasture and was fenced at that point with a rail fence. The whole area was filled with ground squirrels, gray squirrels, crows and other birds that began taking up corn as soon as it started peeping through the ground. It was hard to get a good stand of corn for a full crop.

Pa made a lot of small deadfall traps of the figure '4' trigger type, each baited with a grain of corn. George and I helped with these traps and learned to bait and set them. We caught a lot of ground squirrels and a few gray squirrels which slowed down their taking corn. To control the crows, we mainly depended on scarecrows, but in spite of the traps and scarecrows, a lot of corn had to be replanted to get a crop. Replants very seldom developed good corn, but it helped to have the extra fodder to use as feed. After ears began developing, until harvest, raccoons, groundhogs and squirrels further menaced the crop and were hunted in various ways.

We knew hunters who caught a great deal of fur in deadfalls of the type we used to protect the sprouting corn. Polecats and possums were larger. Much heavier deadfall rocks had to be used to hold them. We could not lift and set the heavy ones we had seen used by other trappers when we first started, and therefore sometimes we lost good fur-bearing animals when they dug their way out from under our lighter rocks. We did catch several good pieces of fur, which made us a little spending or saving money.

Groundhogs were always a menace to the corn crop from roasting ear time until the start of cold weather. They climbed the cornstalks and their weight would break down the corn so they could get at the ears. Those stalks pulled down in this way did not fully develop and usually rotted, lying on the ground. George and I came across a good example of this destruction on a steep bank near some den holes in the middle of the cornfield where they had broken down about all the corn in what would have been a 3 or 4 shock area. This would have produced 6 to 10 bushels of ear corn; it wasn't even worth cutting.

Our dog had chased the groundhogs into their hole before we got there and was barking and digging at the hole. We dug at the

186

hole awhile, but rocks prevented further progress in the digging. We got a heavy hickory stick about 10 or 12 feet long and cut some of the tip off. Then we twisted the end so we thought it would twist up the hair of the groundhog and we could pull him out of the hole, where the dogs could get him. We pushed the stick back to the groundhog. He growled and snapped his teeth at it. We held the end against him and began twisting. It caught in his hair and we pulled him part-way out. Then he got loose and retreated to his old position at the far end of the hole. I took the stick and twisted him in it again and kept twisting as I pulled him out. I lifted him clear of the hole before he could get loose. When he dropped to the ground, old Towser made short work of him. We filled the holes up at that place, but they were soon dug out again. The groundhogs continued eating our corn. It was impossible to get many of them before a lot of damage was done. At that time, George and I were not yet big enough to have guns, so we had to depend on the dog's help. Pa had a mountain rifle that he used to shoot both groundhogs and squirrels, but he did not have much time to spend hunting them.

Later George and I got a 22 rifle and spent considerable time of evenings and at odd times, shooting at groundhogs as they appeared around their holes during the warm weather, especially in areas near crops they were likely to destroy. This sort of hunting was partly for fun and partly to protect farm crops. We have had a few tender young groundhogs cooked but we never hunted them for our meat supply. Some people were able to cook them so they liked to eat them and hunted them extensively for that purpose. Groundhogs seemed to have few natural enemies. They were held in check largely by hunters and good farm dogs.

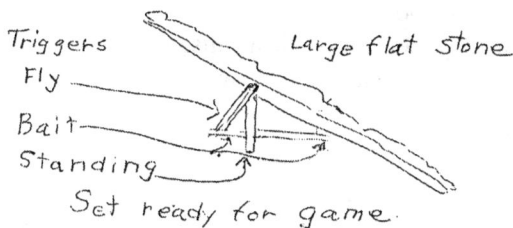

Here is my drawing of a <u>DEADFALL TRAP</u>.

187

"Your Grandma says they had pet groundhogs. We'll get her to tell us about them."

"Oh, boy! She's bringing popcorn this time! We do like your stories, Grandma."

- - - - - - - - - - - - -

GRANDMA'S PET GROUNDHOGS

Very young groundhogs were easily tamed and soon became good pets. One day, Dad brought two very small groundhogs to the house with him as he came in to dinner from work. This was after we had moved down off the hill to the house on Sinking Creek. All of us took turns petting and playing with the baby groundhogs. We kept them in a box for awhile, but they soon got so tame they went any place about the yard and garden and were always present at their feeding place when they were hungry, or at feeding time. We had a lot of fun with them but they soon got big enough to eat and destroy so much garden stuff that they became a nuisance.

When they got to digging through the screen door into the milk-house and upsetting the milk and cream crocks, drinking the milk and eating the butter, that was it! Mama set her foot down! They were pets to all of us, so rather than kill them; we carried them far away from the house and turned them loose near some holes where they soon became wild. We never saw them again. Even though they became such a nuisance, we all had fun with them before we had to carry them away.

- - - - - - - - - - - - -

"You sure had a lot of trouble keeping animals from eating the corn, didn't you, Grandpa?"

"Yes, we did. Ground squirrels did most of their damage to the sprouting corn but didn't do much harm after the corn got larger. Have you seen flying squirrels? And gray squirrels, and fox squirrels. . . ."

- - - - - - - - - - - -

SQUIRRELS

The flying squirrel had webs from the front legs along the body to its back legs which it could spread and glide for quite a distance from high in a tree to a lower position in another tree or to the ground. Unlike the bat, which can flap its web-like wings and fly like a bird in any direction, the flying squirrel has to clumsily climb to a high place, before it can again jump and glide to another lower point some distance away. While we have caught 2 or 3 in deadfalls baited with corn for ground squirrels, we never considered them a menace to sprouting corn. We regarded them more as a curiosity and fun to watch whenever an opportunity presented itself. We never made any effort to hunt them.

Gray squirrels and fox squirrels were plentiful and all were excellent food and very popular for hunting. These squirrels were a menace to sprouting corn and also did considerable damage to the maturing ears of corn. Their damage was usually never as extensive or complete as that of groundhogs. Squirrels depended largely on forest nuts, acorns and other forest food. They were especially damaging to farm crops when such forest supplies of food were scarce.

As years passed, laws were enacted that protected squirrels by permitting hunting in the fall for a limited time only. Dogs were of little use in hunting squirrels since they scared them and kept them on the move, making them difficult to shoot. Good riflemen prided themselves on being able to hit squirrels. Some thought it a disgrace to hit a squirrel anywhere except in the head. Another very few thought it equally disgraceful to damage the squirrel meat at all by hitting it any place with the rifle bullet. They would shoot only when they got in such a position that they could knock the bark off the tree under the squirrel, killing it with the piece of bark as it knocked the squirrel from the tree. This was called 'barking a squirrel.' I was never as selective as the last two,

189

but was well pleased to be able to hit a squirrel with a rifle. Shotguns were used by nearly all hunters who expected to get squirrels, since after a few shots in any area; it was difficult to get a shot except when the squirrel was on the move.

I remember one time in later years, George, Perry and I went hunting during the first part of the open season before much shooting had been done. We had only two shotguns and I insisted that they use the shotguns since we wanted to get some squirrels to eat. I would take the rifle and see whether I could get any with it. We each took a different route and were to get together at a point later along the way. The first gray squirrel was sitting on a rail fence, eating a hickory nut about 50 or 60 feet away. I aimed carefully and actually hit it in the head. The next was climbing a tree and stopped in clear view. I aimed and fired. It tumbled to the ground. A little farther along, I saw a ground squirrel sitting on top a small stump in the sunshine. The chipmunk was no good to eat, so should I take a chance of scaring a gray squirrel by shooting? It was a small target but I shot and scored a perfect hit. I carried the chipmunk along as proof. I was beginning to think I could not miss. One advantage of the 22 rifle was that it did not make nearly as much noise when fired as a shotgun and did not frighten game as much. I was crossing a pasture and saw a squirrel standing on his hind legs looking almost directly at me, about 75 feet away. I did not make a perfect hit but he did not get away.

When I met George and Perry, they each had 4 gray squirrels and wanted to know why I was carrying that chipmunk along. I told them he was proof that in my first four rifle shots, I had four squirrels. We continued our hunt until about noon. I got 2 or 3 more shots at moving squirrels, or at some partly hidden in the leaves but did not add any to my catch. George and Perry increased their catch to the limit of 6 each. This is about the usual result of a successful squirrel hunt. The squirrels we got that day made an excellent meal for all of us, when fried for our supper that evening.

Besides using deadfalls, snares, box traps and steel traps to catch fur bearing animals, some people had trained expensive hunting dogs especially for that purpose. Guy Scott and Earl Heckert had such a dog which cost them either 58 or 98 dollars, which was an enormous price to pay for a dog at that time. They

190

got him late in the season but they said they more than doubled their money on him that season. He was trained to bay animals on the ground, until his master came up, before killing the animal and then, only on command of his master. In this way, they could catch animals alive or by shooting which prevented the hide from being cut in holes by the dog's teeth.

The following summer, the dog would bay fur-animals whenever he got loose. They caught a few and penned them to keep until cold weather when the fur became suitable for sale. They decided to make several pens lined on the bottom with chicken-wire to keep the animals from digging out. They found that, by picking a skunk up by the tail and dropping it gently into a sack without letting it get hold of the edge, they generally avoided getting sprayed with the skunk scent. They even took the dog hunting and in this way, they got several fur animals which kept them busy building more pens and feeding the animals. They were pretty successful with skunk and possum and had one or two pens of coons. In addition to their regular farm work, this kept them busy. Since the pens were bottomed with chicken-wire, they were easy to lift to new locations when necessary for cleaning.

Fur prices were pretty good then. The lumbering business had slacked off. Hunting was the best prospect for extra money to bolster farm income. The summer hunting and fur animal penning paid off well for them. The animals did well and produced good fur by cold weather. The extra income was welcome.

The extra emphasis on hunting throughout the area kept the supply of fur-bearing animals from increasing and caused a gradual decrease over the years. In the meantime, prices of hunting dogs were high. Much money was both made and lost in that field.

- - - - - - - - - - - -

"You must have done a lot of hunting, Grandpa."

"We didn't hunt nearly as much as many of the people did. We weren't as successful in catching fur either. It was a very popular activity and we were successful enough to feel that we were a part of it. And the extra money from the fur was always welcome. Sometimes the hunters were almost as damaging as the animals. . . "

- - - - - - - - - - -

COON TREES

Raccoons were equally as damaging to cornfields as were groundhogs, especially in fields bordering wooded areas. People usually had dogs trained especially for hunting coons. It took a good-sized, well-trained dog to catch and kill a coon on the ground. Usually the coons were treed by the dogs, where they were shot by hunters, unless they went into holes in the trees and escaped.

There was a run, about three-quarters of a mile long, at the back of our farm that was completely in the woods when I first remember it. The name: Coon Run. Few trees had ever been removed, nor were there cornfields near it, but there were always many coons that had their dens in the numerous hollow trees in the area. When coons hid in the den-trees, hunters never hesitated to cut the finest trees, just to get a coon, unless they were too lazy to do so. When the wind was coming gently from that direction on quiet nights, we have often heard hunters chopping, and trees falling. Later we have seen where fine timber trees had been cut on both our farm and the farm joining it. Pa hated to see such fine timber wasted, just to get a coon that was probably worth only a dollar.

Coon hunters, like fox-chasers, were always proud of their coon-dogs and seemed to be well pleased with the results of a hunt if they had chased and treed several coons, whether they caught many or not. Each that got away would be there to hunt another day.

During the fur season, the catch was a very important element of the hunt and added interest and pride to the coon stories told on the hunt and at neighborhood gatherings. Some took special pride in a coon-skin cap or neck-piece for a member of their family when it was made from a coon they had caught themselves.

- - - - - - - - - - -

"Here comes Grandma with some pink wintergreen candy for us. She must have another story to tell."

"Yes, but it's a very short story this time, probably time for just one piece of candy."

- - - - - - - - - - -

MAMA'S NECKPIECE

My dad once caught a coon which he thought was so beautiful that he sent its hide away and had a fur neckpiece made of it for Mama. This cost $14.00 which was a high price for us to pay. As far as we knew, Mama was the only one in the neighborhood having such a fine fur piece. She was very proud of it.

- - - - - - - - - - -

"Grandpa, from the things you have been telling us, it seems that you never had much money to spend when you were growing up. Were you real poor people?"

"Now, Joe, that's really two questions. No, we didn't have much money to spend, compared with now. There wasn't as much money in circulation, nor were there as many things to buy. A lot of money wasn't really needed. . . . ."

- - - - - - - - - -

ABOUT MONEY

We lived in a farming area where people raised nearly everything they needed to live on and didn't depend on buying very much. Pa relied on things other than money to get what they needed, such as exchanging corn for wheat, meat, potatoes or work, as each was needed. For instance, a bag of flour, or a bushel of corn, worth 50 or 60 cents was considered equal to the pay for a day's work. No money was involved many times in such exchanges. This doesn't mean that we did not see things pictured and advertised in magazines and catalogs that we wanted. We did, but we got along without many of them, as did nearly everybody else in the neighborhood, so we did not miss having money to spend.

In answer to that second question, no, we weren't 'Real Poor People.' In fact, Pa was considered a well-to-do farmer. He owned a good productive hill farm of 250 acres on Big Cove where we grew up, as well as another 250 acres of unimproved land in another part of the county. Your grandma's parents, the Morrisons, likewise owned a similar farm of 200 acres on the head of Sinking Creek, where your grandma and her brothers and sisters were raised. While these farms were not the best, or biggest, they were well above the average in the area. People who owned and operated that type of farm, were in no way considered poor people. They were among the best farmers and most responsible leading citizens in the community.

When we were growing up, farmers in our area engaged in general farming and raised nearly everything needed for the family to live on. This included grains, animals, garden produce, berries and fruits, and building materials. Each farm would generally produce more of something than the family needed, which could be traded.

As an example, just after Pa and Ma were married, they bought an old-fashioned foot-pedal operated, reed organ which they paid for with corn. When someone seemed surprised at paying for it with corn, Pa said,

'There are a lot of things around here that were paid for with corn!' In this way farmers were self reliant citizens even though they did not have a lot of money to spend for things they could get along without. They liked to 'save for a rainy day,' as they would say.

- - - - - - - - - -

OUR FARMHOUSE

My grandparents were all born and lived in well-constructed, two-story, 3 and 4 room log houses, built in the period from 1825 to 1850. The cracks between the logs were tightly chinked and daubed with mud to keep out the rain, wind and cold. These houses were floored, roofed and finished according to the construction methods of the time they were built. All four of the ones I have seen had been remodeled and refinished on the inside so that the logs were entirely covered with smooth finished walls. All had cut stone chimneys with good, open fireplaces. They were comfortable, livable houses. In the early days, our part of the country was covered with fine forests, so logs and timber were the most readily available building materials. As wood-working tools and machinery were improved and became available, more serviceable and better-looking houses were built. Other materials than wood came into use. Many of the old log houses were improved and refinished so that they would have to be examined closely to know that underneath that outer finish was an old log house, still silently helping protect people.

The two-story, three room log part of your Grandma's house, where she and her brothers and sisters grew up, had been completely weather-boarded on the outside and 3 extra rooms added. The whole house was then finished and painted inside and out so that it no longer had the appearance of a log house.

Our two-story, three room log house had three rooms added at one end, and the front and two ends covered with unpainted yellow poplar weather-boarding. Two of the log rooms had been nicely refinished inside. Together with the inside of the three added rooms, all were painted or wall-papered. As viewed by people going along the road, the appearance was that of a weather-boarded house, but when viewed from either end or the back, the chinked and daubed log kitchen part stood out. I never knew

195

exactly why that part was left without weather-boarding when the remodeling was done, unless they expected to get it done at a later date and never got to it. It remained in that unfinished state until I was fourteen years old.

I remember helping Pa repair and patch the chinking of the old kitchen every year or so in the fall to tighten it up for the winter. We went out to a red clay bank at the lower end of the meadow. We dug a hole in the ground and mixed the clay with water and stirred it into a stiff sticky mass of mud which we carried to the house in buckets. We filled the holes and cracks in the chinking to make it more resistant to rain, air, and cold. We had to wet the dry mortar between the logs so the new wet mud could be applied and would stick on better.

We never used the old log kitchen in the winter time, but the chinking repair helped the other parts of the house to stay warmer. At first, I am sure, I was not much help, but as the years went on and I got bigger, I became more useful. We had a cut-stone double chimney in the middle of the front part of our house, with an open fireplace in each of the end rooms. A single stone chimney at the end of the old log kitchen, with an open fireplace, helped to keep it warm in the late fall and early spring. In cold weather, we used the smaller kitchen at the south end of the log kitchen which was partly heated by our living room fireplace.

We lived comfortably in this house without any changes until I was 14 years old. By this time, all eight of us children had arrived and the family needed more room. Early that spring, Pa hired a couple of men to help him construct a building at the edge of the yard, about 14 x 20 feet. We were all excited about this building, since we planned to move our cooking and eating facilities out there for the summer while we tore away the old log kitchen and the smaller kitchen, both of which were getting in poor repair. The new addition was to have a new kitchen where the old log kitchen had been located and a living room where the smaller kitchen had been. The living room was to be headed by a small coal stove, and the kitchen with the wood and coal cooking stove. A new roof for the whole house, together with a new porch along the entire front of the house, was in the plans for the summer, in addition to the usual farm work.

All was excitement as we got moved into our new summer cooking and eating house, and made further preparations for our summer's remodeling program. No architects were needed to draw the plans and specifications. Ma and Pa developed them in their heads as the work progressed. We children asked so many questions that they did not have a chance to forget or overlook anything. George and I were big enough to be a lot of help with the building. Our sisters were helpful too, especially in aiding Ma with the extra cooking and housework. Pa and Ma hired two carpenters for the job, Scott Beeson and our Uncle Scipio Lewis, who agreed to keep the work moving as fast as possible.

George and I hauled the tin roofing and roll roofing from the store in Troy on a sled pulled by our oxen. This required more than one trip. We also hauled several thousand feet of cross-tie lumber in the same way, from Big Run, where Pa had bought a big stack of it. This work was mixed in during our regular farm work that spring.

I remember when Uncle Scipio came to help with the tearing away and we started on the little kitchen. George and I were helping tear the roofing and sheeting boards off. George stepped over on the ceiling which let loose and he fell through to the floor below, unhurt. Pa teased him by saying that George's eyes stuck out so much that he was afraid he would rake them off as he went through the ceiling. This fall did not stop us; however, we were more careful where we stepped after that.

The wood shingles were hard to get off the old roof, even if they did leak a lot. We had to go underneath and punch some of them off using 2 x 4's. The weather was hot and the wrecking and preparatory work was especially dirty. We frequently went swimming in the creek of evenings to clean up and cool off.

The remodeling continued throughout the summer and progressed in about the usual manner of such work. One Friday evening, Mr. Beeson had just finished putting in a one-sash sliding window before going home over the weekend. This was almost like the one that had been in the kitchen we had torn away. This new window did not meet Ma's specifications. She wanted a double-hung, two sash window that would let in much more light and air, and also look better. Since the carpenter had left his tools, she had George and me tear the one-sash out, make the frame and install a double-hung window that met with her approval. We used some of his tools but were careful not to damage them. Ma said when the carpenter came back the next Monday, he stood and looked at the window a few seconds before going to work, but never said anything about it. That was her way of having her instructions observed, even if they had never been formally written out.

Later that fall, when George and I were putting up the pipe to the stove in our new sitting room, we let the pipe slip and cut my little finger on the under-side. This cut healed up leaving a black scar from the black soot off the pipe. Lest you think this story isn't true, I have carried the scar here on my little finger for 65+ years.

When we were finishing up the porch along the front of the house, it took so much lumber that Pa said he was afraid he would have no lumber left with which to build anything else on the farm.

Ma thought it would be a good idea to save the logs from the old kitchen to construct a building in the wood lot for storing the wood. George and I built this log storage building later that fall, following the same structural methods as used in building log houses, except that we stripped the cracks between the logs on the outside with narrow boards instead of chinking and daubing them. This made a good place to store our stove wood and keep it dry.

This big remodeling job was completed by early fall. We were able to move our cooking stove and table into our new kitchen before the weather began getting cold. We now had plenty of living and sleeping space. We especially enjoyed the long cool front porch during the hot summer weather.

The house was again remodeled and built onto, at two other times after this, including finishing the weather-boarding and painting the entire outside. These changes took place in 1932 and 1940.

- - - - - - - - - - -

"So by the time you visited the old house, it did have a lot of rooms."

"When did you get electricity? And which remodeling provided the Bathroom?"

"Both electricity and the bathroom arrived in 1940, as did running water. No one lived in the house after 1947, except for a

few weeks in the summer. Our family had scattered by then. We camped there in 1969 with some of the grandchildren. After that, the property was sold out of the family. The house burned in 1972 or 73. That was the last of the four log houses of your Great, Great Grandparents."

"I like these drawings you've made of the old house. We've also seen the picture Grandma has of her old family home."

"It's been torn down too. No one lived in it for many years."

- - - - - - - - - - - -

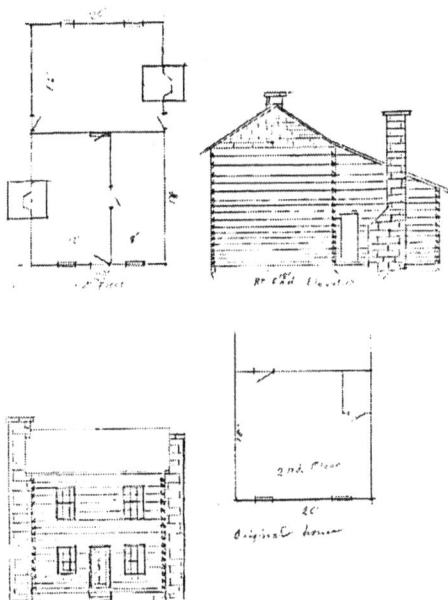

McQuain Log House 1800's

199

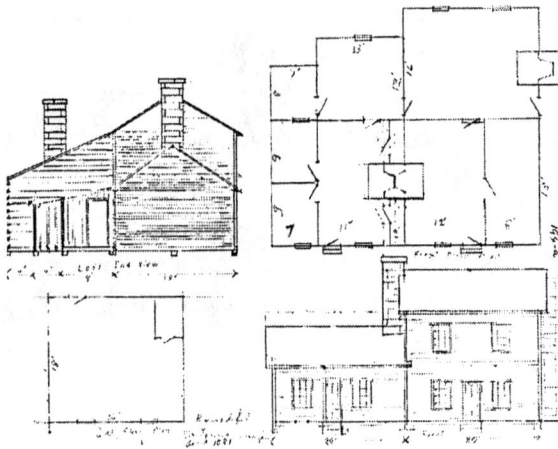

McQuain Log House 1800's

Front view
1911

Front
1911 Remodeling

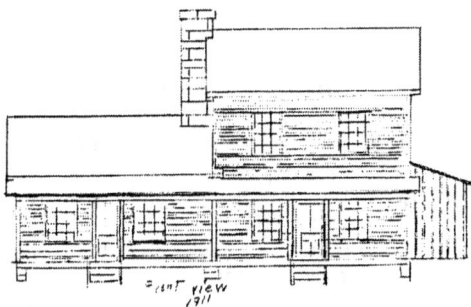

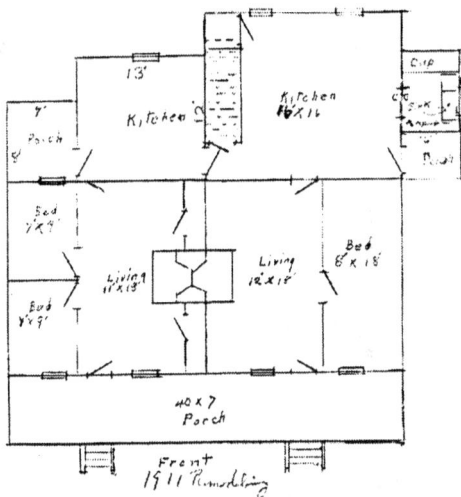

McQuain House, 1911 Remodeling

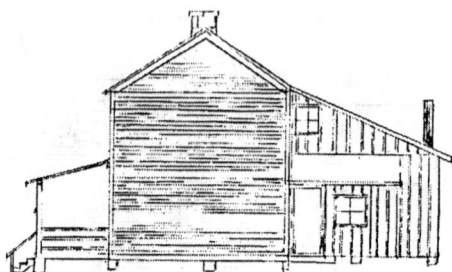

Right end view
1911 Remodeling

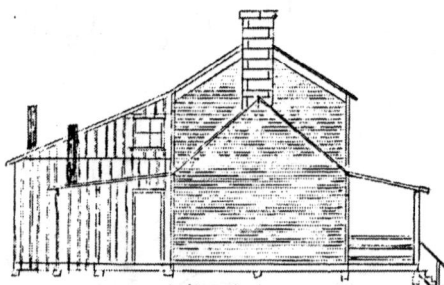

Left end view
1911 Remodeling

1911 Remodeling, End Views

1939 Remodeling, Exterior

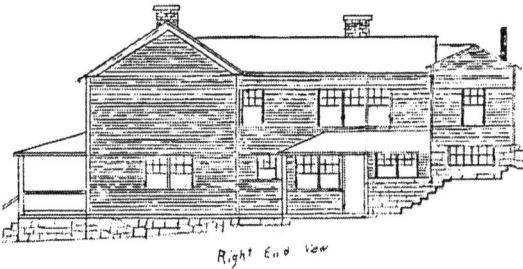

1939 Remodeling, End View

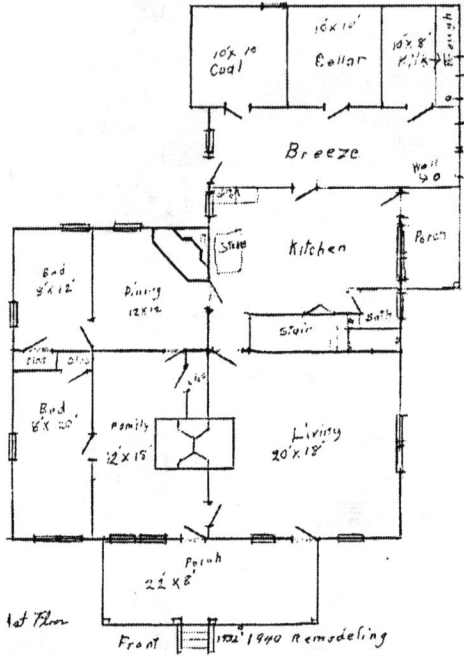

Floor Plan – 1939 Remodeling
1st Floor

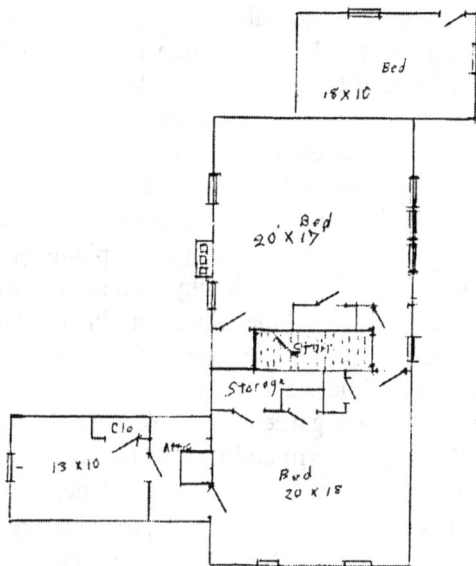

Bed
18 X 10

Bed
20' X 17

Stair

Storage

Clo

13 X 10

Attic

Bed
20 X 18

2nd Floor Front
1940 Remodeling

Floor Plan – 1939 Remodeling
2nd Floor

FARMING

- - - - - - - - - - - -

"Grandpa, tell us more about how you farmed way back then."

"I'm afraid it will sound like a lot of hard work?"

"We liked hearing about the oxen. And you've told us a lot about the good times you had, and the good food you ate."

"Then I guess it's time we talked about the work. First, let's think about what the country looked like before people from across the ocean began farming here."

- - - - - - - - - - - -

When settlements started along the Atlantic Coast, if Miles Standish and John Alden had been able to fly over the country, this is what they would have seen: The Atlantic Coast area, The Appalachian Mountains and the hilly area extending to the Ohio-Mississippi River was covered with unbroken forest. West of the Ohio River, the hills gradually faded into wide level areas still covered with forest, but mixed more and more with grassy, level prairie areas. At the Mississippi, the grassy plains predominated, from there to the foothills of the Rocky Mountains, where forests again became predominate all the way to the Pacific Ocean. They would have seen no cities, except Indian villages and tent encampments scattered here and there. They would have seen no farms, except the squaw gardens, pumpkin patches and meager corn areas of the Indians. In addition to the squaw gardens and patches of corn and pumpkins, the Indians depended on hunting for most of their food, and had no reason for clearing the forests. Thus Smith and Standish would have returned and told their people, there was nothing better than where they were now living, and to continue building houses, hunting and clearing land to raise crops and make a living.

So you see, since all this area was covered with forest, it was necessary to clear away the forest first, before a house could even be built, a garden planted or corn crops grown. So first I shall tell you how this clearing job was done.

CLEARING THE LAND

When I can first remember, a large part of our farm had been cleared and was already in corn, orchard, garden and pasture land. In our area, nearly every farmer had one or more clearings going each winter and spring. People who owned little or no land frequently cleared land for others, for the first 2 or 3 crops, depending on how hard it was to clear the woods again. Many farmers were glad to get extra land cleared in this way, so they would have more meadow and pasture on which to raise livestock. The early spring air was filled with the sound of axes, smoke and the smell of burning wood in the clearings.

While George and I were small, we started helping Pa in his clearings and learned how to do all the different jobs. By the time we were 14 and 15 years old, we were each able to do about as much work as a man, or at least we thought so. Pa did not offer any discouragement to this line of thought on our part. At this age, we started a 6 acre land clearing project in the head of Coon Hollow, on the back edge of our farm, about a mile from our house.

All the big white oak timber and any smaller white oaks, big enough to make a railroad cross-tie had been sold and cut a few years before we began that clearing job. However, many shellbark hickory trees over 2 feet in diameter and 75 to 100 feet in height were still standing, together with many blackjack and red oak trees of smaller size. This made it a heavy clearing job. We missed part of the last month of the 6 month school term that year to start this work.

Our first job was to grub and pile all the small brush, anything up to about 2 ½ inches in diameter. We each used a cutter-mattock to dig around each small bush and cut the roots off about 3 inches under the ground. Sometimes, small bushes could be grubbed at one stroke. Others required more digging and use of the cutter side of the mattock to get them loose from the ground. We usually piled the brush as we grubbed them. Some had to be cut in two with an ax, to fit the brush piles. This grubbing and piling was hard work. We said part of the underbrush along the fence was as thick as the hair on a dog's back, as indeed it seemed to be by the amount of work it took. Pa worked with us at this grubbing part of the time. He had hired a blacksmith to make two new mattocks, one for each of us. These were much better than the old worn-out ones we first used, and seemed to make the work easier. However, there is no way to make grubbing easy.

After about 2 weeks, including bad weather, we had about 2 acres grubbed and piled. Grubbing, rather than chopping off above the ground, was the method most widely favored and used to get rid of brush and small saplings when clearing ground.

In the meantime, some men in the neighborhood wanted a job of grubbing at so much an acre. Pa finally hired them at $6.50 an acre, boarding themselves. They began where we were and finished 4 acres, earning nearly a dollar a day, which was about the average wage at that time. Hiring them permitted us to get started at once on chopping the larger timber.

The little red axes were too small, however we ground them sharp, together with a 3 lb. pole ax and Pa's 4 lb. pole ax, in preparation for starting chopping on the following Monday. We were very much surprised and pleased when Pa brought home with him from the store at Troy, that Saturday evening, two brand new 4 lb. double-bit axes. They were just like the ones we had seen Ben Frymier and other timbermen use in cutting big saw-log trees. We lost no time in grinding one bit on each ax to a keen, sharp edge. We left the other bit less sharp for use in trimming or where there was danger of hitting stones that might dull the sharp bit. We were as eager to get started chopping with our new double-bit axes on the next Monday morning as we had been just a few years before, to get started cutting the 2 trees with our 2 new 'Little Red Axes' which I told you about several days ago.

When we began chopping in the clearing the following Monday, we were sure the thin, sharp axes would chop much easier and faster than the old single-bit ones had. Pa thought maybe their being new had something to do with it too.

We planned to cut both the saplings and the big timber off altogether, completely clearing the land in one operation, before plowing and planting time the coming spring.

Pa had used a different method in most of the clearings, that we had helped him with, up to this time. The grubbing was done first in the usual way, as we were doing it this year. However, the chopping of saplings and big timber was done in two operations, sometimes because of a shortage of time or help, or both. Other times, it was just because of a desire to clear more land and get a bigger area under cultivation the next year. In any event, the saplings and small trees were cut and burned the first year. The remaining heavy timber was deadened and left standing to be cut and cleaned up the following year, thus spreading the work over at least two year.

The deadening process was accomplished on the trees left standing in this way. A notch was cut through the bark and white sap-wood, completely around each tree at stump height. This prevented the trees from leafing out by cutting off the sap supply to the tree tops. The oaks were easily killed this way, but other trees, such as hickory, maple and beech required that another notch be cut around about 2 feet above the first notch, and the bark peeled or hewed off, between the two notches. This usually killed them the first year and prevented leafing out. Sometimes they leafed out incompletely and the leaves wilted and dried up as the

208

hot weather came on. Sometimes additional notching and bark hewing had to be done to get rid of the leaves, the first summer. After all this, sometimes the leaves persisted throughout the summer on some trees.

The corn could be planted and cultivated among the dead trees and would produce a good crop except under trees that leafed out and shaded the crop too much. There was little danger from falling limbs while working among the deadened trees the first season, except in windy weather, when whole trees might break off at the point where the deadening notches had weakened the trunks. Working in such windy weather was avoided for safety reasons.

I had helped Pa cut dry timber the second winter and early spring in several clearings before our Coon Hollow project. The cutting of dead trees, trimming off limbs, cutting logs into lengths for piling, was done in the same manner as the first cutting of green timber which I will tell more in detail a little later on. One difference was that in cutting the dead trees, the tops and limbs broke into many pieces on hitting the ground. They also burned more readily than the green wood. The second year's trash raking and clean-up took about the same amount of work as that of the first year.

Pa told us of another technique used extensively by the early settlers. Since no trees had been cut or removed in those days, the forests were heavy and filled with trees of enormous size. There was no market for lumber in those early days. Since the forest was in the way of building houses, planting gardens, setting out orchards and growing crops, the immediate problem was to destroy the trees where they were in the way. Each settler frequently decided which land he wanted to use in the next few years and immediately began destroying the forest ahead of time. The beginning was to girdle and deaden all the timber of all sizes. Fire was sometimes started in these areas to hold back the growth of small brush. The final clearing then proceeded in the usual way.

Now to get back to our Coon Run job. Pa and George each chopped right-handed, that is, they swung the ax back over the right shoulder in making each stroke. I was left-handed and swung my ax over the left shoulder. Some timber was far easier to cut if one side was cut right-handed and the final or back side was cut left-handed. But George and I had learned both ways because it was often easier and faster to cut both the first notch and the second or final notch while standing practically in the same place and on the same side of the tree. You simply changed hands on the ax handle and swung it over the opposite shoulder, instead of walking around the tree. It was a distinction among choppers to be able to do this equally well either way.

In addition to chopping, we used a two-man crosscut saw in making the second cut in felling many trees, especially the larger ones. We also used it in cutting trees into the log lengths desired. The larger cuts were easier and more quickly made, by sawing. The smaller cuts, and all the limb trimming, were done with an ax. As in chopping, sawyers were naturally left or right-handed, which made little difference on level ground. On hillsides, it helped to be able to saw either way, and was easier to learn than the chopping technique. More important, however, was keeping the saw in good condition by having the teeth even, sharp, properly set and the whole saw free of rust and greased occasionally. I had learned, by this time, how to gauge, file and set our saws so they would cut as fast as saws filed by the best filers anywhere in the community.

Pa and George used the saw quite a lot, while I went ahead, cutting saplings and larger trees, trimming off the limbs and piling them on the brush piles. The logs too heavy to lift were left for later rolling and hauling into log heaps for burning. When there was a lot of sawing to do, I helped with that, and when there was nothing to saw, we all chopped. We sawed the timber that would make posts, into 7 foot post-lengths, which we hauled out of the way at one end of the field for later splitting. Many easy-splitting logs, not suitable for posts were also hauled out of the field, to be cut into stove wood. We made use of our two yoke of oxen in this hauling. Some of the biggest shellbark hickory logs were split in half to keep them from rolling when snaked along the hillside. Some of the finest hickory trees grew here in this cove, that I have ever seen anywhere. There was no sale for them at that time. They did make good stove wood.

We came to a few extra big trees that had died or been blown down and would take a lot of sawing to cut into lengths that we could roll into piles. Pa showed us a different method to use on big logs like that. He went ahead to show us how it was done. We laid a large dry limb across the big log at each point where we

210

wanted it cut and then built a fire against the log at each of these two points. After the fire was started, all that was necessary was to keep a log lying across the big log, at the different burning points, until the big log burned through. If the fire burned out during the night, it was necessary to rekindle it each morning. We burned several of the big dry trees into logs in that way. We tried some green ones too but they burned too slowly to be of any advantage. One or two of the large dead trees burned up completely from end to end before the fire went out after it got started. While it took longer by this method, it was much easier to keep the fires going, than to saw them into logs. There was plenty of other chopping and sawing to be done in the meantime.

Ten hours was the regular day's work then for all kinds of work. Since this clearing was so far from our house, Ma packed our dinner pail each morning for us to carry with us. We carried a jug or two of water with us from the well at home. We had cleaned out a good spring of water in the hollow, below where we were working, from which we replenished our jug during the day. A big spring nearby, at the top of the hill, furnished plenty of water for Molly and the Oxen. We walked to the job and were ready to start work at seven. We worked until noon, when we generally took an hour off to eat dinner and rest before resuming work at one, continuing until six. We then walked the one mile back home, and did the milking and other daily chores.

Our clearing work was interrupted for short periods, occasionally, to do other farm work. For example, some meadow fence needed repairing at the mouth of Big Run, to keep some of the neighbors' cattle from pasturing in our meadow that spring. So one morning, I did not go with Pa and George to work in the clearing, but took my ax, a posthole digger, wire stretchers and tamping stick, together with a hammer, pliers, nails and staples and went to repair the meadow fence.

After making the repairs, I shouldered my ax and other tools and started home, when something whipped about my shoe tops and pants legs. Immediately, I thought of a snake. I let go of all the tools, at the same time jumping sidewise. As the double bit ax fell from my shoulder, the sharp corner edge of one bit, cut through one suspender, my shirt, and into the small of my back, nicking my back-bone. I was scared. There was no snake that I could see, only a few small, short, crooked sycamore limbs that

211

must have bounced about my ankles and pants legs. I was even more scared now, since I could not see how big a gash had been cut, and when I reached back and could feel my backbone through the gash, that didn't help any. Neither did the ends of my fingers covered with blood. I started home, leaving my tools where they had fallen. I decided that I had not been cut very badly when I couldn't feel any blood sloshing in my shoes, or any blood stains on my pants legs.

When I got home, Ma decided the gash wasn't very big and had about stopped bleeding, but she thought we had better go to Troy and let the doctor see it. We drove Molly to Troy, using the buggy. The doctor bandaged the cut and thought it would be all right, but said that I should not work and get hot, for 2 or 3 days. I did as he instructed. It healed properly, but they tell me there is still a scar on my back.

When I went back to the clearing, George and Pa had finished the chopping. They had already raked and burned a fire strip across the upper side and down both ends of the clearing to keep the fire from getting out of control and burning at large in the forest. It was necessary to burn the brush piles out of the way before we could finish rolling and hauling the bigger logs into piles for burning.

If you can picture 6 acres of stumpy, freshly cleared ground, covered with big piles of brush, 20 to 50 feet apart, you have some idea of the size of the fires and clouds of smoke sent up, when all were on fire and burning at the same time. We began lighting the fires late one evening, so the main flash of the burning would be after night when sparks would not fly so far, because there was less wind. There would be less danger of their flying beyond our burned fire-strips and starting fires in the woods beyond. We took these precautions before starting the fires, because once the fire was started, there was no way to stop it.

We lit the fires in many places, beginning near the upper side and working downhill to the lower edge. By the time our fires were lighted across the lower side, the fire had enveloped the whole of the upper side and was rapidly covering the whole field. There was so much dry brush in all the piles, that as the fire got hotter and hotter, the piles each exploded into full flame reaching high into the air. The whole 6 acres in full blaze was an awesome sight. We watched along the lower side and both ends, for any fire

212

outside our control lines, but the smoke and heat along the upper side was so intense and thick, we could see little from either end, and could not venture into the area. Our preparations paid off, and we had no fires outside our control lines. We had little to do except watch the burning spectacle from a safe distance until after midnight, when it burned down enough that we thought it safe to leave and go home.

It took us about a week to ten days to roll and haul the logs into piles for burning. We usually lit the log heaps each evening, although we lit each pile as we completed it, if the fire and smoke would not blow toward where we were working. The log piles made intense heat while burning, but in no way were as spectacular as the burning brush. The burning logs had to be kept rolled together as they burned so that all would be burned up completely. While the logs were burning, we raked and burned all the trash and by the time the logs were completely burned, this new ground was ready for plowing. About 3 months' work was required on these 6 acres.

This gives you an idea of the amount of work required and the manner of doing it, in order to clear the land and get it ready for the cultivation of crops. The tools and methods I have just described were the ones used by everyone then, in doing such work.

- - - - - - - - - - -

"Grandpa, now they'd use chain-saws and bulldozers, wouldn't they?"

"Yes, and more of the big logs would be sold rather than burned. But it would still be hard work."

"What came next? I guess it would be the plowing, wouldn't it?"

"Yes, but I'm too tired to start plowing tonight. All that chopping and sawing tired me out. Can't the plowing wait until tomorrow?"

- - - - - - - - - - -

NEW-GROUND PLOWING

Now take a look at this 6 acres of new-ground burned clean of logs and brush and what do you see? Big and small stumps are scattered everywhere over it. What you can't see are the root systems attached to every stump beneath the ground. This 6 acre mat of green underground roots both large and small, together with the stumps above ground, present problems to new-ground plowing that must be met and overcome by the plowman.

To solve the plow problem, we made a shovel plow, as illustrated in this sketch.

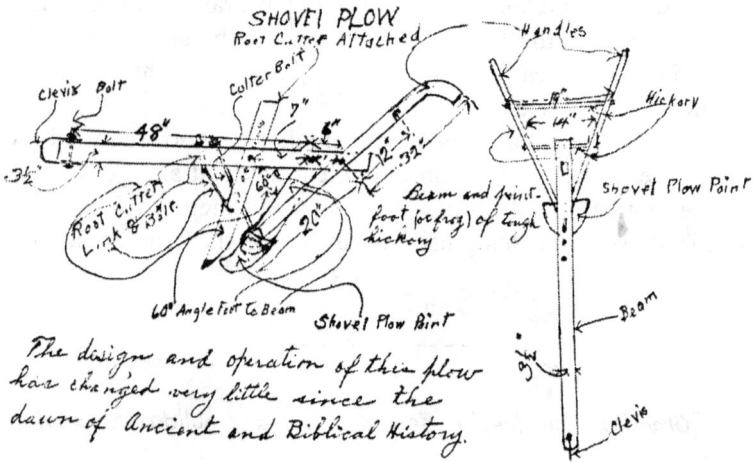

Shovel Plow with Root Cutter

214

The plow was made from a tough hickory sapling, big enough to hew a 3 ½ x 3 ½ inch square piece of timber to make the beam and foot-piece. To this shovel plow, we attached a steel cutter to run slightly deeper in the ground and a little in front of the shovel point, for the purpose of cutting the green roots in front of the plow. Plows equipped with a root-cutter did a better plowing job in new ground. For instance, without such a cutter, the shovel plow was constantly flipping from side to side, or catching beneath roots and diving beneath them into the ground. The team would then stall and have to back up and the plow be lifted and pulled manually from under the roots by the plowman. This added to the work, which was already hard enough. No shovel plowing is easy, but many plows are harder to use than others. The one we made ran the easiest and plowed the best of any that I have ever used. I could easily add pressure on the handles and sink the plow into the ground deep enough to stall a team. The root-cutter stopped the constant side-to-side flipping and cut straight through these roots and the ones that would have caused the plow to dive into the ground and stalled the oxen. On big roots that still stopped the team, the cutter cut into the roots, rather than diving under them. They were then much easier to loosen than without the cutter. Stalling happened much less often.

The power to pull the plow was supplied by our two yoke of oxen, then about 3 and 4 years old. By taking turns with them, one pair could rest while the others pulled the plow. George drove the oxen and I operated the plow most of the time. Before the end of the first day's plowing, I found blisters beginning to form in the part of my palms where the pressure of the plow handles was different from that of the mattock and ax handles. These gave way to tough calluses by the end of the job. We used each yoke of oxen about an hour until it began to get hot, and then tied it in the shade while using the other. In this way we could keep going steadily, except when we ourselves needed a rest. The driver's job was to keep one ox walking in the last furrow and the other on the unplowed ground. He had to get them to straddle stumps and also make the proper turn at the end of the furrow at each end of the field. Our oxen were not broken well enough to do this without a driver, but they were learning. A year or two later, we were able to do some plowing without a driver.

I operated the plow and kept it going as nearly as possible the way it should. Another important thing was to keep my feet and ankles out of the way of loose ends of the roots that were pulled forward by the plow until cut, and then flew back. This was a constant dodging day-long dance and even with the best of luck, all of them could not be avoided. Sore ankles were the result. We averaged nearly an acre a day at this plowing, which was the usual day's work and about the usual rate for the plowing of newly cleared land. Sometimes this type plow was used the second year with even better results.

In addition to the new ground, we plowed 12 to 15 acres of meadow sod for corn that same year. This land was free of tree roots, except near walnut or chestnut trees scattered in the field. We used a swivel turning plow for this work, which locally, was called a hillside plow. The plow was reversed at the end of each furrow on hillside land so that the furrow was turned downhill every time. Where the ground was level enough to allow the furrow to turn over, the ground could be plowed around and around, the same as you see plowmen doing now in level country. We used the spike-tooth harrow and drag in the final seed-bed preparation on this type land. One-row horse-drawn corn planters, riding sulky-plows and riding cultivators were used on a few farms that had enough smooth level land to justify the expense of such machinery.

THE CORN PLANTER

Our best labor saving device was the hand corn planter. The diagram later, shows the planter in the open position, the point stuck into the ground with the grains of corn ready to be left in the ground. When the planter handles were closed, the point opens, leaving the corn. As the planter is lifted, the handles closed, ready for the next place to plant another hill of corn. This was the type planter we used to plant our new-ground cornfield. I have never used any more improved type.

216

Hand Corn Planter

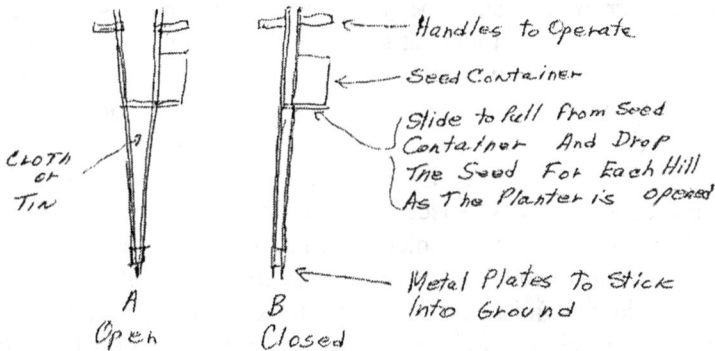

Handles to Operate

Seed Container

Slide to Pull from Seed Container And Drop The Seed For Each Hill As The Planter is opened

CLOTH or TIN

Metal Plates To Stick Into Ground

A Open

B Closed

The cloth or tin secured to each side of the planter keeps the grain in the planter as it falls to the bottom for planting.

"A" The seed for a hill has been pulled from the seed container and dropped between the metal plates ready to be stuck into the ground where it is left when the planter is closed while in the ground as Fig "B". Then it is lifted from the ground ready for another hill.

Hand Corn Planter

George and Pa furrowed or marked the ground for planting, using Molly to pull the shovel plow. She was broken to do such work without the need of an extra driver, thus they were able to take turns at the furrowing. The roots made it hard to keep the furrows going straight and the right distance apart. I followed with the hand planter, planting the hills of corn in the lower edge of each furrow, about 2 ½ feet between each hill. Any extra stalks were thinned out later at the first hoeing. Some operators planted at every other step and others jabbed the planter in the ground at every step. I stepped the right distance for a hill at every step, and that was the way I followed George or Pa furrowing all day long. By quitting time that evening, we had planted the entire 6 acres, which was a full day's work. I was tired and my back ached between my shoulders by the time we were finished.

I remember seeing Pa, a few years before, plant about 4 acres of new ground by using stakes. Some of this ground was too steep to plow or furrow, and some had been plowed with a shovel plow without a root cutter. Since it would have been hard to make straight furrows that could be easily followed in planting, he began on the steep part first and set stakes 50 or 60 feet apart in a line. He set the planter down at the first stake, then moved that stake up to what would be the next row to plant, coming back. Then, looking ahead to the next stake in the row his planter was in, he planted straight to it and moved it up to the next row. He continued to each stake successively to the end of that row. When the first row had been completed, he had his stakes set in line for planting the next row. This process was continued until the whole 4 acre field was finished. It probably took two days. I have heard him tell the neighbors about this many times. He said he made one mistake by going toward the wrong stake at one place. We could easily see the mistake when the corn came up. I have planted small areas in this way.

Pa had used the hand planter for many years. One of his neighbors steadfastly refused to use what he termed 'The new-fangled planter,' and continued the old method of furrowing out the ground for rows. Next, one person would go along each furrow and drop the grains of corn for each hill, by hand. Another would follow, using a hoe, and cover the corn with dirt. This was slow laborious work. One spring, Pa's neighbor was crippled up with rheumatism and his son had gotten behind with their spring planting. He had the last 2 or 3 acres plowed and ready to plant. Finally, the son persuaded his father to let him go down and borrow McQuain's planter to finish the planting. Pa was up at the upper end of our farm while the neighbor's son was planting corn. The father was leaning against the fence watching. Pa walked over to the fence and said,

'Well, Uncle Peter, what do you think of the planter?'

'I'm not sure, Tommy, it may be all right, but it looks too easy!'

Henry, the son, furrowed and planted the whole field in a day with the planter, where he would have been 3 or 4 days using the old way. Where the planter was used, the corn produced as well as that planted by hand, so Henry was able to persuade his father to get a planter for their own use the next year.

218

We got a new planter that had a fertilizer supply box on the side opposite the corn supply box, with a slide to drop fertilizer into each hill. We did not use the fertilizer side and soon took it off to make the planter lighter.

In our area, people always used white corn for bread and would not think of using yellow corn for that purpose. Everyone tried to plant and raise enough white corn for their own use, and if he had enough ground, he raised yellow corn for feed for his livestock. Some thought yellow corn grew better and produced a little more per acre than white corn did.

The 8 row 'Thumbnail White' and 8 row 'Dog-tail Yellow' seemed to do better on thin or poor ground than did the larger corn with more rows to the ear. The bigger types of corn were usually grown on the better ground.

Many pumpkins for both livestock feed and for cooking purposes were planted in every second or third row of corn, and at every second or third hill in the row. This planting was done about the time of the first hoeing, so the vines would not be in the way of the second plowing. Pumpkins were usually restricted to the richer ground, and not grown if the ground was to be sown in wheat that fall. There would not have been long enough growing time.

Sometimes a few tomato plants were set out for use, if needed. These tomatoes were some extra food to look forward to at harvesting time, even if not otherwise needed. Turnips were frequently sowed in open places where corn was missing, especially in new ground where they did well, another way to add variety to the food supply.

We usually planted about an acre of corn-beans with the corn, which vined up each hill of corn. They were excellent to eat while green, or ripe as shelled beans. They could be dried in the hulls, then soaked and cooked in the same manner as green beans. They were called 'fodder beans' when cooked this way. They were usually planted after the first cultivation, so the corn would get started enough to support the bean vines. People preferred not to plant beans in the main corn field, unless other smaller patches of corn were not available.

Corn was usually cultivated two times, or maybe three if it did not get too high before we got to it the third time. No herbicides were used to kill the weeds then, at least in our area.

219

We depended on destroying the weeds between the rows by using a shovel plow, double shovel plow, cultivator plow or cultivator harrow. We have used all of them, depending on the type of ground. We used the single shovel plow in our new ground the first year and plowed about 3 furrows between each row to destroy weeds and preserve soil mulch to hold moisture. But the weeds between the hills in the rows had to be cut out by hand with hoes, along with any weeds missed by the plow between rows. New ground was full of sprouts around stumps. It took 3 or 4 people with hoes to do this work and keep up with one man and horse plowing in such weedy, sprouty ground. It would take 3 or 4 days to cultivate the 6 acres each time. We had older, cleared ground with no stumps or roots that cultivated much easier. On some of our bottom land, we cross-furrowed, so the corn could be plowed both ways, which cleaned the weeds except immediately in each hill. This cut down on the hoe work.

HARVESTING CORN

Both the new ground and the old fields produced a good crop that year. Harvesting corn was usually done in two operations throughout our whole area. First the corn was cut by hand, using a corn knife or cutter about 30 inches long, including the handle. The corn stalks were caught in one arm, and cut until the arm was full. Then the armful was carried to the shock row, where it was set between four uncut hills of corn and all tied securely with a stalk of corn, just above the ears. Additional armfuls were set around this shock heart, until the desired size shock was in position. Another stalk was then tied tightly around the outside, completing the shock. Some preferred tying the 4 hills together first, into a four section brace of shock anchor. Pa called these shock anchors 'galluses' and thought shocks stood up better built around galluses than setting an armful of corn in the middle of them, which was a little faster.

We used the 'gallus' method that Pa preferred. Cutting 25 or 30 shocks was a fair day's work, although some could cut more. About 12 rows were brought together and shocked in the two middle rows of galluses. After standing in shock about 2 weeks, the corn was usually dry enough to store the ears in the open lath corn cribs without danger of spoilage. Shucking started about that time, or by the time the cutting was finished.

Corn required a longer growing season than the improved types now grown. People also needed to save the fodder for feed, since meadow land was not sufficient to produce enough hay to winter all the livestock they wanted. The fodder made better feed if the corn was cut before getting too ripe and especially before getting frosted. For these reasons, most corn was cut and shocked, and then the shocks were torn down and shucked later.

Some types of corn that matured and ripened early, were shucked on the stalk and thrown in piles or rows and then the fodder cut and shocked in the usual manner. The corn was then picked up and hauled to the crib. This required less fodder handling. Sometimes the horses pulled a wagon or sled along and the corn was shucked and thrown directly into the wagon or sled, but this damaged the fodder, making it hard to save. This method was little used in our area.

The shucking I have been talking about was not done by a tractor-pulled picker, driven through the fields as you have seen here in Ohio, nor was it shelled with a huge picker-sheller. The shucking was done by hand, one ear at a time. So likewise was the shelling done by hand, or by a hand-powered hand-fed sheller, one ear after the other.

Here is my drawing of a hand-help shucking tool:

Shucking peg & Hook

Wooden Peg

Round, tough hard
wood peg with a
leather strap or thong
secured in two notches
or rings cut around peg)

Metal Peg

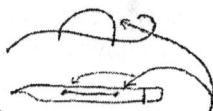

Leather strap,
thong attached
through holes in
metal peg.

Hooks attached to heavy leather
fitted to palm of hand and secured
with light leather straps around wrist
and palm of hand.

Corn Shucking Peg and Hook

    To aid the fingers in pulling the shucks off the ears of corn, a wood or metal peg was used on one hand with a leather strap looped over 1 or 2 fingers. This strap held the peg in position and kept it from flying off the hand and getting lost when throwing an ear of corn toward the corn pile, or in reaching for another un-shucked ear. Pa had a pair of leather, metal-studded shucking gloves with the metal peg attached, for use in cold weather, or when his hands became chapped and sore. These pegs and gloves were a little improvement over the bare hands in getting the husks off the corn. Another improvement was a pair of hooks fastened to a heavy piece of leather fitted over the thumb, in the palm of the

222

hand. It was secured by a light strap, buckled around the hand. I have used all these types, but preferred the hooks strapped to the hand, which prevented finger cramping and made shucking easier and faster. These hooks could be worn over light gloves, if desired.

The fodder from 5 or 6 corn shocks was tied in bundles and shocked into one big shock of fodder. One of these shocks of corn standing up straight that appeared to have a good set of galluses was selected as the center, around which to shock the rest. This corn shock was untied, and the corn laid on the ground in position for shucking. The corn on the galluses was then shucked, leaving the galluses standing, ready to receive the fodder from the other corn shocks as they were shucked, tied in bundles and shocked around them again.

The galluses of the other corn shocks were first cut and then the corn shocks were dragged near to the shucked pile of corn, in position for shucking. The corn tops were placed pointing to the left, as the shucker stood below the shock ready for shucking.

Shucking was done by taking hold of an ear, drawing it, including the stalk toward him, at the same time, pressing the hooks on the opposite hand, into the husk, wringing it away from the ear. At the same time, the thumb of the same hand was passed under the retreating husk, seizing the bare ear, and, letting loose with the other hand, seizing the butt of the ear with that hand, then applying pressure with the other hand to break the husk from the ear, and then throwing the loose ear into the pile of shucked corn. This procedure was followed with each succeeding stock of corn. The fodder from each shock was then tied into about three bundles, using a stalk of fodder for each tie, and this was then set up around the fodder shock. Speed of movement, elimination of unnecessary movements and experience all helped determine the shucking speed and amount of work done in a day.

My speed of movement was about ordinary but I practiced eliminating as many unnecessary movements connected with downing the corn shock and tying and shocking the fodder. Soon I was able to complete 3 shocks to 2 by the others working with me. George and I were helping Earl Heckert with his shucking and something was said at the supper table one evening that I was shucking 3 shocks to each of their 2 shocks. Grant Scott said,

'If anyone shucks 3 shocks to my 2, I'll leave the field!'

We finished Earl's shucking and went up to help Grant and Guy with their shucking. I didn't know if I could shuck 3 to Grant's 2. We went to work that morning, without anyone saying anything. I did shuck 3 to each of their 2, until about the middle of the afternoon, when Grant made some excuse about going somewhere to see about something. He left the field. No one said anything. But that evening at supper, Mrs. Scott said,

'I guess you fellows ran Grant out of the field this afternoon!'

'How's that?' someone asked.

'When Grant came in this afternoon, he said that Bryan was the first man he ever shocked with, who could shuck 3 socks to his 2.'

'We didn't know that was why he left early.' Grant spoke up, saying,

'I didn't say so at the time, but I was getting tired!'

Shocking the fodder from 5 or 6 corn shocks into one fodder shock made it too large to be tied securely with corn stalks. It had long been our practice to use slim hickory sprouts (withes) 2 or 3 years old, for this use. These hickory sprouts could be found in the woods where hickory trees grew and dropped their nuts. They grew tall quickly in the woods, trying to get to the sunlight and in 2 or 3 years would be 12 to 20 feet tall, yet scarcely an inch in diameter. These slim withes were split in halves or quarters and made excellent fodder shock ties. Sometimes a single long length would make a tie, but more often it was necessary to tie the tips of two pieces together to get the right length. One tie was made near the top of the fodder stack, just above the fodder shucks, to secure the top of the shock. Another tie was sometimes made around the bottom of the shock, 2 or 3 feet from the ground to prevent the wind from loosening the bunches and upsetting the shocks.

I have frequently cut withes from stubs that sprouted up from previous cuttings. In this way, several cuttings might be had from the same stub, over a period of years. The withes were thrown into water, or a shady place to prevent drying out before they could be used. Hickory withes and hickory bark were used for many different purposes around the farm, from mending harness and fences, to bottoming chairs and tying meat up for smoking in the smokehouse. Farmers could not see how they could ever have gotten along without hickory withes. They also had a use in the discipline of children.

Later, bailing wire and sea-grass twine met this need, as both became readily available with the developing oil field business in our area.

The fodder was carried or hauled to convenient places for feeding livestock. Corn was fed in the ear, or crushed cob and all, added to the fodder diet, especially for milk cows. Wheat middlings and bran were sometimes added. In our area, little whole wheat was ever fed to livestock, since it was too much in demand for human food. The middlings and bran were left from grinding flour.

Corn, too hard for roasting ears and too green to grind, was often grated by hand on a grater for meal to make bread, before the corn was mature and dry enough to grind on a mill. This grated meal from immature corn made excellent bread with a taste different from regular mill-ground meal.

Pa has often told of the use of hand-turned corn crackers by the early settlers, for making coarse meal, that needed sifting to remove hulls and coarse particles before baking into bread. These corn crackers were used before water or steam mills came into use, or if they were too far away to be used. Perhaps some of the old corn crackers may still be in use, in out-of-the-way places of the world.

I have seen stones with large rounded-out holes in them which were said to have been used by Indians or early settlers to grind corn into meal.

Water and steam powered grist mills were readily available in our area, ever since I can first remember. These ground corn, wheat, or buckwheat, into meal or flour, thus making the older methods unnecessary. Later on, both meal and flour were brought in and sold at the mill and in country stores as they sprang up around the country.

The miller was paid for grinding grain by a toll of the grain, which was usually 1/8th of the grain being ground, or one gallon per bushel. His share was usually taken out before grinding the rest for the customer. In this way, no money was needed to get the grinding done. I am not sure whether the measure used for the toll held a gallon or only ½ gallon, but I have seen the miller dip his share from the hopper before it went through the burrs or rolls to grind our part. Sometimes people accused the miller of taking his toll out more than once, but not to his face, by the small amount left the owner to take home. Pa says he has seen the miller pretending to scare his chickens from the mill porch by taking handfuls of grain from the hopper and throwing at them. His chickens always looked well fed.

The corn was shelled before taking it to the mill for grinding. This shelling was done with the bare hands or by holding a piece of corn cob in one hand and rubbing the corn off the ears, a few at a time. The piece of cob helped, but it was slow work.

Hand-turned shellers were used which had studded wheels that turned the ear of corn as it went through, shelling the corn from the cob, which was thrown out on the opposite end from where the ear had been fed into the mill. The corn dropped into a box below as it was shelled from the cob. This was much faster. The sheller was turned by a crank with one hand, and the ears fed into the sheller with the other.

A larger variation of the first sheller was used that required one or more studded turning-wheels and rough surfaces against which the revolving ears of corn were stripped of corn. A revolving fan-wheel forced a current of air through the corn as it was shelled and fell toward the box below, removing all chaff or pieces of cob. The corn was then clean and ready to be take to the mill or stored in bins until needed. This sheller had a revolving, heavy-rimmed flywheel about 3 feet in diameter, to equalize the sheller speed as each ear went through. One person could turn and feed this sheller, but it was much faster and easier if 2 operated it, one turning the crank and keeping up the speed, while the other fed the ears into the sheller.

We used all these methods of shelling corn, but I remember best using the small sheller and the large flywheel sheller. I have helped shell seed corn by hand where we did not want the tips of ears shelled in with the seed corn. Sometimes we shelled these small grains at the tips and then ran the remainder of the ear through the sheller to shell and clean the seed corn.

We selected our seed corn as we gathered the corn by picking the biggest and best-developed ears of the variety we wished to continue raising. This corn was stacked in single rows, between the overhead joists on boards nailed to the under-edges of the joists in the granary. The air circulating about these ears dried them out so they would not freeze during the cold winter weather.

Freezing would prevent their growing when planted the next spring.

We learned in school, how to test seed corn by the 'rag doll tester' method so as to determine which ears would grow and which would not. Five grains were taken from numbered ears and placed in testing spaces on a cloth. They were similarly numbered, then rolled and tied, forming the 'rag doll.' This was then kept damp and warm until the corn sprouted. Those ears sprouting perfectly were stored for planting, the others, for use if needed in an emergency.

One fall was especially poor for drying corn in cribs and the following winter was extra cold and froze crib-stored corn so that little, if any, would grow the following spring when planted. Our tested seed grew as indicated by the tests. We had a good stand of corn at first planting. Many people planting crib-cured seed got very poor stands which required a lot of replanting. Many fields had to be furrowed out and completely replanted. People came to buy our extra, tested seed. Even that which we had laid back that tested imperfectly was bought and planted it was far getter than crib-cured corn.

When we found that people were having so much trouble getting corn that would grow, we ran some tests on 3 or 4 bins of shelled corn we had left over from the year before when all corn grew well. This 30 or 40 bushels tested out good. People quickly found out about it and came from all over the county to get it to plant and replant with. Soon it was gone. Pa sold this corn at the usual price, even though he might have doubled the price on it and people would have been glad to get it. He thought it better to let them have good seed so they could raise something to eat the next year. It was trouble enough for them to go so far to get seed without having to pay extra for it when they got there. Pa met and talked with many people whom he had known when he was Gilmer County Sheriff several years before. This was a renewal of old acquaintances and seemed to be enjoyed equally by both Pa and the people coming for seed corn. This was white corn. Some only needed 2 or 3 gallon to plant as many acres for bread corn; others wanted as much as a bushel, or more, to plant larger acreages. It required about a gallon of seed corn to plant an acre.

"So that's the story of how Coon Hollow got to be a cornfield."

"It really took a lot of work to clear the land and plant it. Grandpa have you seen my garden this year? I won a prize at the fair last year with my green beans, but my cabbage wasn't very good."

"Your sweet corn turned out OK, didn't it?"

"Yes, it was fine. I'll be glad when it's ready this year."

"We didn't grow a special type of corn for the roasting ears I mentioned. We ate the regular field corn when it was young and tender. It tasted good to us, but I agree that the sweet corn you grow now is better."

"My garden was plowed by a tractor but I planted it by hand. I can use a hoe too. I bet weeds still grow as fast here in Ohio as they did back then in West Virginia."

"You don't have quite as many animals eating your produce, although rabbits are hard on lettuce. Birds still like strawberries and raspberries as well as people do."

"Did you always grow corn in Coon Hollow?"

"We grew 2 crops of corn and then we planted our first wheat. . ."

WHEAT

The story of our first crop of wheat on our Coon Run new ground will be a fairly good example of wheat-growing methods in our area for the period of 1900-1914, the year this crop was harvested.

In the fall after cutting and shocking our second crop of corn, we decided the sprouts and weeds were sufficiently under control to grow a crop of wheat. We broadcast the wheat over the ground by hand. Pa did the sowing by carrying a sack containing wheat

228

slung over his shoulder, from which he took the wheat by the handful and scattered it before him over the number of corn rows that he could cover. The corn rows made it easy to sow without overlapping or missing strips. We cut the corn stubs and sprouts with a hoe before plowing. Then George and I followed with shovel plows, plowing the ground to cover the wheat. We tried to use a spike-tooth harrow to level the ground more after plowing, but this ground was too rooty and stumpy. We gave that up. We did use broad-hoes to dig the wheat in, around the stumps and between the corn shocks. By plowing shallow and evenly, the wheat was covered to a fairly even depth and came up and made an even stand of about the correct thickness on the ground. From 1 to 1 1/4th bushels of wheat to the acre was needed to get a good stand. The wheat got a good start before cold weather set in, and there was considerable snow during the winter to help protect it from winter freezing. The growing season was good the next summer, and we had a good crop.

Pa tried to get someone to help us cut the wheat but good cradlers were already engaged to help others. We thought of exchanging help with some of our neighbors, but it seemed that wheat all ripened about the same time that year. All were wanting help with their own wheat, rather than having any time to help anyone else, until they got their own wheat cut.

Since there was no chance of getting any immediate help and our wheat was just right for cutting, we decided to start cutting it ourselves the next Monday morning. I was 17 and had cradled enough in earlier years to make a hand at cradling with experienced cradlers. Pa and George were both good at tying or binding the wheat into sheaves ready for shocking.

I used the ordinary grain cradle, or cradling scythe, which was then widely used throughout our part of the country. Horse-drawn reaper-binders were used little, because of the lack of smooth-lying land. The old time crooked sickle blade with the wood handle was used only on blown-down wheat that could not be cut with a cradle. The sickle was slow for an expert to use, and dangerous for a novice, so I used it very little.

The cradle-scythe had four curved, wood fingers following the scythe curve, to catch the grain as cut by the scythe and carry it through the cutting stroke. The cradle-scythe left the wheat in a straight, even swath with the heads all pointing away from the cradler and the straws parallel with each other, ready to be raked into sheaf-size bundles for binding into sheaves. Cradlers could lay the wheat in even swaths, or they could lay it in bunches of three cradle strokes each when desired. This was a little more difficult and more tiring, however it was a help to the binder if he had no one to rake.

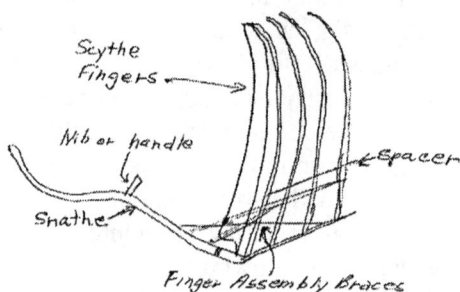

To operate the cradle, seize the nib in the right hand and grasp the free end of the snathe in the left hand.

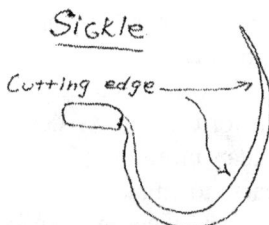

Grain Cradle

We started in the ripest wheat the first day. George and Pa raked and bound the wheat in sheaves after me, but did not keep up. This let the wheat dry a little in the swath before binding. Toward evening, they decided it would be better to let it lie in the swath overnight. They stopped raking and binding, and shocked the sheaves that had already been thrown in groups of a dozen each. The tops of two sheaves were broken down to the band so

230

that the sheaf lay on top of the shock, and would shed the rain and allow the wheat to cure and dry out in the shock. The next day, Ma and the whole family came out for a picnic dinner. Eunice and Lois helped rake the wheat into sheaf-size bundles; this permitted both Pa and George to bind.

This second day was a nice cool day for working and we were cutting in the best part of the field. I decided to see if I could cut 100 dozen that day. I marked carefully where I began that morning, and worked steadily all day. It looked like rain about noon, so I helped shock what we had done to keep it from getting wet. It did not rain after all. However, even with this delay, by quitting time, I had cradled 100 dozen. I had heard Pa frequently tell about Jimmie Lamb and other good cradlers cutting 100 dozen a day. They had done their good cutting on smoother ground where they could cradle around the tract without having to walk back to the bottom of the field after each swath cut to the top. He thought I had cut as much or more than they would have cut on the kind of ground we were working over. It was too steep to cradle in any direction except up-hill. We finished the 6 acre field of 425 dozen in a little over 4 ½ days, averaging about 80 dozen a day.

I was so tired the evening that I cut the 100 dozen that I thought I would not be able to eat any supper. That would not do, for I did not want any of the family to know how tired I was. I took my time and was able to eat a fairly good meal so that none noticed my slowness getting started. By the time I had finished, I was feeling pretty good, and considerably rested.

After the wheat cured in the shock for a week or two, we hauled it from the field and stacked it on a flat, about halfway down from the top of the hill, where a portable steam horse-drawn threshing machine could easily be hauled up, to do the threshing. Pa showed me how to turn the sloping butt end of the sheaves with the long side up, to let the stack bulge out, and to hold the bulge until ready to draw in, then to top the stack when the short side of each sheaf was kept up. He said we had to use care in securely placing each sheaf so as to prevent slipping, especially when expanding the stack for the bulge. I guess I was lucky in following his instructions, because when we had finished stacking, we had two nicely-shaped, bulging stacks that were almost twins in appearance, and as well shaped as any stacks in the neighborhood. We felt pleased that our stacks compared favorably with those of the best recognized stackers in the community.

After wheat in the stack went through a sweat, it was ready to thresh and store. A new set of threshers made their way through the neighborhood this year with a well-equipped, steam-powered threshing machine. When they came to our place, they doubled their teams to take the steam engine up the hill. We pulled the thresh box up with our one yoke of oxen. No time was lost in getting on the hill, and they were ready to start threshing by 1:30 PM. They had been served their dinner at the neighbor's before coming to our farm. They said they would be through by early suppertime and would eat with us before going on to the next set. Four or five men owned and operated the mill. Ten or twelve other men were needed to get the wheat from the stack to the thresher, measure and sack the threshed wheat, and stack the straw as it came from the straw carrier. The extra help was secured among the neighbors who had threshing to do, by exchanging help with one another. The threshing machine men were paid so much per bushel in cash for their work, plus their board and lodging.

They finished threshing our 125 bushels and were off the hill by early suppertime. Another set was threshed after supper, and they went on to the next farm and set up that evening so they would be ready to thresh, first thing the next morning. They were completely out of the neighborhood in less than 3 days.

This was much different from the first threshing machine I can remember. These threshers, too, said they would be through by suppertime and would go on to the next set to stay overnight. Their equipment was in poor condition. Belts broke and had to be repaired. Babbet bearings burned out and had to be re-poured. Steam pressure would get low and they would have to wait for the fireman to get up steam. The fan and sieves failed to separate the chaff and dust from the wheat, and it too, had to be repaired. The straw elevator broke and would not carry the straw to the stack. It seemed everything that could go wrong, did. That evening a few sacks of threshed wheat was brought in on a sled. They had scarcely got started! The men with the mill stayed with us all night. One of the owners had a long gray beard reaching nearly to his belt, which interested us children very much. All seemed to enjoy the evening, talking and having a good time.

Everyone was sure they would be done before noon, when they went to work the next morning, but noon came and they still were not done. More breakdowns and more repairs had delayed them. One of the neighbor women helped Ma with the dinner for not only the 4 or 5 mill men, but for the extra 10 or 12 neighbors who were helping with the threshing. There were 2 tables full of men. We children waited while the men were eating, before it was our turn. Again, they were sure they would be done before evening.

Ma told them she would get supper for them, but they should bring the threshing machine off the hill with them, together with the un-threshed wheat, to be stored in the barn. Supper would be the last meal she would prepare and they could go on to the next farm after supper.

When suppertime came, they still weren't done. Pa told them to take the mill off the hill with them and make repairs later. He loaded the un-threshed wheat and took it in with him to the barn. I think they had a little over 100 bushels of wheat threshed and 10 or 15 bushels not threshed. This was extra bad luck, but threshing was always expensive and time consuming. If neighbors had not exchanged work, it would have been impossible.

Women usually helped each other with the cooking on such occasions, and prepared plenty of good substantial food to satisfy the appetites of the hungry threshers. The expression, 'Like cooking for threshers' came from these occasions. Threshing-time came at the most plentiful time of the year and was one reason women took such pride in preparing such good meals. Such things as new potatoes, green beans, ripe tomatoes, cabbage, onions, fruit and berries, eggs, fryers, milk, cream, butter, cottage cheese, and roasting ears all appeared on the tables during the rounds of a neighborhood threshing season.

But that time, Pa said the 16 men could have threshed the wheat out with flails in less time than that threshing crew.

I have heard Pa tell of an earlier type portable threshing machine which was horse-powered, before the steam-powered type came into use. These were powered in much the same way as the old cane mill or portable stationary hay bailer. A horse, or other animal, was hitched to a shaft and went round and round, turning a power unit, geared to transfer the horse power to the threshing unit. Some of these machines did not separate the wheat

233

or grain from the chaff which required another winnowing operation. This mill was easier and faster than flailing the grain from the straw by hand as had been done before this improvement. The chaff-piler, horse-powered machines had gone out of use in our area before I was big enough to remember or help operate them, but I saw one in operation between Brest and Paris, France when I was there during the First World War. I am sure it was that same type machine, since it was operated in much the same way as Pa had described the operation of the old machines in this country.

The flail is a much older tool, used to separate grain from straw and is sometimes used yet today. To make one, take a hickory, willow, or other tough green pole the right size, for a handle, with the butt end used for the club to pound the grain straw. The pole should be pounded at a point about 18 inches or 2 feet from the end, soothe club end will hang freely when used. Here is my drawing of a flail:

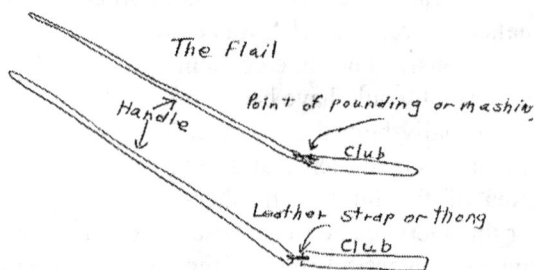

The Flail

Another way is to tie the club to the handle by boring a hole through the end of each, and tying them together with a leather thong, which allows the club to swing freely when striking the straw. This kind can be saved for future use.

I have used the flail to thresh out seed oats for planting when we raised oats to be fed to the livestock in the sheaf, or when we did not raise wheat. I remember one such year when we needed to flail out enough oats for seed to sow. Pa made a flail for his own use and helped make two smaller ones for George and me. These were made from green hickory poles and pounded to mash the wood pliable between the handle and the club, and yet hang together while using.

We untied the sheaves and laid the un-threshed oats straw on the haymow floor where we beat it with the flails to loosen the grain from the straw and chaff. At first, it was great fun, beating the oats and hearing the muffled noise from the haymow floor. I am not sure how much flailing fun we had, but Pa examined the straw a time or two and rearranged it and we flailed some more. Finally, he decided that we had flailed this enough to get the oats out. We then took forks and gathered the straw up from the floor, shaking each bunch, to leave the oats and chaff on the floor. We could flail 2 or 3 turns before having to gather the grain off the floor and sack it. As I said, this was great fun at first, but after a while, it became more like work.

We tried throwing the chaff and oats into the air on a windy day to separate them, but this did not prove successful. We borrowed Simon White's grain windmill to do the job. We turned it by hand with a crank to develop the power to shake the sieves and blow the air through the falling grain, which cleaned out the dust and chaff from the oats. George and I had difficulty at that time, developing speed to make the mill clean well, so Pa took longer turns than we did.

Later, we raised a few crops of buckwheat and used flails to thresh it, and the grain windmill to clean it. I believe the miller had a way to clean buckwheat before grinding. Buckwheat was grown extensively in parts of West Virginia, but was not a major crop in our area.

One winter day in Germany, the first winter of the Army of Occupation, immediately after the close of the First World War, I heard a noise in a barn loft just across the street from my billet, that sounded very familiar. I went across the street and climbed up to the barn loft to see what was going on. Sure enough, they were flailing out grain just as we had done at home not many years before. There were 3 or 4 women and an old man or two, flailing out rye. They used flails tied with leather thongs which had worn smooth over the years from regular use. They, too, threw the rye and chaff from the mow high into high wind and separated it in part, but had to complete the job with a hand-powered grain windmill, not too different from the one we had used. They made use of the long rye straw in tying grape vine trimmings into bundles which they stored in ricks near their houses, together with other tree trimmings, for use in heating their ovens for baking bread. The rye was ground and much of it used in making coarse bread.

- - - - - - - - - - - -

"Let's stop our threshing for awhile and eat an apple. How many kinds can you name, Joe?"

"Well, there's Red Delicious, and Yellow Delicious, and Winesaps."

'And Cortlands, Rome Beautyss, Red Romes. But did you ever hear of Sheep Nose apples? Or Red Astricans? We had some very unusual varieties."

"Why did you have so many kinds?"

"Let me tell you about our orchard. . . . "

- - - - - - - - - - - -

OUR ORCHARD

Ever since I can first remember, and for many years afterward, we had a large apple orchard of 6 acres. They were some of the finest varieties of apples that I have seen any place. There were several trees of each variety, some of which ripened very early, while others continued throughout the summer and into fall, even including some late winter apples. The trees were past prime bearing age when I first remember them, but they produced a lot of all kinds of apples, nearly every year. Some of the varieties were Early Harvest, Yellow Transparent, Paw-paw Apple, Plate Apple, Grindstone, Maiden Blush, Red Astricans, Russett, Sheep Nose, Bell Flower, Rome Beauty, and York Imperial. Others we gave names such as the Turkey Apple, because the turkeys roosted in the tree, Porter apple from the name of the man who gave us the tree, the Spice Apple, because it had a spicy apple flavor. The Apple Butter tree was a wild tree out in the pasture which made good apple butter. A large red, sweet

236

apple we called Jim Sigh Sweet, and another juicy, well-flavored apple we called Micky Jack, neither of which were so called for any particular reason.

Before catalogs were put out, agents went through the country taking orders for nursery stock to be delivered later. Grandpa may have bought these trees from such an agent, or he may have gone directly to the nursery and put in his order for the trees to be delivered when he needed them. Nearly all the trees had rings of bulged wood under the bark completely around each tree a foot or more above the ground, which Pa said was caused by grafting at the nursery. The grafting rings are not as noticeable in later orchards.

I have heard Pa tell many times about holding many of the trees while his father filled the dirt in around them when the orchard was set out. And that he was five years old at the time. That would make the date the orchard was set out to be 1858. It was a pretty big job and must have extended over several days.

We asked Pa why they set out such a large orchard all at once. Pa told us that his father was planning to go into the distillery business as soon as he could get enough trees bearing apples to make the business pay. This was the reason for planting so many at one time. Nearly all farmers had apples planted near the house, usually about an acre, for family use, thus there was no local market for apples, since nearly all would raise their own. The laws were changed in Virginia or West Virginia, soon after this first orchard planting that either prohibited the distillery business, or put into effect so many regulations that accomplished practically the same thing. The result was that Grandpa did not pursue the distillery business further, nor did he make further orchard plantings as he had intended to do. Even though his plans did not work out, 2 or 3 generations enjoyed plenty of fine apples from this orchard.

Another orchard was later set out on Uncle Zan's part of the farm just across the creek above the mouth of Little Cove. Still later, another small orchard was set out in a low gap up across the creek above our house, on another part of the farm. We had plenty of apples as we were growing up, even if some of the trees were past prime bearing age.

Most country houses were built without basements or cellars in which to store fruits, potatoes and canned foods through the winter to prevent freezing. Apples, potatoes, turnips and cabbage were buried in the ground for such protection. We would select a well-drained section of the garden in late fall and rake 2 or 3 inches of the topsoil off a space about 5 or 6 feet in diameter, piling it in a circle around the area. We then spread some straw or hay in this depressed area and then piled the apples or potatoes in a conical pile on this straw as steep as they could be piled. Straw or hay was added to the sides of the pile, and then about 10 inches of dirt was piled on the whole thing, resulting in a conical shaped mound. This was quite a safe way to prevent freezing the produce thus stored. Apples and potatoes could be had throughout the cold winter months, by digging a hole through the dirt cover at various places to take out the fruit. Then the straw would be pushed back and the hole filled with dirt. When winter freezing was over, plenty could be taken out and stored, which in many cases would be kept for use until something came on to take their place. Seed potatoes were kept for early planting in this way. Often potatoes would run out before the new crop came on, but it was a goal and a challenge to work toward.

Cabbage did not keep too well, but was stacked in long rows on straw, one head after another, with the roots sticking up, covered with straw and dirt, piled in a ridge over all. Heads of cabbage could be removed from the end of the ridge for use through the winter and some could be saved for early spring use after the cold weather. Several conical holes of apples and potatoes, and ridges of cabbage might be necessary to store the entire family crop of each. There would be some spoilage and loss, to be sure. Apples always had an earthy taste when stored in holes.

'Air tights,' canned fruits, berries and sauces that might freeze were often stored in boxes wrapped in paper, with paper surrounding, but more often dry oats were under and around them, since paper was a very scarce item in most cases. Even dry leaves were used and then the boxes kept in a room that had heat in it, to prevent extra cold exposure. These boxes could be, and often were, stored in the living room and under the beds. Basements and cellars were a great improvement as they became available for this sort of storage.

Our first effort at making a cellar was in 1914 when we converted the old smokehouse. It was about 12 by 18 feet, sided with upright boards, nailed to 8 inch square oak sills. The cracks were stripped and a 2 by 6 inch plate was nailed around the top. To make this wall cold resistant, we studded and sealed it on the inside of the sills and filled the 8 inch space with wheat chaff for insulation. This chaff was from our first Coon Run wheat threshing. The wall chaff was dry and tamped down. Over the ceiling more chaff was filled in to more than an 8 inch depth. A ventilator was installed through the ceiling and more chaff was added to the attic space formed by the gabled roof.

We mixed concrete in a box, using hoes, for the concrete floor. It was our first experience with concrete. We did not know concrete was so heavy. It was hard to stir with either a hoe or shovel. We tried to mix it both dry and wet, but it was hard either way. If we did not keep it moving, it settled quickly and was hard to stir. Before we got done, we learned the proper amount of water to use, and to keep each mix moving until out of the box into the form. Then we could rest a little if needed before starting the next mix. We could not rest much or the mixes would not join, so there was not much resting until the job was done and troweled to the desired finish. In all, our first concrete job turned out pretty well and was used for about 25 years until replaced with a stone milk house, cellar and coal house, all combined, in the 1939 remodeling.

Our new cellar made it much easier to store things and not have to bury in the ground. It was much easier to get at things for use through the winter. Canned things kept well here and were out of the way more than in the house or under beds. We set a lighted lantern in the cellar in extra cold weather to further insure that nothing froze. We sometimes buried some apples and potatoes if we had more than we could store in the cellar.

We built shelves and bins so as to make the best use of the storage space. George and I used up all the crating material that we had sawed to make into crates. We had made several potato crates and 25 or 30 one-bushel apple crates. I shall never forget our surprise that fall when we took our crates and went to pick apples. We began with a big Rome Beauty tree. It was full and the best apple in the orchard. We had scarcely finished picking that one tree when all our new crates were full. It had taken us considerable time to make these crates and we had scarcely got started picking and all were full. We had not thought much about the total number of bushels they would hold. We made other bigger rougher crates and had to use big storage boxes and other smaller ones, before the cellar was full. Some space had to be kept for daily storing of milk. In all, the whole family was very well pleased with the amount of food we were able to store in the cellar.

- - - - - - - - - - -

"Even the door is thick on a cellar like that one, isn't it, Grandpa?"

"Yes, the door was about 8 inches thick and was also filled with chaff. It was always cool in our cellar house in summer because of all that insulation helped keep out the heat."

"And in winter, it worked just the other way, didn't it? That's what insulation does in our houses too. Did you make cider from any of the apples? We like cider."

"Oh yes, we always made our own cider, because we always had plenty of apples. Almost every farmer made his own cider, and if he didn't have his own cider mill, he borrowed one from his neighbor. . . ."

- - - - - - - - - -

CIDER MAKING

One year, about as far back as I can remember, Pa and Ma got a cider mill, corn sheller and a rocker-type washing machine, all at one time. I was not big enough to operate any of them at first, but I tried to and was not discouraged in my efforts by either Pa or Ma, in fact, they seemed pleased at my eager efforts. All too soon, I became big enough, and still Pa and Ma continued encouraging my efforts, which sometimes were not as eager as when I was smaller. I became proficient in operating all three machines.

The cider mill had a hopper to help feed the apples into the grinder where the apples were mashed into a rough pulp. This fell into a round container made of strips of wood bound together with metal bands with slight openings between each strip. These round containers would hold about a bushel of mashed apples and were set on blocks of wood with many slits through them to let the juice pass through. After this slotted container was filled with the mashed apples from the grinder, a round follower block was placed in the top, which was forced down by a large metal screw. This forced the juice from the mashed apples. This juice ran out through the bottom slits and through the cracks between the side strips. It was caught in a slanting wood trough which carried it to a bucket or other container. The wheel at the top of the screw had 4 uprights about 4 inches high, and in a square, 4 inches apart, on the wheel for hand turning. A 3 foot long lever with a 4 inch square end, which fit between the uprights, was used to further tighten the screw down on the mashed fruit to get more juice. While the ground apples were being squeezed, more apples were being placed in the grinder.

The apple grinder was turned with a crank by hand and had a heavy fly wheel on the opposite side which helped keep the momentum up and the speed more even than without such a wheel. When the second mashed apple container was full, the screw on the first one was released and the dry apple pulp emptied. The second container was moved under the screw where the juice was squeezed in the same manner as the first.

The cider in the bucket from the press was strained through a cloth as it was poured into a larger container, such as a large stone jar, wood tub or barrel, where it would be allow to work, or ferment for a few days. Some put it into a wood barrel and set it out in the sun where it would work quickly and soon became what they called 'hard cider.' Cider made in this way had the power, but little reddish color, and was not as good a flavor as made by the method Pa used.

After the cider had started fermenting in the big containers in which it was first kept, Pa skimmed off what scum had risen to the top. Then he put the cider into a 15 or 20 gallon kettle and slowly brought it to a boil, removing any skimmings that came to the top in the process. He did not keep it at the boiling point very long. The cider was then poured through a cloth, removing any apple pulp, into the charred oak cider barrel where we kept it for use as needed. Getting rid of the solid matter in the cider and keeping it in the shade, allowed it to ferment more slowly and gave it a better flavor than could have been gotten with less care. A pitcher of this cider not only tasted good but had a pleasant amber color. Many of the neighbors praised the flavor of our cider and they could easily drink enough to get high. We did not encourage that kind of use. The part in the middle that did not freeze into ice in the winter looked and tasted even better.

Some people put wild cherries into their cider to raise the alcoholic content, but we never did this to ours. Our cider was also used to produce excellent vinegar when we needed it.

Pa told us about many apple peeling, coring and stringing parties at which neighbors, men, women and children, would gather to do this work, and at the same time have a good time during the evening. In earlier times, the peeling was done by hand but later it was made easier by the small machine, the apple peeler. It was still necessary to cut and core the peeled apples for cooking and making into apple butter, or for stringing and drying.

Often the apples used for stringing and drying were simply cored without peeling and then strung on long twine strings to be draped from side to side on drying racks or boards. These were dried on screens over the stove or in the sun on roofs. Apple peelings were often used in making delightful jelly. Cooking of the peelings for jelly, and the apples for making apple butter, was usually started during the evening on the stove by some of the workers, which permitted the completion of the jelly and apple butter to be delayed until the next day.

Much useful work was accomplished in the course of the evening. During the social hour following the work with apples, music, singing, dancing, games, stories, gossip and other entertainment. Refreshments made it an evening of enjoyment and helped develop better neighborhood spirit. Such parties and bees were had for doing various kinds of work and served as an excuse for getting together for an evening of entertainment, as well as to accomplish some necessary work at the same time.

- - - - - - - - - - - - -

"We really like the apple butter Grandma makes. Do you suppose we could have some on a slice of bread right now?"

"Maybe that's what your Grandma will feed you the next time she wants to tell one of her stories. Many times we cooked the apple *butter outside, stirring it with wooden stirring paddles. It was cooked a long time, until it was as thick as Ma wanted it. And sometimes it would go 'plop' and splash on you. You could make peach butter that way too and we usually had lots of peaches. . . ."*

- - - - - - - - - - - -

PEACH ORCHARD

From as far back as I can remember, we had a bearing peach orchard on the steep hillside facing the Big Run ford over Big Cove Creek. It began at the edge of the woods bluff, 300 or 400 feet from the creek and extended about 250 feet wide to the woods at the top of the hill, perhaps 1500 or 2000 feet, 2 ½ acres in all. The land had been cleared and tended in corn. Seeds from the best peach trees on the farm, which included both nursery and wild trees, were used to plant the orchard in 1900, when it was first cleared. The trees were in rows across the field, but in addition to the rows, seeds had been planted beside nearly all the big tree stumps. These stumps afforded protection for the small trees and helped enrich the ground for their later growth. The seeds did not reproduce trees that bore the same kind of peach that the seed had come from, so the orchard contained many different kinds of peaches. They were well distributed in ripening times from early summer to late fall. There were clings as well as freestones, large nursery type and the smaller white delicious flavored wild type. Of course there were some less desirable kinds too. Since the orchard extended from low, down next to the creek, to high, near the top of the hill, some sort of crop was fairly sure. If frost or freeze killed those low down, frequently those at other levels escaped and produced. It was beautiful to see this orchard in full bloom in early spring. The ripening fruit, during the summer and fall, afforded a closer view equally beautiful, if not more pleasing than that of early spring. Before they stopped raising corn in this field, about 4 crops, many of the trees began to bear. The orchard was sowed in grass and kept fenced from the pasture for several years. The grass was cut for hay during this time, even though the ground was so rough and steep that the hay could not be cut with a mowing machine, but had to be cut by hand with mowing scythes, gathered up with forks when cured and ready for stacking.

When the peach orchard was fenced and sowed in grass, Pa cleared another cornfield just beyond it. This field extended from the wooded bluff at the lower edge of the peach orchard, along its west side, to the woods at the top of the hill. It was about twice as wide, equally as steep and rough and contained between 5 and 6 acres of rich north hillside land.

Although George and I were too small to be of much help working in the corn during the next 4 years that corn was raised there, we were there working in our two small play fields a great deal of time, and maybe helping Pa a little. At least we had time in between working and playing to find where the early-ripening peach trees were located and where to find the trees having the best ones. By the time this new field was ready to be sowed in grass and made a part of the pasture, the peach trees were big enough so they were not bothered much by the cows and cattle pasturing among them. Sometimes we took the cattle out of this field for awhile, if they went to damaging the trees too much when the peaches were ripening. This orchard lasted 12 or 15 years and furnished a lot of fruit for our use. Whether working in the corn, cutting filth, or hunting the cows, it was a memorable pleasure to drop by the orchard and get a peach to eat, and some to take home for the rest of the family to enjoy.

- - - - - - - - - - - -

"Here comes Grandma with that bread and apple butter for us. She must have a story ready!"

"Yes, she wants to tell you about their peach orchard."

- - - - - - - - - - - -

We had a small peach orchard of nursery trees that had a lot of fine big peaches on them, but did not bear nearly as regularly as many of our other trees did. We had also planted seeds near stumps, and also in the fence corners in some of the meadows. I can almost taste the delicious white peaches that were tinged with pink and red which extended through the peel to the peach pulp inside.

We made jelly from them, and peach butter as well as peach preserves and spiced peaches. We also canned them and dried them for later use.

- - - - - - - - - - -

"Peaches are too expensive now to use for making peach butter, but how would you like some peach cobbler?"

"That would be just peachy!"

"Oh, Joe, that's quite a joke! On the other side of the peach orchard, we cleared some more land where we had our first experiences with logging and sawmill work. . . ."

- - - - - - - - - - -

LUMBERING

We had a 6 acre tract of rich north, sloping woods land, the south-west corner of which met the north-east corner of our Coon Run clearing at the top of the ridge. George and I began grubbing this tract after we finished planting corn. We worked at the grubbing throughout the summer of 1914, between the other farm work. We finished it in the early fall. The reason I know so well that it was 1914 is that it was the summer of the 17 year locusts. They were thick in the woods where we were working and their constant singing noise rang in our ears the whole summer all around us. I was born in locust year 1897; this was my second 17 year locust year.

This tract of woods had had only the largest timber-size trees removed and was yet covered with a good stand of white oak and chestnut oak timber, together with other less marketable timber. White oak and chestnut oak railroad ties were readily salable at a price of as much as $1.50 per tie.

Pa and Ma decided to have a saw set and cut the crosstie timber into ties for immediate sale. The other lumber would be cut into 2 x 4's, 2 x 6's etc that could be used for farm buildings or house repair about the farm, or sold should a market develop. It would have been too much of a waste to burn such timber in log heaps.

We began cutting the tie timber first, which included the largest trees, so they could be hauled out before we cut the other timber. We got a new two-man lance-tooth crosscut saw with which to do the sawing. George and I began this timber cutting in the fall, and like the grubbing, it too, was worked at between other fall farm work, and late into the winter before being completed.

Lan Butcher came in the winter, before we were quite done cutting, to see about hauling the crosstie timber to the mill. He said he had two teams of horses doing nothing which he could use, and get a little pay toward their keep by doing the skidding job. He and Pa came to some sort of an agreement; he did the work and we boarded the two men driving the teams as part of the agreement.

George and I did the skidding of the other timber to the mill site with our yoke of oxen, Tob and Log. We had already sold Buck and Barry, the other yoke we had raised. The tie logs were hauled by hitching a chain to one end and dragging endwise on the ground, which we called snaking. These big logs were rolled down the hill and then snaked across the creek to the mill site in the upper end of the bottom at Big Run. Some of the biggest logs would cut 8 or 9 ties each, and made a load for two horses to snake or skid.

George and I cut the other timber from the clearing and hauled out the saw timber first. We notched and cut the trees without splitting any at the butt as they broke from the stump. We thought we did a good job, since some of the good trees leaned considerable which made it more difficult to keep them from splitting. The biggest tree was a chestnut oak that stood straight with no problem to keep from splitting, but since it was about 4 feet in diameter at stump height, we had less than two feet to pull our 6 foot saw back and forth in cutting it. Many large and small chestnut oaks were hollow at the butt, which continued up so far as to get little usable lumber from them. Many of these hollow logs, together with other trees too small for lumber, were hauled out into the pasture for later splitting into fireplace and stove wood.

The main difference in the Coon Run clearing and this 6 acre job, which was ready by corn planting time, was that we saved the good timber, which made about 2000 railroad ties that were readily sold. Some timber was also cut from other parts of the farm at this time. Other lumber was cut and stacked for later use. Your Grandma and I bought some of the lumber which had not been used, when we built our house in Glenville, a few years afterward.

THE SAW MILL

The mill was moved in and set up in the spring, but since the owner was a farmer and operated the mill as a sideline to his farming, the sawing proceeded intermittently during the summer. There were mill breakdowns, and when the mill was ready, sufficient help to operate it, was not always available. I helped by filling in when help was scarce, sometimes by wheeling sawdust away from the saw pit, off bearing (taking the slabs and lumber away from the saw,) tail sawing, as block setter, firing the boiler and even helping to file and condition the saw, together with helping make other repairs.

Pa and George did the best they could to stack the ties, and haul the other lumber away from the mill for stacking, when I was helping run the mill. When all three of us worked together, we could easily do our work taking the lumber away and keeping logs on the skids for sawing. This was not a very rapid mill. It remained there until fall.

We cut some extra trees and brought them in for sawing after most of the sawing was done. Earl Heckert and Guy Scott hauled several sunken logs out of the creek for the Log and Tie Co., which they had cut into ties. These logs could not be floated to market. The ties were stacked and let dry so they could be floated.

When the mill was finally shut down late in the fall, they let the steam and hot water blow off into the swimming hole, which made it warm enough for a last swim of the season. It was certainly a drawn-out sawmill job that may not have been very profitable for the owner.

Later that fall, Piercy, an agent for the Log and Tie Company, came, counted and paid Pa for our ties. He hired George, Guy, Earl and me to brand our ties and to go with him to brand ties at

247

other sets that he wanted to take up that day. It did not take the four of us long to brand both ends of each tie in our set, including the ones cut from the sunken logs. They already belonged to his company, but had to have the company brand on each, the same as the ones he was buying for the company. Earl rode his horse and went along with Piercy to the next tie set on Crane Run, but George, Guy and I walked, taking a near-cut, up Board Cut Run and over the ridge down into Crane Run. We arrived a little before Earl and Piercy, who went around by the road. This was a much larger set than ours and took longer to brand. We were through branding well before noon.

Our next branding job was at Spurgeons above Conings on Bear Fork of Cove Creek. Again Earl and Piercy went on horseback around the road, taking the branding hammers, or irons, with them in their saddle bags. (These branding hammers were about two feet long, with the wood handle near the middle and the brand figure on each end of the hammer. Long branding hammers were needed to brand the end of each tie when they were not evenly stacked.) Once again George, Guy and I took a nearer way over the hill to Conings where we thought we might get with them for the rest of the way. They did not overtake us until we were in sight of the ricks of ties. It was nearly noon and Piercy arranged for dinner for all of us at Spurgeons, since none of us had brought with us, anything to eat. It was a good dinner and I think Piercy paid for it.

We began branding ties while dinner was being prepared and I can assure you that we had no lack of appetite when called for dinner. This was not a large set of ties and we finished it after dinner.

Piercy said we were getting along fine, but he thought the next and last set, at the forks of Rush Run, gotten out by Barket and Frank Schulte, was the largest set of all. We took a narrow road over to the Schulte ties on Rush, which was about the shortest route there. We all started out together. We walkers kept along with the riders without much extra effort and all arrived at our last branding site by a little after 2:00 PM. It was by far the largest batch of ties we had faced that day. There were three long, high ricks. All had not been sawed at this point. Some had been hauled from other sets and were stacked here, since all could be floated from this point on. There may have been as many ties as there were at all the other locations combined. We branded as far down as we could, from the top of each rick, and then finished from the ground, where we had to scaffold in places, over low ground, in order to reach all the ties.

A little after 4:00, Winnie Burton, who was teaching the Upper Rush School, a little farther up than where we were, walked down the road past where we were working, on his way home. We all knew him. Some of us said that he made his $2.00 a day teaching, far easier and quicker than we had made whatever pay we would get for our day's work. And $2.00 was what we each got later in the evening when we had finished the branding.

We were sure we earned the $2.00, even if it was high pay for that kind of work. In included a lot of branding and walking. Although already tired when through branding, we each yet had 6 dark miles of walking before we reached home for our suppers. We did not try to keep up with Earl and Piercy on their horses on the way home. Our noon-day meal was getting low, long before we got home for supper.

This was probably the only paid day's work for any of us that week, since hired work was scarce and the pay low, when any was to be had.

- - - - - - - - - -

"That was a lot of walking, Grandpa. Was that when you decided that being a teacher was a good idea?"

"I'd already taken the teacher's examination, and had the same grade certificate Winnie Burton had, but I hadn't started teaching yet. Getting an education was the only way we could see to improve our positions. All of us children became teachers at some time or other during our lives."

"Yes, we've heard about aunt Lois teaching veterans in VA hospitals. She would organize classes in anything they wanted to learn, even if she had to learn it herself first."

"Edna became a high school teacher, and Helen spent many years teaching in Miami, Florida. She taught many Cuban children to speak English."

"George became a lawyer after teaching a few years to earn money to go to law school at West Virginia University.'

"Myra started nurses training after teaching. Even Perry, the only farmer in the family, taught for about 5 years."

"That's only seven. Who is missing?"

"Eunice was the oldest of the girls. After her years teaching, she worked in Washington D.C. and Chicago for the Census Bureau. It was teaching that gave all of us a start."

- - - - - - - - - - -

HUNGRY DAN

- - - - - - - - - - -

"We've been talking about how we traded work around the neighborhood. Whenever you worked at someone's house, you usually got your dinner too."

"You must have known where the good cooks were."

"Yes, we did, but usually we were hungry enough that it didn't matter much. Have I told you the story about Hungry Dan yet?"

"No, I don't think we've heard that one. Was he especially hungry?"

"This is really one of Pa's stories. . . ."

- - - - - - - - - - -

This all happened when Pa was in his teens, about 1868 or 1870. Pa said to his mother,

'Mother, what news did Mrs. Williams have this morning when she was here?'

'Oh, nothing much unusual. She was sort of on her ear about the way the neighbors had treated her son, Dan, last Sunday. She said after breakfast, he went to preaching up at the schoolhouse and went over on Cove after that. He was gone all day and came home after dark, hungry as a wolf. She got up and got him some supper and asked him if Sniders invited him home for dinner. He said they didn't. She always feeds the Snider boys when they're around at mealtime. She said she didn't like it and was going to tell them so.!'

'Mother, you know Dan would be hungry if he had been eating all day. I saw him up on Cove at the picnic and he was helping himself to the grub when I saw him,' Pa replied.

251

'I couldn't think of him going all day without eating, even more than at the picnic. You'll be seeing more people from up around there this week, Tom. Ask more about this.'

'I will,' said Pa. During the next week or two Pa found out more. Sniders said he didn't go home for dinner with them, but had gone home with Woofters, who had an early dinner and Dan left for the picnic right after that. When he got over to Hinters, he stopped to see if their boys had started to the picnic. They were just eating a late dinner and asked him to join them. Then Dan and their boys went on to the picnic, where Pa had seen him eating again.

Pa was sure that if Dan did not get home until after dark that he must have eaten again somewhere. So he kept asking around, and finally Thornt Norman said,

'He ate supper with us. He ate like he had eaten nothing all day.'

'That was the 5th meal Dan had that day!' Pa told Mr. Norman.

'I don't see how a boy could eat the way he did, if he had eaten that much already!'

'Well, this you won't believe. When he got home late that night he was so hungry, he let his mother get out of bed and get him a good supper.'

'You don't say! That boy ought to have a good thrashing. He could not have been hungry.'

'However that may be, Mr. Norman, you are just getting acquainted with Daniel Webster Williams, as we in our area already know him,' Pa replied.

'If that is the real Dan, I know him well enough now.'

When Pa got home, he told his mother about all Dan's meals. And when Pa told us this story, our next question always was,

'What became of Dan, Pa?'

'Well, when Joe McQuain and his family went west not long after this, Dan went with them to the railroad and got on the train with them. When the conductor came along collecting fares, he asked Joe how many he was paying for. Joe said, 'All but that one,' meaning Dan. When the train pulled out, Dan was left standing on the platform.

After they had been out west 3 or 4 months, they looked out across the prairie and saw someone coming that looked a lot like

Dan. Sure enough, it was Dan. They were all glad to see him. He stayed with them a little while, but there was too much work to be done there, and not a chance for a lot of extra eating. Dan soon drifted on and they lost track of him.

At one time Dan was sent to the pen, but his two brothers and father, who had been in the Union Army got him out. They had a lot of pull. His discharge from the pen was written on sheepskin. He teased his father and brothers by saying he was more important than they, since their discharges from the Union Army were written on Paper.'

- - - - - - - - - - -

"Hungry Dan got his meals without even exchanging any work, didn't he?"

"People in the neighborhood liked to tell and re-tell the story of Hungry Dan. There was always a lot of work connected with farming, but Hungry Dan didn't want to do any of it to earn all those meals."

"I wonder how he got way out west. Too bad we don't know that story."

"I haven't told you much about milk and how we took care of it, have I?"

"No, but you've told about going after the cows and feeding them."

"Milk was an important farm product to every farm family. I think you'd like to hear more about it, and about the good things to eat that milk provided."

- - - - - - - - - - -

MILK

Nearly every family had at least one or two cows to provide fresh milk and butter for daily table use. We always had cows, in varying numbers up to as many as 10 or 12 at a time. Most of the cows had their calves in early spring, but we also tried to have 1 or

253

2 good milkers with young calves in the fall, so as to have milk throughout the year. A few times we had very scarce amounts of milk and butter from midwinter until early spring.

We generally had plenty of good grass pasture from early spring until late fall and depended on this pasture for the feed for our cows during that time. We allowed the cows to suckle their calves until weaning time, about the time the calves were 2 or 3 months old. At first, the milk was the calf's main food, but as they learned to eat more and more grass, we cut down on the amount of their milk supply by shortening the sucking time so that by weaning time, they depended almost entirely on the grass they ate. There was always some sort of market for good calves so it was important that they get a good start.

At times, we had 1 or 2 cows that gave extra rich milk and were easily milked. We let their calves suck them only a little but pulled them away and let them suckle another cow giving poor milk. This was more bother and was done only when there was plenty of help at milking time. We let the cows into the calf lot to suckle their calves and put them out when we thought they had been in long enough. This was a part of milking, morning and evening, each day, until the calves were weaned.

After the calves were suckled, we finished milking each cow by hand. Sometimes cows were gentle enough that the bucket could be set on the ground under them and milked into it with both hands. When this could not be done, a person held a cup in one hand and milked into it with the other. Small boxes or 3-legged stools were used to sit on while milking. Some used one-legged stools if they wanted to perform the balancing act at the same time. Some cows kept stepping about all the time. One had to bend over and keep following them along while milking. These constant steppers soon got tied up to the fence while being milked. No matter what cow you were milking, her tail, wet or dry, would swing into your face, or drag across your neck in a disagreeable fashion. Sometimes it would dip into the milk and then brush it on you wherever it switched. Holding the end of the tail in the hand holding the cup that you were milking into solved the problem, until the cow got to jerking the tail, trying to switch it, spilling the milk.

Then too, there was the cow with the scratched teats, from going through a briar patch, which would kick and move around while being milked. Her teats would be treated at milking time or just afterward. These are a few of the difficulties encountered in milking, with which any milker is familiar. However, aside from these slight disturbances, most of the cows seemed to enjoy being milked and would stand quietly, chewing their cuds during the process.

At weaning time, after the morning meal, the calves were shifted to a new lush pasture such as a meadow of second-growth grass after the first cutting of hay had been harvested. It was better still if such a calf pasture was out of sight of the milking lot and cow pasture, so that the morning and evening mealtime experiences were more quickly forgotten by both calves and cows. In no way was it possible to prevent the cow-calf mooing and bawling for each other, beginning with the first evening's separation and continuing almost incessantly for as long as a week or more. Even at night, from the milking lot, the night silence was broken by the intermittent mournful mooing of the cows for their absent calves. Often there was a less audible answer from the calves in their distant pasture, to their absent mother's plaintive calls. This was a somewhat sad farm experience, which time and absence soon blotted out for both cow and calf.

After the calves were weaned, our job of going after the cows was harder because they usually didn't come in by themselves anymore. We were big enough to go after cows, even when we were not big enough to help milk. It did not take long to get big enough to milk! The milking took more work, as did the care of the greater amount of milk obtained when the calves did not get any part of it.

After the milk was carried to the house or cellar, it was poured through a milk strainer having a fine mesh copper screen which removed any dirt or foreign matter that may have gotten into it during or after the milking process. This was done as it was poured into the stone crocks or other containers for storing in the cooler or cellar. Sometimes a white cotton cloth was used in addition to the strainer or when a regular strainer was not available.

It was necessary to carefully wash and dry the strainer and straining cloth as well as all other milking utensils and storage containers. If we add to these the churn, butter molds, ladles and all utensils used in further processing, this washing and drying became quite a large and necessary chore in itself.

A clean, cool place to keep the milk for table use, while the cream raised, and to keep part of it from souring had always been a problem at our place. We improved the situation in several ways as time passed. Your Grandma says that her parents had a cellar dug into the hill close to their house where they set their milk in crocks on the cool dirt floor. They sometimes lowered buckets of milk and cream into their dug well, in extra hot weather to be sure of having sweet milk and cream for table use. Butter lowered into the well stayed solid and pleasing to use.

We had no cellar dug into the hill, but had a smokehouse with hard dirt floor where we stored our milk when I was very small, even if it was not very cool. We too, lowered milk, cream and butter into the dug well to keep it better in hot weather. This was a general practice in our area.

When I was about 7 years old, a man came through the country selling a cooler for milk. Pa and Ma bought one of these coolers. It was about 3 feet wide by about the same height and 5 or more feet long, enclosed with about 3 inch thick walls containing some insulating material. It had a zinc-lined water-tight compartment in the top part, about 10 inches deep, covered with a thick lid over the top, that could be lifted up while putting in or removing milk crocks. This top, waterproof space was arranged so that cold well-water could be poured in at one end through a large funnel and the warm water drawn off at the water level at the other end. This made use of the principle that cold water is heavier than warm water and sinks to the bottom, forcing the warm water to the top.

This cooler worked pretty well, but more cold water frequently had to be added in hot weather to maintain the cooling effect desired. In the space below were two cool compartments with shelf space and close-fitting doors to each, for storing butter, cheese, pies and food that needed cool storage. Changing the cooling water was quite a chore in hot weather, but it did keep the milk and cream sweet longer. The smokehouse was still used for processing many milk products that did not require cooling.

We later dug a milk house into the bank across the run from the house which cut down on the well-water pumping and carrying to the cooler. When we changed the smokehouse into a cellar, the cooler and bank milk house were used less and less, until both were replaced completely by the new cellar.

BUTTER

Butter was always salable at some price at the store in Troy. Ma usually made more than we needed for our family, especially during the summer when pastures were good and the cows gave lots of milk. The cream would rise to the top of the milk in the crocks before the milk soured and was skimmed off. If this was done just before the milk turned to clabber, the cream layer could be loosened from the container sides by passing a knife blade around the edge and then tipping the crock and pushing the layer of cream over the edge into a cream container, in a continuous sheet. This left the skimmed milk, which we called 'blue john,' in the crock. At this stage, milk was starting to sour and was not good to drink. The cream was likewise turning sour and was not good in coffee or over cereal. When skimmed before starting to turn sour, the milk contained a little butterfat which was left in the skimming, and was better to drink. In skimming after turning to clabber, all the cream could be skimmed off. This sour cream, together with any sweet cream left over from table use, was all put into a container, where it was kept until ready for churning into butter.

This butter cream was put into a churn where it was shook and agitated until the butter separated from the buttermilk and gathered together on top, where it was dipped off into a butter bowl. It was further worked over with a wooden butter paddle to remove any remaining buttermilk. A little salt was added, enough to bring out the flavor. The butter was then shaped in molds or pats and stored in a cool place for later family use, or for sale.

The first churn that I remember our using was the dash type in which the container was made of wood staves, surrounded and held together with metal hoops, all tightly fitted to a round bottom. This had a removable round wood lid at the top, with a hole in the middle, through which the dasher was operated by hand. The dasher handle was lifted and lowered in the cream to agitate it, until the butterfat separated and floated to the top. After removing the dasher and lid, the butter was removed to the butter bowl. Ma had a round butter mold with a fancy flower design in the bottom, into which she forced enough finished butter to fill it. Each mold full, when forced out by the loose bottom, weighed about a pound and the top had the imprint of the fancy design left by the butter mold. This was a fancy way to prepare butter for either sale or table use.

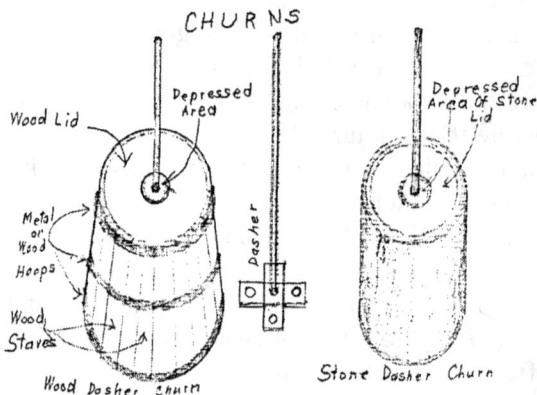

CHURNS

Wood Lid
Depressed Area
Metal or Wood Hoops
Wood Staves
Dasher
Wood Dasher Churn

Depressed Area of Stone Lid
Stone Dasher Churn

Two Churns

I have seen other similar wooden churns, some of which had wooden hoops. When the cream that worked up the dasher handle through the hole in the lid, began to show tiny bits of butter in it, it was time to slow down and operate the dasher more slowly. We were always watching for this time to slow up. Ma could tell from experience whether butter cream was at the right temperature for proper churning, and would often add a little hot or cold water to get the right temperature.

A similar dasher churn had a container made of stoneware and fitted with either a stoneware or wooden lid. Perhaps the wooden lid was a replacement for a broken stoneware lid. This churn was fitted with a wood dasher and operated the same, whether made of wood or stoneware.

We later got a wood barrel churn, in which the barrel was fitted with pivots on opposite sides, which rested in slots in stationary upright supports. The end of one pivot was extended beyond the upright support and fitted with a crank, which was

258

used to rotate the barrel, end over end. The barrel was fitted with a lid securely clamped to the top with small levers to make it water-tight. A 2 inch glass view-hole in the top helped to determine when the butter began to form. A screw and eye was used to fasten the churn to the upright support to make it more stable when the lid was removed from the top to put in cream, or remove butter. The barrel could be tipped over to pour out the buttermilk, if desired.

I am not sure whether this was a better churn than the dasher type, although it may have been a little easier to operate. We children liked to turn it end over end, and hear the cream and butter splash around. We also enjoyed stopping from time to time to see if butter had started to appear on the inside of the glass view-hole in the lid, the signal to turn more slowly and that the job would soon be completed.

I am sure many other different type churns have been used in making butter. Perhaps no churn is more unique than the one discovered at the same time of the discovery of butter. It is said that long ago, an old Arab camel driver, in preparing for a long camel journey, filled his goatskin container with rich milk to take the place of food and water. It served well, but by late evening of the first day's travel, it began to sour and he drank little as he continued his journey throughout the night. Next morning, on trying to take a drink, nothing would come out. Yet, from the weight of the skin, he knew it was not empty. On opening this skin, he found that part of the milk was almost solid and clogged the drinking spout. The thick part tasted good, and the sour, thinner part was more pleasant to drink than before. He had discovered butter, buttermilk and the churn, all at the same time. They finally found that they did not have to take a long camel journey, carrying a goatskin filled with milk to get butter and buttermilk.

We made use of buttermilk in various ways, both drinking it and using it in preparation of other foods. Any extra was fed to the chickens and hogs.

- - - - - - - - - - -

"Maybe you are getting tired of all these details. I've made a drawing of our churns so you can get a better idea of how they were."

"Grandpa, a lot of work goes into our glass of milk. I'd like to try making butter with that barrel churn. If the lid came off while you were turning it, that would be some mess!"

"We also made cheese from our milk. . . . . "

- - - - - - - - - - -

CHEESE-MAKING

Perhaps the most widely-used easy method of making cheese was that in which skimmed, clabber milk was used to make smear-case or cottage cheese, which we children frequently called 'daub-case.' The clabber milk was heated gently to about 100 to 125 degrees. This caused the whey and cheese to separate. It was then strained through a cheese cloth, or run through a strainer to get rid of the whey. The cheese could be allowed to hang and drain to get rid of more of the whey, or squeezed by hand to force the whey out. The right amount of heat made soft curd; more heat made harder curd cheese. The heat used was never to the boiling point. A small amount of sweet cream was mixed with this cheese and salted to taste. Since milk is about one part solid matter to four parts liquid, a gallon crock of clabber milk would make a little less than a quart of cottage cheese, enough for a small family. The whey left over was used in mixing feed for chickens, or was added to the swill tub for the hogs. Nothing was wasted. We always had cottage cheese when milk was plentiful.

Ma made another kind of cheese for table use which we all liked. She also made some to sell. A lot of sweet milk was needed to make a relatively small amount of cheese. She added rennet to the sweet milk so it would curdle in the making process, and the whey could be drained, strained and pressed from the

260

solids that were left, which was the cheese. She got the rennet from the store and also from parts of the stomach of calves butchered by people in the neighborhood. I have heard Pa and Ma talk of getting it from both sources at different times. The cheese-making was not continued when I was big enough to do much of the actual work, so my information is from what I saw being done.

Sometimes the cheese was hung up in a cheesecloth to drain and then taken down and put away to cure for awhile. When it was brought out to use, or put into the basket to take to the store, it was still in the same rounded shape in the cheesecloth as when stored away to cure.

Ma had a cheese press she used part of the time. The form for putting the cheese in, for shaping and pressing dry, was round, made of wood staves about 12 inches long, bound together with hoops, making a container about 10 inches in diameter and 12 inches in height, set on a board for a bottom. A round wood top was fitted loosely inside so it would move up and down freely without sticking. After straining as much of the whey through the cloth as would go through easily, the balance was poured into the cheese form, where it was pressed by hand, squeezing out more whey. Then the top was placed in, and levers, blocks and weights were added, pressing out more and more of the whey and moisture. It was left with pressure on for awhile as more was pressed out. The cheese took the form of the press and was the thickness to which it had been compressed. We children crowded around to eat the little bits that Ma cut off the cheese, which had formed in the drain holes in the cheese form. This was as interesting as licking molasses from a splinter at molasses-making time. This cheese, like the one made in the cheesecloth had to be put away where it aged for awhile before it was ready to eat or sell. Sometimes Ma set the cheese form in the new cider press and used the large metal screw in it to press the cheese. This was easier and quicker than using the levers, blocks and weights of the old cheese press.

- - - - - - - - - - - - -

"I didn't know that kind of cheese could be made at home. I thought cheese factories always did it."

"Oh, yes, but it's more work than cottage cheese, so that's what we made oftener."

"Mom remembers the ice cream you used to make when you took them to the old farm visiting."

"We always had everything you need to make ice cream, except the ice. After your Grandma and I were married and living in Glenville, we would take ice from the ice house to the farm, to make the ice cream."

"Mom says sometimes they got to help turn the freezer, until it got too hard to turn. Mainly she remembers licking the dasher and eating the ice cream. Why don't we go to the Dairy Queen right now."

"Did thinking about ice cream make you hungry? Call you grandma and let's go!"

"What's your next story about?"

"Did you know that we butchered our own hogs? But let's go after that ice cream first. . ."

- - - - - - - - - - - - -

HOG BUTCHERING

Hog butchering usually took place in the late fall about Thanksgiving, after the weather had gotten cold enough to cool the meat quickly, so it could be salted away for winter storage and curing. It was also a yearly event that was worked toward throughout the year.

We usually bought 3 or 4 pigs each fall to keep through the winter for butchering the next fall. Each of them dressed out from 300 to 400 pounds of meat, depending on the breed, and on the care and feeding they had received during the year. Sometimes we got early spring pigs for fall butchering, especially if we did not get as many fall pigs as we thought we needed. It was a matter of pride among farmers to have well-developed hogs for butchering, regardless of their age. That was one reason Pa always took such great pride in slopping and feeding his hogs, and seeing that they had good water holes to wallow in during hot weather, and warm straw nests for cold weather. We bought our pigs from neighbors who raised pigs for sale.

We kept our hogs in areas of as much as an acre or more so they would have plenty of room to exercise and grow. About a month before butchering, we would put them in a small pen where they could not exercise as much, and would put on fat much faster. They were also fed as much corn as they would eat. By butchering time, they were in excellent condition. They had eaten bushels of corn in fattening, but they were worth it in the meat produced.

Hog butchering day was an exciting occasion on any farm. Dry wood, for heating water, was made ready in advance as well as sufficient kettles in which to heat the water. A sled covered with boards usually was the platform to work on, and a large barrel, or hogshead, tilted against the sled and securely fastened, was used to put the boiling water into, for sousing the hog up and down, to scald it so the hair could easily be removed.

Neighbors usually exchanged work on these occasions, so there was sure to be enough help, equipment and knives to get the butchering done in less than a day.

Pa had 3 or 4 sets of hog hangers and gambrel sticks stored under our house for use from year to year. These were gotten out and made ready for use.

Often our butchering was done on Thanksgiving Day, when there was no school, and we children could be at home to be of help. All was excitement and everyone was up and had breakfast before day-light. The kettles had been filled with water and fires built under them to start the water heating, by the time breakfast was called. The water was generally boiling and ready for use by a little after daylight when our neighbors arrived. Pa got his rifle and carefully loaded it. Then all went to the pen to get their first hog. When we were very small, we children watched from a distance near the house, but as we got older, George and I took a more and more active part in the work. Pa rested the rifle on the pen, took careful aim and when the rifle cracked, 2 or 3 of the men jumped into the pen and stuck the hog so it would bleed freely. (At first we could not see what was being done. And it seemed to take a very long time for Pa to aim and then fire.)

The men emerged from the pen, pulling a hog to the sled-table for scalding. While the men were doing this, Pa reloaded his rifle and was ready for another hog. All went back to the pen and brought another hog down. I never heard Pa make a hog squeal by poor excited shooting.

The barrel was filled about half-full with boiling water, so that when the hog was slid into it, the water just about filled the leaning barrel, without spilling much. The hog was slid into the barrel, head first and pulled up and down a time or two, and turned over at the same time. Then it was pulled out to air and to see if the hair had been scalded enough to pull and scrape off easily. If not, it was slid back into the water briefly. When tested again, the hair would usually come off easily. The hog was immediately turned around and the other end slid into the barrel in the same manner, until it could be scraped easily. Sometimes extra boiling water had to be added to the barrel to get the proper scald. Sometimes patches here and there had to have boiling water poured on them. Plenty of boiling water had to be added to the scalding barrel for the second and each succeeding hog, to insure good scalds.

After the hair had been removed, the hog was made ready to hang up. A 3 inch slit was made in the back of each hind leg just above the hoof spurs, exposing the two large tendons. Each end of the gambrel stick was inserted under these two tendons, spreading the legs wide apart in the process. The hog was then pulled on a hand sled to the hanging spot, where the gambrel stick was placed above the wooden pegs on 2 of the hanger legs. While the lower ends of the two legs were held on the ground, at the proper distance apart, the third leg was hinged at the top end to the other two, by inserting a bolt or pin through a hole in the tops. The three top ends were raised into the air with the third leg acting as a brace to hold them in position when the hog was raised high enough to clear the ground. The head was usually removed at once and rinsed in clean cool water and hung up by the nose to dry.

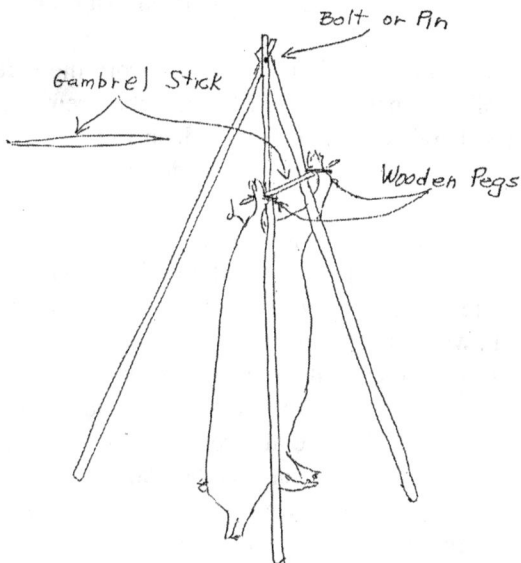

Hog Hanger

When all the hogs had been hung up in this manner, they were then gutted and the clean gut lard removed, before the less desirable gut soap lard was taken off. Ma supervised and helped with this work. This gutting was done before noon, if possible so the hogs would cool off during the noon hour. It was seldom that butchering moved rapidly enough to have fresh meat for the noon meal.

The scalding sled was cleaned off after lunch and moved to a convenient place to use as a table on which to cut the meat. While still hanging, the hog was slit down the middle of the back to the back bone, which was loosened from the tail down to the ribs, before placing on the sled where the ribs were cut from each side of the backbone with an ax. The entire backbone was removed and cut into cooking lengths with the ax. This method left the tenderloin fastened to the side meat, hams and shoulders. The tenderloin was removed from the side meat, and cooked separately, or made into sausage. Thus we had no pork chops as we know them now. The backbone would have had to be cut in

265

the middle with a saw, leaving the tenderloin fast on each side and then sliced crosswise to get pork chops.

We cut the hams and shoulders loose from the sides, peeled the leaf lard off the inside of the ribs, and then removed the ribs from the sides, leaving on some of the lean meat. The feet were cut from the shoulders and hams at the desired length and stored for later processing.

As the meat was cut in pieces, it was carried to the smokehouse and laid out on tables and boards to cool out for a day or two, until the animal heat had left it. Then it was ready to be salted and put away for salt curing.

Pa carefully applied salt to each ham, shoulder and side of bacon. As much salt was rubbed on the hide side of the meat as would stick to it, and likewise all around the edges and over the top part of it. Each piece of meat was then laid in a large tight box or barrel with the hide side down. The bottom of the storage bin was covered with salt before laying the bottom pieces in, to be sure that there was enough salt to fully preserve the under side of each bottom piece. In addition to the salt already rubbed into it, the top side was covered with extra salt until it was white. This was to make sure there was plenty of salt to penetrate and cure the meat properly.

Additional bins were used as needed to hold all the meat. Pa said it was better to have more salt than needed than not to have enough, which must have been right, since we never lost any meat by spoilage. The bins were tightly covered and the meat allowed to cure here for a month or two before the final hickory smoke curing was started. After a month or two, or when Pa thought the meat had salt cured in the bins enough, he took it out and hung the pieces up to poles or 2 by 4's arranged cross-wise in the smokehouse about 7 feet off the floor. When I first watched Pa and Ma hanging the meat up, there were a few hickory withes already tied up to the cross pieces with hooks on them, formed by cutting off a small limb long enough to make a hook. These had been left tied fast to overhead supports and had been used over and over. All they had to do was to make a hole through the thick part of the hide, lift the piece of meat up and hook it. Pa had new green withes to be used in place of the old dry ones that were without hooks and could not be retied. There was a little advantage in using the new ones, since they were made fast to the ham first, then lifted up and tied to the overhead support. Galvanized fencing wire gradually took the place of hickory withes for this tying.

The hanging up of meat for smoke curing was a considerable chore. As George and I got older, we were able to relieve Ma of helping hang the meat, and of some of the smoking chores.

The meat was allowed to hang in the smokehouse for most of the cold winter weather, during which time the salt dampness dripped and dried from the meat and further curing and drying took place. In the late winter or early spring, when the weather began warming up and before any bugs or insects were crawling or flying about, we began the final hickory-smoke curing process. Up until now, the air had been allowed to circulate freely through the smokehouse, but now all screened areas and openings were closed to make the smoke build up thick and dense inside the building to hasten the curing. We kept a supply of green hickory chips and short green hickory sticks cut from limbs, on hand in the smoke house to produce the hickory smoke.

Three or four small fires were started with dry kindling on the dirt floor directly under the hanging meat, which had been moved close together, but not touching each other. After the small fires got started, the green hickory chips and sticks were placed on the fires, sparingly, so as to produce as much smoke as possible, with little blaze. The smoke and fumes passing up and between the pieces of meat did the curing and added the aroma and flavor to the meat that made it so desirable. At times, ashes or water had to be put on the fire to keep it smoldering and smoking. Green wood, soaked in water, helped at times. These smoking fires required constant attention during the curing period. The dirt floor and the small fires, along with our constant attention during the curing process, kept the danger of the building catching on fire, to a minimum. We all felt that it was better to have too little fire, than too much. I have often opened the door to look about the fire, and found that it had gone out completely. The building was still so full of smoke one could scarcely see. At other times, only a few live coals remained and still the dense smoke prevailed.

The smoke cure continued ten days or two weeks, or until the color, texture and general condition of the meat indicated that it had been smoke-cured sufficiently. Pa and Ma depended on their knowledge and experience in determining when that point had been reached. It seems that their knowledge and experience was very dependable since our meat always kept well and the taste was memorable.   Meat cured in this way would keep almost indefinitely in all kinds of weather and retain its excellent flavor.

We made lard from the clean gut fat, rib leaf fat and other fat parts trimmed from the meat, which were put together in kettles and cooked over fire to render. The lard was then stored in stone jars or other containers for use in cooking and baking.   The cracklings left from rendering lard were good to eat, and were also used in cooking, as in crackling bread.

Bits of fat not readily or easily rendered into lard, such as that sticking to the shoulder, ham and head bones after the meat had been sliced off, including that left on the meat rinds, were all saved in a tub until they could be made into soap.

In addition to the three main cuts of meat discussed above, the shoulders, sides and hams, there were ribs, backbones, heads and feet to be cared for. The ribs and backbones were cut in suitable lengths and cooked for table use. Those not immediately needed were salted and stored for later use.

Pig feet were considered a delicacy, but had to be processed and used right away. Later on, we learned to pickle or can them, but many pig feet found their way into the soap tubs before better ways of using them were learned.

The heads went several routes. The brain was a delicacy when cooked and eaten right away. The lean meat of the heads went into the sausage meat. The fat was rendered into lard, while the bones with the attached fatty parts went into the soap tub.

The sausage meat which had been accumulated during the cutting-up process was ground and, if more sausage was needed, some shoulders were also ground. I remember one sausage grinder very well, that we used. We had a lot of sausage meat to grind that year, so we borrowed a rather large grinder that was fastened to a long board. This board was laid across two chairs and the one turning it, sat on the long end of the board which helped hole the board and mill from moving about while in use. When Pa or Ma sat on the board and turned the grinder, it moved about very little, and appeared to turn very easily, as the ground meat dropped quietly from the grinder into the pan below. When I eagerly sat down and began turning, the board and mill would not sit still at all, nor did the crank turn as easily as it had appeared to when Pa and Ma were operating it. The ground meat came out unsteadily and then stopped all together. I was holding to the board with my left hand and turning the crank with my right, and was not feeding any more meat into the grinder. At that time, neither George nor I was able to turn the crank and feed the meat into the grinder at the same time. When one of us did the turning and the other the feeding in the meat, we did a fairly good job. As we got bigger over the years, the work was less difficult, but was never more exciting than those first attempts when small. Pa and Ma later got a new grinder of their own that fastened securely to the edge of a table, which made the work easier.

Ma cooked the sausage in gallon stone milk crocks after seasoning it with salt, pepper and sage. The grease that cooked out of it was usually enough to cover over the cooked sausage, and the whole thing was allowed to cool in the crock. It was then ready to be set away in a cool place, with a cover over the crock to keep it clean. It would save a considerable length of time, and was sliced from the crocks and fried in the skillet as needed. Another way we kept sausage was to fry the patties, pack them in mason jars, cover with hot grease and seal immediately.

- - - - - - - - - - -

"Grandpa, making sausage was a lot of work, wasn't it?"

"Yes, but when it was served at the table, we all agreed that it was worth every bit of it."

"I don't think I'd like to eat brains. They just don't sound good."

"We didn't waste very much of the pig. And the expression, eating 'high on the hog,' probably comes from the abundance of meat available to eat just after the hot was butchered."

"I liked that sausage we had for supper, didn't you? And the molasses and butter on those hot biscuits that Grandma made! Ummmm! Good! Grandma got the sausage and the molasses at the supermarket and didn't have to grind the sausage herself. Did you have molasses when you and your brothers and sisters were growing up, Grandpa?"

"Oh, yes, we ate a lot of molasses, as did almost everybody then."

"But you couldn't buy it at the supermarket, so how did you get your molasses?"

"Remember I told you people raised nearly everything they needed, on their farms or in their gardens. Molasses was another item of food that nearly all farm families produced for themselves. . ."

- - - - - - - - - - -

SORGHUM MOLASSES

Sorghum molasses is made from the juice of sorghum cane which grows very much in the same manner as corn and requires about the same type of cultivation. It is planted in the spring in row, about the same as corn. We had no planter for cane seed, so we dropped the seed in furrows, in hills about 30 inches apart, and used a hoe to rake fine dirt over the seeds, about an inch deep. The small seed did not come up as quickly as corn, nor did it start growing as rapidly.

The first cultivation was very tedious with a lot of weeds to be pulled out of the hills by hand so the cane could get started ahead of the weeds. This was a slow back-breaking job, not popular with anyone. After the first cultivation was over, succeeding cultivations were more rapid and much easier. The usual cane patch contained about one-half to one acre of land and would produce from 50 to more than 100 gallons of molasses, which would be enough to satisfy the sweet tooth of an average family for a year or more.

The sorghum cane growing season is about the same length as that of corn and the two are of similar appearance during the early growing season. When the corn starts to shoot and tassel, the big difference appears. Cane forms no ears. It heads out in the top and forms its grains there in its tassel-like head. These heads of grain develop and ripen in the fall about the same time as corn.

270

The cane head grain is excellent for chicken feed, birds like it, and other farm animals learn to eat it. However the grain heads were not the main reason for growing the sorghum cane. The stalks are filled with sweet juice which we used in making molasses. Sometimes it was grown for fodder for animals.

Throughout the farming area and small towns of our part of West Virginia, many families raised cane every year, others every other year or so. As a result, molasses making was a regular fall activity, beginning as soon as cane was ripe enough, about the first of September and lasting over a period of 4 to 6 weeks or more. A few people had cane mills and boiling pans and traveled from home to home, making the molasses, since few farmers had the equipment to the work themselves. Since the price and quality of work was considered in hiring, both were competitive and stable. Some had reputations for making excellent molasses.

We hired Algie Thompson, who did good work, and his son Ray, to make our molasses several of the last years we raised cane. I remember one year in particular that Algie said he would not be able to get to us until late, but that he would do our work if we wanted to wait for him. We waited. In the meantime, we had a supply of wood ready and drying in the sun, to use in making the fire under the boiling pan.

That year, our cane patch of about 3/4th acre was in a piece of new ground about half way to the top of the hill behind our house, where the early fall frosts were sure to hit first. It was better not to let cane get frosted with the blades on, before cutting. We bladed our cane and left the stocks standing. Blading was a tiring process which caused our hands to cramp before the day was through. We used sticks to knock the blades off, on part of the patch, but still we had to remove some blades by hand. We even thought we could taste the early weeding and late blading work in the molasses. The blades were fed to the calves to get them started eating fodder in the fall. Later in the fall, when frosts were sure to come anytime, we cut the cane off close the ground and clipped the heads off near the tops, with our corn cutters. We then laid the cane stalks crosswise of the rows being careful not to let the ends drag on the ground. This helped keep sand and dirt from getting into the juice. This precaution, together with all the straining processes along the way, kept the molasses free of sand.

Pa, George and I hauled the cane off the hill and piled it in the barn lot next to the garden fence, where we covered it with fodder to keep it from freezing when the weather began to get cooler.

The big day came. Early one morning, Algie and Ray drove into the barn lot, lifted the molasses boiling pan and their new sheet metal furnace from the wagon, on which the cane grinding mill was securely fastened. The wagon was staked and blocked to the ground and the tongue and double-trees removed. The long crooked shaft used to turn the mill was put in place and one of their horses hitched to the end of the shaft. The horse walked round and round the mill, furnishing the power to operate the mill and squeeze the sweet juice from the cane. Algie immediately began feeding the cane stalks into the mill and the green foamy juice started running into the juice tub beneath the mill. The shaft was fastened to the top of the mill and would pass over the man feeding the cane into the mill. It sloped downward to the end where the horse was hitched, where it was about 2 feet off the ground and a convenient height for pulling. A lead pole was fitted in a hole in the shaft and extended out in front of the horse. A strap from the horse's bridle, which was fastened to the lead pole, made sure the horse would continue in the proper path all the way. All went round and round together. When the horse stopped, the mill and everything stopped. The power shaft was about 20 feet long and formed the radius of the circle the horse traveled around the mill.

This mill had guards in front of the rollers where the cane was fed into them, which protected the man feeding it, from getting his fingers caught between the rolls. Cider mills had not had such guards and many people got their fingers caught in cane mills. Sometimes cane was bladed as fed into the mill. This made it more dangerous, even with guards in front of the rollers. Pa said it was a common sight to see men with their fingers off one hand, or an arm off up to the elbow. Some were pulled into the unguarded mill rollers and killed. I remember seeing one of our neighbors who had four fingers of his right hand off up to his knuckles, and the tips off four fingers on his left hand. He said he grabbed at his right hand to try to pull it out and caught the left one too. He said the only thing that kept from grinding them off farther up, was that he yelled, 'Whoa!' and the horse stopped.

272

They backed the horse, and pushed the shaft backward to unwind the mill and let his fingers out. He was lucky to stop the horse so quickly.

After Algie got started on the mill, Ray set up the pan and furnace. This sheet iron furnace was mounted on two rockers which made it unnecessary to dig a furnace out of the ground, and also made it easy to level this one. With the help of Pa, George and me, Ray soon had the furnace and pan set up, a skimming hole dug, juice in the pan, a fire started and the boiling under way. The rocker furnace put the pan at a convenient height for skimming, watching, and tending the boiling operation, which was done by Ray, who was a grown man at that time. Algie and Ray relieved each other at the pan for dinner, supper and during night boiling, which was necessary to finish. It took until after midnight to finish that crop of about 80 gallons.

Pa, George and I kept the cane carried over and piled handy for Algie to feed into the mill and also piled the wood nearby for Ray to keep his fire going. The boiling pan was about 12 feet long, 4 feet wide and 8 inches deep. It was divided crosswise with partitions about 8 inches wide and about 6 inches deep, with openings first on one side and then on the other, in succession to the end, where the molasses was finished and let out of the pan. These openings in the partitions were equipped with removable gates so the juice could be moved forward toward the finishing end as it neared completion. The fire was fed from the end where the raw juice was put into the pan since it would take more heat without scorching, than after the juice became thicker near the finishing end of the pan. The smoke and heat flowed away from the main fire through the furnace to the smoke pipe at the finishing end, making an even heat at that end. Knowing how to fire, skim, and move the juice through the maze of passages toward the finishing end of the pan was the secret of making good molasses.

About the middle of the afternoon, one of the other Thompson boys, who was a photographer, came by and stopped to take a picture of the molasses making. He wanted some pictures for themselves and of course, wanted us to buy some, which we did. We formed a group near the molasses pan, which included both Algie and Ray. Ray wanted the picture to show him tending the molasses pan. It did, and even showed the steam off the pan about his face.

273

We had Ray dip some foamy molasses out on a plate to cool for us children to eat. We also had long flat splinters which we sometimes dipped into the boiling foam and let cool to lick. It was a big day that year, as were other days on such occasions in other years. Sometimes, neighbors would gather to play games, or simply just to talk and see someone step into the skimming hole.

Molasses was used as a sweetening in many different ways. Ginger cookies, cakes, and gingerbread were special treats. When the molasses was boiled down even more, it made excellent taffy. I am sure no one would ever forget pulling taffy of evenings when that was the principal entertainment, together with the pleasure of eating it, and having a supply left to last for several days. This was often a means of entertainment when neighbors got together for a period of enjoyment.

Grandpa Lewis told of another use he ran onto while surveying. The surveyors were seated at the supper table and the lady of the house was waiting on the table, helping each to get what he wanted to eat. As she poured Grandpa's coffee, she asked,

'Do you want long or short sweetening?"

Grandpa was a little uncertain just what she meant, but since he liked his coffee sweet, he replied,

'Long sweetening, please."

To his surprise, she stuck her finger into the pitcher of stiff sorghum molasses and came up with a bounteous finger full, which she let drip into his coffee, and wiped the remainder from her finger on the edge of his cup.

- - - - - - - - - - - -

"That must have surprised your Grandpa. I think I'll ask Grandma if we could make some taffy when the rest of the cousins come."

"Yes, that would be a good thing to do at the lake some evening when it's too rainy to be out. Or perhaps when one of Indian Lake's storms comes up and the fish aren't biting."

"Mary Ruth and Karen would probably get it in their hair!"

274

"See what Grandma says if you ask her for 'long sweetening' tomorrow on your cereal."

"Grandpa, there's something else I want to know about. Grandma gave us horseshoes for Christmas last year. They're real ones, with some nails left in one of them. Did you ever shoe horses?"

"Yes, I have, but it has been more than 50 years ago."

"I want to know about the nails, and why they don't hurt the horses' feet."

"You realize the horse's shoe isn't used to keep his feet warm, but in other ways, it is similar to yours. . . ."

- - - - - - - - - -

HORSESHOES

The horseshoe protects the horse's foot in much the same way as the sole of your shoe protects your foot. Horses, mules or cattle out in the pastures do not need shoes to protect their hoofs, but when they are used day after day to carry or pull heavy loads, their hoofs wear down and their feet became too sore for them to continue walking or working. Shoes of iron are used to protect their hoofs from wear. If you look at a horseshoe, you will see a series of 4 holes, beginning about the same distance from the toe (round end) of the shoe, and evenly spaced on both sides to about the same distance from the heel (open end) of the shoe. These holes are used to fasten the shoe on the horse's foot, with nails. If the nails are not properly driven, the horse will flinch or pull away when the nail hits the tender part of the hoof. The outer part of the horse's hoof is covered with a thick hard covering similar to your fingernails. This part has no nerves in it and can be pared or trimmed much the same as you trim your nails. The hoof covering is thick enough to drive nails into, without hurting the horse, if driven into the outer part. The holes in the shoe are punched through the shoe close to the outside edge for that reason, and for the same reason, each shoe must bend so it will fit the shape of each hoof. These iron shoes have to be heated red hot in the forge so they can be bent to the proper shape when held with tongs, and shaped on the anvil with a hammer until the correct fit is obtained, before nailing it fast.

A farrier begins by paring the hoof down level, ready to fit the shoe. Then the right size shoe is selected. Shoes come in many sizes to fit big and small feet. We had several nail kegs, each filled with a different size horseshoe, from which to select the right size. New shoes had neither corks nor toe pieces and all were bent alike with the 4 holes ready punched on each side. The extra toe piece and heavy corks were used on heavy draft horses for road use. The shoe was plain at first, and then the farrier bent it to fit the hoof, if the original bend did not fit. Then the corks were bent and shaped on the anvil after heating to a white heat. The toe of the shoe and a piece of toeing iron were both brought to a white welding heat and sprinkled with welding powder, put together, and then welded together. A little hammering was necessary in the process, after which the toe piece was cut even with the edge of the shoe, as cut from the bar of toeing iron. The toe piece was further shaped while hot if necessary. I never did much shoeing where the toe piece was used.

We had a heavy cowhide apron which we used when working about the forge to protect our clothing from flying sparks. We also used the apron when shoeing horses, to protect us from being cut with the points of shoe nails, should the horse suddenly jerk his foot while we held it between our legs while nailing the shoe on. This would happen if a nail was driven too deep and hurt him. Such nails had to be pulled out and re-driven so as not to go so deep. The nail had to go through the hoof at the right height above the shoe so it could be bent and clinched. I always bent each nail down as soon as it came through the hoof, to prevent it being jerked back into my leg if the horse kicked. After all eight nails had been driven and bent down, the horse's foot could be let down on the floor, or set on a foot-high block, while the ends of the nails were nipped off. After this, the horse's foot was raised up backwards and held between my knees while a clinching iron was held on the end of each bent, nipped-off nail. Each nail-head was struck with a hammer to draw the clinched nail tight.

After completing this operation on all 4 feet, the horse had his new shoes on, and was ready for work, riding or racing.

- - - - - - - - - -

"So my horseshoe must have been used on a heavy work-horse, because it has this extra toe piece on it."

"Yes, he was ready for pulling heavy loads. This may help you realize that horse-shoeing as a whole, is a rather complicated trade. There are different techniques for different purposes."

"Just as we have different shoes for different uses, Grandpa. There's work shoes, and football shoes, and baseball shoes and. . ."

"And tennis shoes. Let's put on a pair and go see if the fish are biting. That's enough horse-shoeing for one day!"

- - - - - - - - - -

GRANDPA LEWIS' STORY

- - - - - - - - - -

"I wasn't going to tell you any more stories about work on the farm, but I do remember one more. This one was told to us by Grandpa Lewis and happened before the Civil War."

"Your Grandpa Lewis was in the Civil War, wasn't he?"

"Yes, he and his four brothers, also his father. Three of the brothers were killed. I'll tell you more about them next, but first, one more work story."

- - - - - - - - - - - -

Grandpa Lewis and his brothers were helping their father put up hay at the edge of the Tygart Valley River, near the town of Beverly, Randolph County, Virginia, later West Virginia. About noon, they all ran for shelter when it began to sprinkle rain, but it was only that, just a sprinkle. They all got back to stirring the hay so it would dry faster, for it was nearly ready for stacking. The weather remained threatening, and farther up the valley, they could see that it was raining. There was closer thunder and the boys were watching the clouds, listening to the thunder and doing little work. This did not suit their father who wanted to get the hay put up. He said to them,

'Come with me!'

They followed him eagerly toward the house, thinking they were going for shelter, but when they reached the run crossing, he ducked each one in the water, after which he said to them,

'Now that you don't have to worry about getting wet if it rains, let's get back to work putting up that hay!"

- - - - - - - - - - -

"And now are we ready for your Grandpa's Civil War stories?"

"Yes. I've been writing Grandpa's war experiences, and I'll just tell you the ones he used to tell us when we were small. You can read the rest for yourselves."

- - - - - - - - - - -

CIVIL WAR STORIES

Many families in our area of West Virginia, although still part of Virginia until 1863, were divided on the question of the Civil War, some favoring the North and some the South. But the children of John and Susan Lewis were not divided at all. Four of the boys, including my grandfather, Oliver Hazard Perry Lewis, enlisted at the beginning of the war. Their father also enlisted, and the younger brother, Steven, joined them about 3 years later. They fought in many battles; John and Thomas were killed in action, and Walter died of 'fever' while serving in the army. All of them were fighting for the South. Grandpa and Steven spent part of their service in Northern prisons.

Grandpa told us that on one cold winter day, they were hiking from their overnight camp to a new location for an expected battle. On their way, it became necessary to cross a deep stream of water where there was no bridge. Their commanding officer was of a rank high enough to be supplied with a horse to ride. On arriving at the water's edge, he turned to the men of his command and said,

'Men, it is necessary for us to ford this stream. I will not ask you to do anything I would not do myself!"

With this, he dismounted and waded into the stream waist deep, breaking the thin ice on his way, as he led them to the other side. He continued walking to keep warm and to dry off, thus sharing the same discomfort as his men. Such acts of sharing and leadership are the kind to be expected of such leaders as Early, Jackson, Pickett and Lee.

- - - - - - - - - -

On another occasion, a considerable number of soldiers were bivouacked for the late afternoon and night in the woods at the foot of a long low ridge that lay between them and the northern soldiers. They were sure this hill would protect them from artillery and small arms fire. Grandpa said some soldiers thought they had to smoke and make coffee, regardless of what else happened.   They felt pretty safe; so many little groups were smoking, making and drinking coffee, and sort of enjoying themselves. All at once, a shell whizzed overhead and burst a safe distance away. No one worried, for they were still sure the hill between them would be protection enough. Let them waste their ammunition! Suddenly, Crash! A shell hit a tall dry tree, cutting it off as the shell burst. The falling tree killed one soldier and wounded 2 or 3 others.

'The damn Yankees can hit you where you aren't!' was the exclamation that followed.

'   'How did they know we were here?' The smoke from the coffee fire had drifted up between the dry tree and the Yankee artillery position. They figured that if they could hit the tree, they would hit those near the foot of the tree, and they did!

- - - - - - - - - - - -

The movement of artillery and army supplies over long distances was by rail and water where these facilities were available, but the final distribution to the soldiers on the battlefield was by mule, horse and manpower. The artillery pieces, together with the supply wagons, were constantly getting stuck in the mud holes in the roads and fields over which they traveled. Teams were doubled up to pull them out. This slowed the movement of guns and supplies.   Too often, rather than unhook and double teams, when infantry men were near, they were ordered to supply the extra power needed by putting their shoulders to the wheels to roll and push the stalled artillery and wagons through. The infantry men were able to hike around many of the bad places, but not the teamsters and mule skinners.

Grandpa said they could not miss the mud holes, and just followed each other, and all got stuck. The infantry men thought them the poorest drivers in the world. Each succeeding one got harder to push through, as the mud hole got deeper and deeper. Infantry men got dirty hiking over either dry or muddy roads. Supplying the extra manpower to get the stalled vehicles moving, made their clean-up job even harder.

There was a friendly rivalry between the cavalry and infantry that found expression in ribbing each other at every opportunity. A cavalryman riding past a column of infantry on the march would call to a tired looking prospect,

'Tired of walking, Buddy?'

'Tired as a dog,' came the reply, thinking of getting a ride.

'Well, just try running awhile!' came the response with laughter.

Of evenings after supper, when cavalrymen were wearily currying their horses, they were often asked by infantrymen, who came near,

'Are you tired of currying?'

'You bet I am,' thinking of getting a little help.

'Why not use your brush, while you rest?' Such simple inquiries were good for hearty laughs, even though used over and over.

- - - - - - - - - -

We never got any direct answer when we asked Grandpa whether he ever killed a man in battle. When we sensed that he did not want to answer directly, we did not press the question. We were satisfied with such answer as,

'When so many men are running, shooting and yelling, all around you, it is hard to be sure who was shot by whom, or where. I have seen many wounded and killed around me in several battles.'

The answer was different when we inquired whether he had ever been wounded.

'I was with 'Stonewall' Jackson at the Battle of Cedar Mountain, when a partly spent Minie ball struck me in the hip. It lodged there and I was sent to the General Hospital at Staunton to get the bullet taken out. My brother, John, was killed in the same battle.'

Grandpa soon recovered and returned to his regiment, where he was in many more battles, the most important of which was the Battle of Chancellersville. Grandpa said that many of the Southern victories were the result of long hard marches, ending in surprise attacks of hard fighting. They were often in full attack before the enemy knew they were near. That sort of soldiering got results, yet it was exhaustive on the troops. When they were given an order saying,

'We move at gray day tomorrow,' they knew it meant exactly that and not nine or ten in the day.

- - - - - - - - - -

Another experience I remember of Grandpa's was at the Battle of Gettysburg, not so much because of his description of it, but that he was in Pickets Charge at Cemetery Ridge. Across the valley and up the hill went the 5,000 men, in the face of the artillery and musket fire of Meade's army, even penetrating some of Meade's first lines of defense at the top of the ridge. The saddest part was that their losses, about 3/4ths of the 5,000 men, had been so heavy that they were unable to hold on to their hard-earned gains and had to withdraw. Sadder still, for the Confederates, General Lee began, the following night, his retreat back to Virginia. With that retreat began the gradual loss of the Confederate cause. They did not lose easily. Many battles and much hard fighting remained to be done.

Grandpa's part in the fighting ended when he was captured about 6 months later in Highland County, Virginia on Nov 9, 1863. He had been recommended for promotion from 1st Lieutenant to Captain just before that and had been given a short furlough to visit him home before receiving and entering the duties of that new rank. On his way back to his outfit, he rode around a sharp turn in the road in Highland County where he met General Averal, a Union officer, accompanied by several aides. Escape was impossible, and fighting, certain death. The officer took him into custody saying,

'I outrank and out-number you, so we'll just take you along with us!' And so he became a Prisoner of War, and never got back to his outfit to receive the promotion to Captain. Although he never actually received the earned promotion, after the war, he was often referred to by his relative, friends and neighbors as 'Captain Lewis.'

Immediately after capture, he was sent to the Military Prison at Wheeling and from there was sent to Camp Chase, Ohio,

282

through the winter of 1863-64. Next he was sent in the spring of 1864 to Fort Delaware, Delaware, where a group of 600 Rebel officers were being assembled to be sent to Hilton Head, S.C. His war records say, 'THESE PRISONERS OF WAR WERE SENT FROM WASHINGTON TO THE DEPARTMENT OF THE SOUTH FOR RETALIATION.'

I talked to Grandpa Lewis about his year and a half in prisons, not long before he died on April 30, 1917. He said war prisoners were treated differently in different prisons, but that prisoners of war were not sent to prison to be treated good or bad, but to keep them from getting back to their outfits and again entering the fighting against their captors. The guards were soldiers, sometimes recovering from battle wounds and unable for battle duty, but always armed and ready to shoot anyone trying to escape, refusing to halt, or breaking any prison regulations. Food enough to sustain life was generally provided, even though the quality at times was poor. Winter clothing and blankets were scanty, and little fire was permitted. Conditions had to be silently endured.

Conditions were made far worse for Grandpa and the other Rebel officers when they were sent to Hilton Head and placed deliberately, in an open field stockade within the fortified area. They were directly under the fire of their own Confederate guns, which were bombarding the whole fortified area. This, together with the harsh treatment, was done under orders from Washington in retaliation against treatment received by Union prisoners in Southern prisons, Grandpa said conditions were bad in Confederate prisons, but not the result of deliberate orders to make them that way. Discipline was severe and quick in both Northern and Southern prisons, and harsh too, were the living conditions on both sides, including scarce and poor quality food. By the winter of 1864-5, there was no question but that both clothing and food was far scarcer and of poorer quality in Southern prisons, but this was not as a result of any direct order on the part of the South that conditions be made that bad.

Almost all the battles of the Civil War were fought on Southern soil, together with all the destruction and waste they caused. Things got worse and worse, not only for the Southern armies and their prisoners, but for the civilian population as well.

Grandpa's treatment at Hilton Head was deliberately done under orders inflicting harsh and unusual punishment that accomplished nothing of any benefit. A starvation ration was immediately imposed on arrival, thus starting hunger and malnutrition on their devastating course. All developed ravenous appetites with too little food to satisfy them. Even wormy corn grits, stale moldy bread and tainted meat were devoured when mixed in their ration. Food for a day in prison was ½ to a pint of corn meal; often with so many bugs in it they could see the meal moving before boiling it to turn it into mush and 'meat.'

One day a man went through camp with a fat little dog which the prisoners caught and had in the frying pan when the man came back looking for him. He didn't find his dog, for he didn't look in the frying pan. Grandpa said it was mighty fine eating.

Things got so bad that rats killed about the compound were skinned and roasted or boiled on the tiny fires allowed, and then eaten, often after a struggle among the prisoners for that privilege. Bugs and worms, found in digging out stumps and roots for firewood, often met the same fate as the rats. Cramps, diarrhea, dysentery, scurvy, sores and other diseases accompanying such a diet were prevalent. Care of the weaker by the stronger was a critical uncertain chore, performed with greater and greater effort as all became weaker.

Stumps and roots found in the compound were constantly dug out by the prisoners throughout the winter, to make more fire than could be had from the small amount of fuel furnished. Then even the stump supply within the compound was exhausted. Fires were allowed only at certain times during the day. When the guards yelled,

'Fires out!' the prisoners were required to put out all fires at once. Any delay caused the guards to shoot directly at the fire until all were extinguished.

Constant suffering from damp winter cold was always a problem because of thin, worn-out clothing, fireless nights, and the shortage of straw bedding and blankets.

The Southern forces were notified that the prisoners were confined in the open compound within the fortifications. If they expected this to reduce the southern artillery, they were disappointed. It was slower for several days while the Southern artillerymen carefully checked their ranges, after which the answer was shot for shot, with a few extra shots added for bad behavior. Seldom did a shell miss its mark and land within the prison compound. The long nervous waiting strain was harder on some than others.

Prisoners developed a game that was played with two or more contestants, in which the winning point was to be the first to see each shell as it whined overhead toward its target. It was necessary to look ahead of the sound to see the shell. Some worried that they wouldn't hear the one that hit them. There was always a joy-killer, no matter what the game was. Others relaxed and dropped off to sleep part of the time and failed to make a high score.

The shelling ceased after about 2 months when the Southern forces were driven from their positions near Hilton Head. After still another month of continued retaliatory punishment, that, too, came to an end. With better food and living conditions, the prisoners' health and physical condition improved enough so that they could be moved north about the middle of March to Fort Delaware. After about 2 months more, the war having ended in the meantime, the prisoners were released from prison, by taking and signing the Oath of Allegiance to the United States of America. That oath and signing that restored their citizenship, took place for many of them on June 12, 1865.

Uncle Steve was released that same month, so only the oldest and the youngest of the Lewis boys, and their father, came home from the war.

- - - - - - - - - -

CIVILIAN WAR STORIES

"I shall tell you of some incidents that took place during the war years in our part of West Virginia."

"Were most of the people for the North or the South, Grandpa?"

"The sympathies of the people in Gilmer and Randolph counties, where our relatives lived, were divided. There were about an equal number of men serving in each army, although West Virginia as a

285

whole supplied far more soldiers to the Northern Army than to the
South. . ."

- - - - - - - - - - - -

That border area, which became West Virginia in 1863, was
claimed by both North and South, but controlled and occupied by
neither, until the North gained control. It was subject to raiding
parties from both sides. The part west of the mountains to the
Ohio River was more easily accessible to Union forces and
influences were the mountains and valleys farther to the east. It
was a divided insecure area filled with fear and apprehension.
Rampant divisiveness of family against family, of father against
son, brother against brother and neighbor against neighbor
prevailed.

One McQuain family, living on Little Cove had two in the
Union Army. Our family, whose sympathies were with the
Southern Cause, had no one in the army, which might be
explained by the fact that both brothers were over 40 years of age,
with growing families. The oldest of Uncle George McQuain's
family was somewhere in his teens, while Grandpa McQuain's
family of seven, ranged in age from 11 years down to a babe in
arms. Thus both were needed at home with their families.

- - - - - - - - - - - -

"Your Grandma has some stories to relate about her
grandparents treatment during the Civil War."

"What's she going to feed us this time? I hope it's her Pumpkin
Nut Cake."

"And she's put ice cream on the top too. We're ready to
listen?"

- - - - - - - - - - - -

My grandfather, William Dexter Morrison was only about 15
at the start of the war and was not old enough for army service.

286

My other grandfather, Joseph Matthew Wood, was about 26 and just right for the army, but he was married with a family of two small children who needed him at home. Both the Morrison and Wood families sympathized with the South.

Not long after the war got under way, the Union authorities began arresting civilian men having Southern sympathies and sent them away to prison at one of two military prisons, either Athenium Prison in Wheeling, or Camp Chase, Ohio.

Grandpa Wood was among those picked up on Sinking Creek and sent to prison at Wheeling where he was held during the time he was a prisoner. We don't know how long he was held, but whatever the time; consider the plight of Grandma Wood. She was left alone in a log cabin in a small cleared area with woods all around and with the two children to care for. (My mother, Minnie, had not yet been born.) It was a wilderness area then. She had a garden to tend, corn to hoe, firewood to cut, meals to cook, as well as her children to care for.

The exact reason for Grandpa's arrest was never known, but the family thought some of their neighbors on the creek had made a complaint. Another reason was that he could and might join the Southern Army, since he was of acceptable age. It might only have been a neighborhood argument, but there was little he could do to defend himself, since this was divided country.

I always wondered just how Grandma Wood managed. She was a little woman, only 5 feet tall, but she was very strong-willed and perhaps that was what helped carry her through.

- - - - - - - - - - - -

"Is she the same Grandma who gave you the big French doll for sleeping at her feet to keep them warm? My mom told us that story."

"Yes, she's the one. That doll cost $10. which was a very large sum to pay for a doll. Mary Ruth has the doll now, if you'd like to see it. We kept it hanging on the wall and only got to take it down now and then to play with."

"Well, Grandpa, how did the McQuains fare during the war? You've told us a lot about your Grandpa Lewis and his family."

"My Uncle George McQuain's difficulties were about the same as your Wood ancestor. . ."

MORE CIVIL WAR STORIES

Uncle George McQuain was picked up and sent to prison at Camp Chase where he said prisoners were harshly treated, poorly fed and that it was generally a bad place to be. Again we don't know how long he was confined. His wife was left with a family of 4 or 5, but the oldest boy was big enough to help in caring for the family. They, too, lived in a log cabin surrounded by woods, but they lived near relatives who could be called on to help out, if needed. Uncle George was over 40 and too old for the army, but he was a pretty free talker in expressing his views on subjects. No one had any trouble knowing his feelings on the war or other topics, which might have gotten him into trouble. Or again, it could have been a disgruntled neighbor who wanted to get him into trouble by complaining to Union raiders.

On another instance, near Glenville, a band of Union soldiers removed a Southern sympathizer from his home and family in the usual manner with little or no reason and sent him on his way toward prison by way of Weston. One of the soldiers was selected by lot, to act as guard and escort him on the way. The soldier and prisoner proceeded on their way. The soldier was reluctant to have to make the long trip. About 7 miles out of Glenville, on their journey, at the head of Stewarts Creek, they came to a long turn in the road that wound up a hollow and came back near itself, but higher up the hill. The soldier told the prisoner they would take the short cut and walk across the run and up through the brush to the road and save time. The prisoner, who was walking in front, took the path as told and walked but a short distance when the soldier shot him in the back. The soldier, thinking his prisoner was dead, left and returned to his comrades, to whom he reported that the prisoner tried to escape, ran from the road, and he had to shoot him. However, a man living nearby, saw the incident and said there was no running. Another version was that a man heard

288

the shot and got to the dying man, who said that the soldier told him to take the short cut.

Local indignation ran high for a time, but nothing was done to punish the soldier. The murdered man was buried in a small graveyard just above the road in front of the short-cut path on which he was murdered. Shortly after the war, a monument was put up at the grave by friends and relatives, bearing this inscription:

IN MEMORY OF   (victim's name)
MURDERED BY UNION SOLDIER   (murderer's name)

together with the date and other information.

I had heard this story many times, so one day about 1930, your Uncle Page and I stopped at that graveyard to see if such a stone marker really existed.   It was there.   We copied the inscription, and noted that it was a sturdy monument, 2 or 3 feet in height and securely set in place. This marker was unique in that it was a monument to the Victim and an indictment of the Murderer.

- - - - - - - - - - - -

"Grandpa, why didn't the Sheriff do something to protect the people?"

"It was one of the results of the Civil War conditions of controversy and divisiveness.   The part of Virginia west of the Allegheny Mountains was opposed to seceding from the Union with Virginia.   They organized a provisional government for that part of the state with headquarters at Wheeling, which finally led to the admission of West Virginia as a state on June 20, 1863."

- - - - - - - - - - - -

About 28,000 men from West Virginia joined the Northern armies and about 18,000 men enlisted in the Southern armies. This is a partial indication of how seriously the state was divided, and how difficult it was to maintain law and protection on an equal basis for all.

Gradually a homeguard organization to assist with local defense was established in many counties under Northern direction, as their power and influence was extended in the area. Southern sympathizers were often treated harshly and unfairly. Some more incidents about Grandpa McQuain's family may help to understand the situation.

When Grandpa McQuain learned the Union authorities were arresting men in the county who were known to favor the Southern Cause, he left home and hid before they got to him. Pa always said he was sure his dad was near home part of the time, because he had seen his mother preparing food that never was put on the table. He was away a good while the first winter, and for short periods at other times when Union raids were made. Pa said he was 8 and his brother, George, about 10, and they were kept busy cutting firewood and helping their mother take care of the family of 7 children. His family endured hardships, but not as bad as if he had been sent to prison, as happened to so many.

- - - - - - - - - -

"Grandpa, were there any battles on your farm?"

"Mostly there were just raiding parties but have I told you about the Battle of Pine Knob? That was across the creek from our house, and I don't think it's been written in the history books."

"Oh, yes, we'd like to hear it. Just think, a real battlefield right there at your farm."

"Well, wait until you hear the story before you make a park out of it, or put up a historical monument. . ."

- - - - - - - - - -

BATTLE OF PINE KNOB

Early one drizzly morning, 6 or 7 musket shots pierced the morning stillness from the direction of Pine Knob, which was across Cove Creek from our house. No one could be seen anywhere. Not long after hearing the shots, members of the Home Guard, stationed at Glenville, came by, inquiring if any Rebel soldiers had been seen. Grandpa said that some were reported to be in the area. When the shots were mentioned, the Home Guard members said they had heard the shots and thought the Rebels might be near.

Later in the day, when Pa and Grandpa went across the creek to get fodder from the shocks in the wheat field, they saw tracks in the soft ground where two or more people had jumped over the fence and had run down the point to the lower side toward Big Run. People were excited, but little more was known until later one of those who had fired off their muskets that morning, stopped by for something to eat. (It was generally known that Confederates could get a meal at Grandpa's.) He told this story.

About 6 or 7 had got together to visit their homes in the general area, thinking they would be safer in a group. They were sure they had been spotted and reported to the home guard, so they put one man out to watch the road while the others slept or rested at Pine Knob. The man watching came running to them and said he had seen men coming up Cove carrying guns, whom he was sure belonged to the Home Guard. They were not sure whether their guns had drawn too much dampness to fire, so they decided to fire them to be sure, and at the same time, cause the Home Guard to slow up and concentrate on that area while they scattered and left the vicinity in 2 or 3 directions, to delay pursuit.

Thus, they had shot into the air, one at a time, making as much noise as possible, and then had scattered. Two had gone down through the wheat field, all leaving tracks in crossing the roads nearby, to confuse and delay pursuit. All reassembled at a prearranged place the next day in Braxton County, from which point, they returned to their outfit. Thus happened the Battle of Pine Knob, which was no battle at all, but only an exciting event in our part of the county.

- - - - - - - - - - -

"So that's why the Battle of Pine Knob isn't in the history books. I was thinking that they had slighted us!"

"There's another similar event that could be called the Battle of Glenville. Your Mom was born in Glenville. You can ask her if she ever heard about that battle.

- - - - - - - - - - -

THE BATTLE OF GLENVILLE

Another exciting event happened at Glenville, which was the headquarters for the Gilmer County Home Guard. Some defensive trenches and breastworks, called Fort Moore, were on a high knob overlooking the town, later called Tank Hill. Since little water was available on the high knob, the courthouse, farther down the hill, with plenty of water, was used as part of their main defenses. Both afforded a fair view of the surrounding low ground and the more distant encircling hills. Early one morning, a musket shot or two called the Home Guard and the people's attention to Confederate soldiers leaving the road and disappearing behind a hill extending closer to town. Fear and excitement prevailed as the Home Guard ran for their defense positions. The townspeople cautiously watched to see what was going on.

Soldiers had been stationed along the Staunton-Parkersburg Pike at Troy and Linn, 10 or 12 miles away, and others at Weston, still farther away. The Home Guard telegraphed for help, saying they were surrounded and attacked.

The Confederates continued running, 1 or 2 at a time, across the open space to assemble behind the hill extending nearer to town. To make things more dangerous, they were seen dodging from behind one hill to another, much nearer town.

'Would the soldiers never come?'

'Would they all be killed or captured?' Such was the thinking of many of the surrounded Home Guard as they waited for the soldiers.

When the soldiers arrived they were greeted by a scared Tuckahoe, who exclaimed,

'We're sure glad to see you! We've been having a pretty scary time around here!'

'Where are the Rebels attacking you?'

'Behind the top of that ridge across the river!'

'How many of them are there?'

'We don't know. It took them more than an hour to get through that open place over there. There must be a lot of them behind that ridge.'

There had been no shooting. Not more than 2 or 3 had been seen at any one time, and none were in sight when the soldiers arrived. The answers made less and less sense as the questioning progressed.

The soldiers, together with their commander, were as mad as hops, at making the trip when it became apparent that the Home Guard had been in no danger at all. However, they ordered the Home Guard accompany them in searching the area to make sure. The facts, as came to light then and later, was that a group of 6 to 10 Confederate soldiers had been there. They had gone through the open place to cover behind the ridge, but in reality, continued out of sight and around into view again, over and over, creating the impression of a much larger and more dangerous force.

It was made perfectly clear to the Home Guard that they were to defend themselves and be absolutely certain that they were in real danger before calling for help. This, together with other stories and incidents where members of the Home Guard used that power and prestige to further their own personal benefits, lowered the standing of that organization and its members in the eyes of many people in the area.

THE WOUNDED REBEL

A Rebel soldier was on leave to visit his home near Glenville and was wounded on the way. He escaped and finally got home. It immediately became apparent that a doctor would be needed to get the bullet out and dress the wound. Only his family knew of his presence in the area. It was important, for his safety, to keep it that way. They knew a doctor in Glenville who could be trusted, but the wounded man could not be taken to the doctor without being seen. The doctor said he would come after dark. They had sterilized bandages, hot water, and an oil lamp ready when the doctor arrived. Two or three helped the doctor while the others remained in the adjoining room. They began by cleaning the wound with hot water, and continued by removing the bullet, together with a small piece of his coat that had been carried in with the bullet. The soldier soon recovered.

The doctor scarcely got started when the soldier's brother, sitting in the adjoining room heard the water dripping into the pan while they were cleansing the wound. He thought it was blood, fainted and fell off his chair onto the floor. The others in that room dashed cold water in his face to revive him, and then got him out of the house where they walked him about in fresh air to keep him from passing out again.

That illustrated the dangers encountered by Southern soldiers when visiting relatives and friends in that area. In other parts of the border area, it was the Union soldier who was in more danger.

Another story was circulated of a Northern soldier visiting his own home, or that of a neighbor, who felt he was in little danger. He was out in the yard in the sun, one cold winter day, carrying a small child, which he put down on the ground to see it toddle around. Just as he straightened up to watch and enjoy the child's eager efforts, a shot rang out from the nearby woods. He jumped to cover behind the house, having felt the bullet pass. It had passed through part of his uniform and had been deflected by several thicknesses of paper, which he had wrapped around his body underneath the coat, to help keep out the cold wind. Thanks to the paper, he was safe. The child, who was in no danger, was brought into the house by another member of the family. They never learned whether the sniper was a Southern soldier, or a neighbor trying to get revenge, but whatever the reason, it added to the neighborhood fear and mistrust.

- - - - - - - - - - - -

FEEDING UNION SOLDIERS

I've heard Pa tell several times of two Union soldiers who were on furlough visiting relatives and friends in the neighborhood. These two soldiers stopped at Grandpa's house for a visit. After dinner, the soldiers and some of the family were out in the yard, talking. In response to some of the children wanting to hear the guns shot, the soldiers decided to shoot at a large oak tree that stood at the far end of the field below the house, about 250 yards away. They shot at a light spot on the tree, and all could see where the bullets hit, by the bark each knocked off. The children ran to the tree for a better view and to probe the depth of the bullet holes.

Pa said that some years afterward, they cut the tree and split clapboards from it, and at that time, when splitting the block that had the bullet holes in it, they could not find the bullets. There were no bullets in, or at the bottom of either hole. Pa decided that, since it was cold weather and the tree was frozen when the bullets hit, that they had bounced out.

I was always intrigued each time I heard the story that they did not find the bullets. It was even more interesting and impressive, because the big stump, about 4 feet across, was still there for us to see and play around when we were small. George and I put the final touches to the story by splitting off pieces for firewood, until the last decayed roots were chopped and dug out; about the time we got the two red axes.

- - - - - - - - - - -

"Grandpa, why did your Grandpa McQuain feed Union soldiers? We thought he favored the South."

"He did favor the Southern Cause, and this was known by nearly all in the county but, on the other hand, he tried to be neutral in the way he treated soldiers. Union soldiers from the area felt safe to talk to him or to visit and share a meal. At the same time, they knew that Southern soldiers of the neighborhood felt equally safe. Since the North was pretty well in control, it was the Southern soldiers who had to be careful.

"There's another story about our cousin Zan. That's short for Alexander. Every generation of McQuains has had an Alexander, named for the first one who came from Scotland."

"He was the one in the Revolutionary War, wasn't he?"

"Yes, that's the one. Well, this Alexander. . . "

- - - - - - - - - - -

Zan McQuain, Uncle George's boy, in his mid-teens, was at Troy one day while several Union Soldiers were stationed there. One of the members of the squad complained to some of the local people that one of their squad was such a good shot that the others had been keeping him in chewing tobacco, so they would like to see someone out-shoot him. One of the local people, knowing that Zan was a good shot, said,

'I wouldn't be surprised if that boy,' indicating Zan, 'could out-shoot him.'

Zan protested, saying he had no gun and when told they would let him have one of their guns, said,

'But I have never shot your gun!'

'It shoots where you hold it. Here try a shot at that piece of ice over against that cliff.'

Zan took the gun and aimed a little to one side of the ice. The bullet hit where he had aimed. The soldier said,

'I can come closer that that. How much do you want to bet?'

'I've only this much money,' Zan said, holding it out in his hand, 'besides how do I know I would get the money if I won it?'

'Oh, we'll see that you get it. He's been chewing off us too long. We want to see him lose,' assured the other soldiers. The soldier shot first and came closer than Zan's free shot. Zan shot and splattered the ice in all directions.

'He was just lucky! He can't do it again.'

'I have no more money,' Zan said.

'You just won this. Bet it all!' exclaimed the soldier holding the money

'Well, I'll shoot only once more, regardless of who wins.' Another outstanding piece of ice on the same cliff was selected to be the new target. Again the soldier came close and again the piece of ice flew to pieces when Zan shot.

'You weren't just lucky. You're a good shot!' said the soldier as he handed Zan his winnings. When the match was over, old Mr. Heckert said to the soldiers,

'If that boy was old enough to be in the army, he'd shoot all of you before you could touch him!'

- - - - - - - - - -

On another occasion, a circus came to town for a showing where several soldiers were in attendance. A small tent near the main tent housed a small sideshow which began attracting attention of the soldiers. Those coming out, after seeing the show, were laughing and kidding each other. When asked by those outside, they would tell them nothing. Their indefinite comments only roused the others curiosity and desire to find out what it was that caused so much hilarity and so many unrevealing remarks, such as,

'You won't believe it!'

'I never saw anything like it!'

'It's a laugh!'

'Don't miss that!' Both soldiers and civilians coming out after seeing the sideshow, revealed nothing except unrestrained amusement. It was the most popular sideshow at the circus. What was it?

I'll tell you before you start for the tent. As each entered the tent, right in front of him, lying in a nest of straw was an old sow, contented suckling her 12 or 14 hungry little pigs. In a rocking chair nearby, sat an old woman with a bonnet on her head, which partly covered her wrinkled face as she gently rocked back and forth, constantly whittling on a piece of wood and repeating over and over the warning,

'Cut from you and you'll never cut yourself.' It was a complete sellout, and may have been among the first efforts at army entertainment.

- - - - - - - - - - - -

It was always difficult to keep in communication with headquarters and other units. Advanced units had trouble keeping telegraph lines open. A detail of soldiers were checking a line that had gone dead. They came across an old woman who had cut the wires and was sticking the ends into the ground, when she was asked,

'Why are you sticking the ends of those wires into the ground?'

'I want to see if they have room in hell for any more ' Damn Yankees!'

As she made an effort to escape, a soldier was ordered to prevent the escape. This was a problem for the soldier. Should he grab her and hold her, shoot her, or use his bayonet? He chose the bayonet. Thrusting his bayonet through her heavy, long-flowing dress, he pinned her to the ground. She was held securely, with little effort on the soldier's part and no harm to the woman. While mending her dress, she probably thought of more cutting remarks that she wished she had said.

297

- - - - - - - - - - - -

While Ran Philips, a relative in Randolph County, was away from home in the Southern army, one of his nearby neighbors stole Ran's big iron kettle and took it to his home to use. Ran's wife and family knew where the kettle was, but were afraid of further reprisals or thefts if they tried to get it back while the war was still going on, so they got along without it.

After the war, when Ran learned about the theft and saw his kettle being used by his Yankee neighbor, he was furious, but he, too, was unsure what he could safely do. He was not physically afraid of the kettle thief, but as a defeated Southern soldier, he was not sure what the victorious Northern authorities might do. After considerable though while getting more angry all the time, he walked over and confronted the neighbor with something like this,

'I see you are using my iron kettle out there in the yard. I need that kettle at home. I want that kettle set inside my front gate by not later than day after tomorrow morning!' Not waiting for any reply, he turned and walked back home.

He did not have to wait until the second morning. The kettle was inside his gate the very next morning.

- - - - - - - - - -

Many years after the war, at the end of a heated political campaign in which people had been worked up considerable by fiery speakers on both sides, everyone was interested in how the voting was going and who was voting for whom. Some young men were standing beside the road talking, when they saw Mr. Cain, an old Confederate veteran, riding toward them. They decided to find out how he had voted. They asked,

'Mr. Cain, how did you vote this time?'

'The same way I shot!' came the answer without hesitation for thought, or slowing the pace of his horse as he rode past.

- - - - - - - - - -

I have heard this story told several times, about a boy hunting his cows one evening in Randolph County. He saw his cows across on the other side of Tygart River, and went up the river a little way to a wooden bridge to cross. Several Confederate soldiers were preparing to cut the bridge down and set it on fire to slow the advance of Northern soldiers, who were expected at the bridge soon. The boy said to the soldiers,

'You can't cut that bridge down until I get my cows across.' He was told to hurry and get his cows across. They waited until the cows were safely across before it was cut into the river and set afire.

That boy, Lieu Fiddler, grew up and moved to Gilmer County on Big Run. He worked for Pa, hoeing corn and during hay harvest. Such insignificant incidents are often better remembered because they are about people you know.

- - - - - - - - - - -

A Union soldier named Moneypenny from our area, who was stationed in the vicinity of Washington at the time Lincoln was shot, told this story. He was arrested for Booth and had to go to considerable trouble to prove that he was not Booth, who shot Lincoln. It took statements from his buddies and officers to convince the authorities that he was not the man they wanted.

He said that Booth was a fine-looking man and that he looked so much like him that they thought he was Booth disguised in a uniform of a Union soldier. Moneypenny was a good-looking man and seemed pleased to be mistaken for Booth. Some thought he would not have been so proud to have been mistaken for Lincoln instead of Booth.

- - - - - - - - - -

John Lamb, one of our neighbors who lived over the hill on Little Cove, less than a mile by the road around to his house, told several stories of incidents that happened during his service in the Union Army.

While serving as Company Cook, his company wanted to have steak for a meal and asked him if it would be possible. He told them that they would have to save the best part of their beef ration a day or two to get enough steak to go around, and he would need some extra help in preparing it.

The evening for steak came. His help was well along with hammering the steak to tenderize it. He had a lot of steak stacked on a board. He was starting to cook some of the steak when some soldiers from another company came by. They wanted to know how it was they were having steak and none of the other companies had any. After they had explained how they managed, the visitors were not satisfied and upset the steak pile on the ground. This caused fighting between the men of the two companies. After the fighting, they cleaned their steak off and went ahead and enjoyed their well-earned meal.

Mr. Lamb was a good story teller, and it was almost like being there when we listened to him telling about it. At the time he was telling us, he was an old white-haired man with a long, flowing white beard.

- - - - - - - - - - -

Benton Queen, another Union soldier, lived about a mile above our house on big Run. He would haul logs past where we lived on a bobsled, through the snow, to Troy to be cut into lumber. The thick, bobsled runners had been sawed from a big log with a crook at one end that turned up enough to easily slide over the snow without catching on objects in the road. He sat on the front end of the logs, driving his team of horses through the snow. Often the falling snow, blowing in his face, stuck to his long beard until it was white with snow.

We heard him tell of living in his little sod house on his homestead on the prairie out west. He was glad that he was given some credit for service in the army, which cut down on the time he had to live on the claim to make it his. He said it was a lonesome life out there by himself.

He never talked much to us about being in the army, but George and I were very much impressed when he told us that he fired the last shot at the Battle of Richmond, which resulted in Lee's surrender to Grant at Appomattox Courthouse on April 9, 1865. They were glad the shooting, killing and crippling had ended. Mr. Queen never forgot that day.

- - - - - - - - - - -

Elmer Burton, a crippled Confederate soldier and neighbor lived about 2 miles farther beyond us up Big Cove at the mouth of Crane Run. He had been crippled in both hands in a battle during the war. It was a hard fought battle in which the two armies were charging toward each other, shooting as they came. The soldier coming toward Burton shot at him as they came toward each other, hitting him in one hand. As they clashed bayonets, his bayonet, deflected by Burton's gun, cut into his other hand as Burton's own bayonet found its mark and closed the struggle. A comrade nearby heard Elmer shout during the brief encounter.

'You're trying to kill me!'

I have been at Elmer Burton's home a few times and was impressed to see how twisted and scarred his hands and fingers were, and yet how well he was able to use them as he went about his farm work and chores.

- - - - - - - - - - - -

SOUTHERN HOSPITALITY

Five or ten years after the war, Grandpa Lewis took a trip into Virginia. Where he ate his dinner at noon the first day, he asked what his chances would be at finding a place to stay overnight. He was told there was a little town on up the valley where he would have no trouble finding a place to stay. As he rode along, he thought he would rather stop at a farm or plantation than in some little town. Some of the homes and plantations appeared well-kept and prosperous looking; while others looked little better than many he had seen damaged during the war.

About the middle of the afternoon, he stopped at one of the more prosperous homes and asked to stay for the night. He was very graciously informed that they were in no condition to keep him, but that there was a small town a few miles ahead where he could easily get overnight lodging. He repeated his inquiries 2 or 3 more times during the afternoon and early evening with the same results and more references to the town just ahead.

Grandpa was tiring of such flimsy excuses and his horse needed rest and food more than he. He came to a prosperous looking, well-kept plantation with the buildings located back away from the road at the end of a tree-lined lane among the trees. Again he was given the same brush-off. This time he replied,

'I've heard that lame excuse and story about that little town just ahead all afternoon. I spent 4 years of my life helping Jackson, Lee and Jeff Davis try to set up the Southern Confederacy. If I'd known Virginia was like this, I'd have given Abe Lincoln a quit-claim deed for the whole thing without a single protest!'

'Were you with Jackson and Lee?'

'Yes, I was.'

'Come right in! Drop your rein over that post. One of the boys will look after your horse.' It turned out that the man and his family had all been involved in the war. They had a good visit that night.

Southern Hospitality had suffered from the destructiveness of war and from the influx of thieves and carpet-baggers during the Reconstruction.

- - - - - - - - - -

UNCLE STEVE

"Uncle Steve, the youngest of those 5 Lewis brothers, visited us in Glenville. This was about 1924, after your grandma and I were married and some of our brothers and sisters were living with us while attending college.'

"Then you got to hear him tell stories of his own experiences, didn't you? Was he very old when you were talking to him?"

"He would have been about 77 then. He died in 1933 in a Confederate Soldiers home in Richmond when he was 86. Here is one of his stories. . . ."

- - - - - - - - - -

One of Uncle Steve's assignments was to destroy and block the roads of an advancing Union Army which was coming through a mountainous area. They were preparing to blast some tremendous rocks into a canyon-like passage through which the army would have to pass. Before their blasts were ready, the advance part of the army came up the canyon into view of their outposts. Some of the wagons were immediately below when the blasts were set off, completely blocking the road. Two wagons were mashed by the falling rocks. The army would have to take time to clear the road, or take a roundabout way to get by. In either case, it would delay their advance and that was what Uncle Steve's unit was to accomplish at this particular place. They left unseen on a mountain trail, away from the canyon top, to continue their tactics of obstruction and delay.

- - - - - - - - - - - -

"Uncle Steve gave us a clear description of this incident and I wrote it up for an English assignment at the time. I have been looking for that account so I can give you more of the details, but haven't been able to find it yet."

"Grandpa, there have been a lot of our ancestors in wars, haven't there. You've told us about the first Alexander in the Revolutionary war. And now all those Lewis boys in the Civil War. Was anybody in the War of 1812?"

"Grandpa McQuain's father, another Alexander, was in the War of 1812."
Then Ma's brother, my Uncle Warren, was in the Spanish-American War."

"And you were in the Marines in the First World War and the Navy in WW2. My Dad was in the Army then and served in Germany."

"Five of our family were in WWII. My brother Perry was in the Air Force in England. That's when he went up into Scotland looking for McQuains. When he found some, he said he was sure they were McQuains, because first they showed him their horses, then their dogs, and finally took him to the house where they showed him their guns. After all that, they introduced him to their wives."

303

"You and Uncle Perry make two. Who else was in?"

"Eunice, Lois and Edna were in the WAAC. Edna was serving in New Guinea when she drowned while swimming. She's buried in a national cemetery in the Philippines."

"The Korean War, was any of our family in that?"

"Our son, Thomas, was in the Air Force during that war, but he stayed in this country. No grandchildren were in the Vietnam War, so that's one we missed."

- - - - - - - - - - --

AUNT EUNICE'S STORIES

"Your Aunt Eunice sent us a few family stories. These were in her last letter."

"She's your sister who lives in Oregon, isn't she?"

"Yes, she worked in Washington D.C. for many years, and after retiring, has lived in Florida and Portland. Her husband died many years ago."

- - - - - - - - - - - -

Cove 'Crick' was high and muddy. Bryan and George were hanging on the picket fence, watching drifts go floating by, when unexpectedly a big wheel from a mill came along. George had never seen its likes before and knew he must not let it get away. For the first time in his life, the yard gate had been left open. He bolted through the gate, scurried across the mare lot, dived under the bars and was racing down the meadow before Ma saw him. She entered the race in pursuit. She caught him before he reached the point where the creek and meadow merged.

After that he was called "George W. Millwheel."

- - - - - - - - -

Pa overheard Bryan and George expressing thoughts awakened by Ma's Bible reading. George said, dolefully,

'It's going to be so crowded in Heaven; a feller can't run around when everybody is resurrected!'

'No,' Bryan said, consolingly, it won't, for a lot of them will go to damnation.'

- - - - - - - - - -

'Diggin' the taters' was an inescapable family affair. Pa, with old Moll, plowed the potatoes out, row by row. The children picked them up, one by one, and put them in a bucket. Each child had a bucket. Ma also picked up, in fact, most of them. She emptied all the buckets into a sled body so they could be hauled into the garden and be stored in a 'tater hole' for winter. The digging of 1904 is the best remembered one, because Lois, at age 2, picked up more than did any of the 3 older children.

- - - - - - - - - -

With the help of 4 year old Edna, Ma was baking a cake. It was no one's birthday and, since we seldom had cake except on such occasions, Ma told Edna not to tell and the cake would be a surprise for the boys, Bryan and George, at supper. The secret was safe until the boys came through the cow-lot bars, then Edna went into action.

She rushed to meet them, excitedly telling them that there was a big surprise in the cooler in the old kitchen. She practically dragged them into the old kitchen. There, to her consternation, stood Ma sifting meal for cornbread. Edna was literally frozen in her tracks. The boys, sensing that she was about to spill some beans, chided,

'Well, go ahead and show us the big surprise!' This she did with summary and dispatch. Turning to them she said,

'Scott Varner's little girl fell down and skinned her a--.'

- - - - - - - - - -

All of us children were in school except Helen, who was seated at the table with Pa. She was waiting for him to get through eating and leave the table, and hopefully leave his piece of pie as he usually did. Pa was a very slow eater. The waiting and silence became too much for 3 year old Helen. She voiced the opinion that Edna would have already eaten his pie if she were at home. Still Pa was unimpressed, so she reached over and picked up Pa's pie and said,

306

'I'll 'showed' you how she would gobble it down.' She did and left Pa speechless, as well as pieless.'

- - - - - - - - - -

One day Myra said,
'Pa, your boys,' meaning Bryan and George, 'are up there in the apple house cussing!'
'Well,' Pa said, condescendingly, 'you tell them they must not be cussing.'
'No,' Myra objected. 'Just let them go ahead and they will be burned up on the Judgment Day.'

- - - - - - - - - -

Ma made Myra a dress and Perry a playsuit out of the same piece of yard goods. Lace was used on Myra's dress, but there was no lace on Perry's suit. When he saw the difference in adornment of the 2 garments, two-year old Perry's countenance fell, but his voice didn't. It rose in a loud adamant demand,
'I want something with 'wace' on it!'

- - - - - - - - -

Early one crisp fall morning, a knock came on our kitchen door. Bryan opened it and there stood Grant Scott, who was in a hurry. He made known his reason for being there without delay.
'Can your Pa come up and help me butcher another hog?"
That Bryan had not been named in vain, for the man who became famous by a speech depicting a Crown of Thorns being pressed down on the brow of labor, was apparent in his reply to Grant,
'Don't know if he can help you, for he's not got all the goose s--t off his boots that he got on them when he helped you the last time!'

- - - - - - - - - -

Once Myra and Perry, our youngest brother and sister, were discussing heaven and how far away it might be. Perry wondered,

307

'If we climbed to the top of that highest hill, do you think we could touch Heaven?'

'Maybe we couldn't,' Myra replied, 'but I'm sure Bryan could, he's so tall!'

- - - - - - - - - - -

"What are you going to tell us this evening, Grandpa? You never did tell the one about the counterfeiters."

"I've been thinking about that, Joe. Since Myra is visiting with us, I think we'll let her tell the story. She wrote a rather complete account of the story once. Let's let her tell it."

"That sounds great. Would you do that Aunt Myra?"

"Yes, but I can't compete with the TV, so you'll have to turn it off first."

"Jane, you turn it off, you're closer to it than I am."

"Say, Joe, how come you're always so far away when something needs to be done?"

"There, that is much better. You kids sound much like we often did at home, 60 or more years ago. It makes me feel right at home. Your Grandpa has told you about picnicking at Jackson Rocks on various occasions and that these rocks were named for Cummins Jackson, who was an uncle of the famous Civil War General 'Stonewall' Jackson. . ."

- - - - - - - - - - -

JACKSONS ROCKS

Our grandfather and great-grandfather knew Cummins Jackson well, because in their boyhood, they had lived on neighboring farms. Even when the McQuains migrated to Gilmer County, they remained friends and visited whenever in the neighborhood. Cummins was born near Weston, at Jackson's

Mill, and took his two nephews to raise after the death of their parents. These boys were Warren and Thomas ('Stonewall.')

As the story goes, Cummins made a very good grade of counterfeit money and the money poured from his mint in great quantities. He was very shrewd and it was several years before federal authorities caught up with him. He would take long trips into neighboring states, Ohio, Kentucky and Tennessee, and in fact, had learned the counterfeiting business from a group in Tennessee. One time, when things were getting hot for him, he brought his minting machine to our great-grandfather's home there on Big Cove, and asked him to hide it until it would be safe for him to resume his money making. But Cummins bought a newer type machine later, and never came after the old one. It remained in our family's care until 20 years or more after the Civil War, when my uncle and aunt took a sledge hammer and knocked it to pieces, fearing it might cause trouble. The legislature had just passed an act declaring it unlawful to have such a machine in ones possession.

The family story says that Cummins had also brought the melting pot and silver, together with a great deal of his minted money, and had hidden them among those large rocks on the hill behind our house. Those are the ones we called Jackson Rocks. We have searched for hours in vain, trying to find this treasure.

Cummins Jackson joined the gold rush to California and died a few months after he reached the Pacific Coast.

- - - - - - - - - - - -.

"That was a good story, Aunt Myra! I wish we could look for that silver. What we need is a metal detector."

"Perry tried using one of them and it didn't work either. I have more information on Cummins Jackson that you may read if you wish. Tonight's story is the part that affected our family."

"Yes, we've really been talking mostly about the McQuains and how it was when Grandpa was a little boy."

- - - - - - - - - - - - - -

THE BAPTIZING

"There was another story Pa told, about a Baptizing that he attended once. He was a young man then. Have I told you that one?"

"No, I don't think we've heard that one. Just his deer stories."

"Well, I'll tell two more stories about Pa and then we'll go on to some other subject."

- - - - - - - - - - -

Pa must have been in his late teens when he went to a church up toward the head of Big Cove where several people were to be baptized after the morning preaching. In those days in our area, the baptizing was done out in the creek where a hole of water could be found that was at least waist deep. This was such an occasion. Those to be baptized, together with their relatives and friends, gathered at the water's edge. The water gradually got deeper so that it was easy to get to the right depth for each, although the water was over a person's head in a large part of the hole.

A big log extended out over part of the deepest water and as the spectators gathered around the water, one young man walked out on that log, the better to see the proceedings. He had on a brand new suit, topped off with a new broad-brimmed hat, all of which he was sure he could show off much better from his position on the log. Perhaps he was trying to impress the pretty girls.

Up on the headwaters of Cove, there was a difference of belief among the members of some of the churches as to how the rite of baptism should be administered. Some believed one should be immersed three times, once as each name of the trinity was mentioned. Others believed the person should be immersed and held under during the reciting of the three parts of the ritual. There were also differences as to whether the immersion should be face forward or backward, but whatever the method, all believed in total immersion, which was used on that day.

The day was very cool and the spectators could almost feel the cold water themselves as each candidate waded into the cold water and was baptized. As each came back to the bank, he received a heavy coat or blanket for warmth.

As one emerged from the water with a gasp for air, the young man on the log took a long sympathetic breath as he stepped backward with a splash, where he sank beneath the water, leaving his new hat floating gently on top. He immediately came splashing to the top, gasping for air. He grabbed for his hat, put it on his head and pulled himself back on the log, amid laughter and a few handclaps from the crowd. Hurriedly, he made his way back along the log to the bank, looking like a drowned rat with his wet clothes clinging to him in disarray. He started running for home, and with no more visions now of pretty girls admiring him.

The baptizing continued with no further disturbance.

- - - - - - - - - - -

PA'S NEW BOOTS

Another time, Pa went with other young people up on Cove to a church gathering which lasted all day, including dinner served on the grounds. The dinner always assured a good attendance at such gatherings, even though the interests of many may not have extended further than the dinner itself. At the close of the morning speaking, the meal was served on tables in the shade of the trees.

When the tables were cleared off after dinner, the chairs and benches were rearranged so the speaking could continue outside in the shade, where they would all be much more comfortable than inside the church. The speakers' table and chairs were arranged so all could face that way.

Pa was wearing a new pair of fine leather Sunday boots with vine-like decorations in red on the top of each. This was a nice pair of boots of which he was very proud, and wanted as many people as possible to see them. With these thoughts in mind, he seated himself in the best place he could find for that purpose.

Just before the speaking got started, they moved the speakers' table to another location because of how the sun was shining. This made it necessary for all to turn their chairs toward the new speaker location.

Pa thought this new arrangement did not give him and his new boots as good a location as he thought they should have, to get the attention they deserved. He got up and quietly started moving around to a better place. As he was nearing a point where he and his boots could receive more attention, he heard a sudden swishing noise! His new boots were splattered with thin cow manure; even the red decorations on the tops of the boots had not been missed. He had stepped on a pile of manure hidden by the grass, and it had developed gas under the thin outer crust, from the sun shining on it. This had caused it to scatter so much when he stepped on it.

Many nearby saw his plight, but he felt as though all were looking at him. This was not the sort of attention he had in mind. He moved out of sight as quietly and quickly as he could and then went to the creek where he cleaned his boots so they again looked very nice. He was glad to take a seat at the back of the congregation. The less the attention, the better!

- - - - - - - - - - - -

"Why did our ancestors ever pick West Virginia to settle in? And why did they go so far up those little creeks, Little Cove and Crane Run?"

"Many of them came from Scotland, and perhaps the hills reminded them of home. They all had an independent streak in them. Perhaps this story that Ma used to tell about the Lewis family will help us understand."

- - - - - - - - - - -

MA'S FAMILY DODGES PROGRESS

Ma's grandfather lived in the Tygart Valley area where he had a fairly good farm and raised cattle as his most prized product. As the coal industry and the city of Elkins developed, the railroad came through or near his farm. With all the rail traffic, locomotive noise and whistling, he was sure his cattle would be kept stirred up and excited so they would not develop as they should.

He sold his farm in Randolph County and bought a farm lying along Grave Creek near Wheeling, Virginia (now West Virginia) where he resumed his cattle farming, free from the railroad and other noises of progress.

Scarcely had he got started in this new location, and 2 or 3 of his older children been born here, when disaster hit again! Another railroad was built along Grave Creek to Wheeling, splitting his farm from end to end, with no place to raise cattle, except right along the railroad, in this narrow creek valley. He just could not keep out of the route of progress. The railroad bought his farm and he returned to the Tygart valley where he purchased a farm a safe distance from the railroad and again resumed farming. That's where those five Lewis boys were raised who served in the civil War.

Ma said that when her family moved to the head of Crane Run in a covered wagon, when she was 10 years old, in 1880, that they had no such luck at her Grandfather had in getting in the way of progress. No railroad ever got near the head of Crane Run, in fact, the highway never got nearer than 4 or 5 gates away (about a mile.) Ma said she never could see why her father and mother ever moved way up there on Crane run. Grandpa Lewis had already served 4 years in the army and had seen much of the East during that time. He had worked the harvests on the western plains after the Civil War for a season or two before he was married. He was a surveyor and must have known a lot about various lands available. And yet he picked Crane Run!

His farm on Crane Run was a good, woods, hill farm, partly cleared and may have been cheap in price but, like many West Virginia woods farms, by the time it was cleared out and in grass, it was often about worn-out due to cropping and erosion. And by the time the owner had raised his family on it, he too, was about worn-out, and ready to take it a little easier.

Most West Virginia farms would not support more than one family, so other members of farm families had to take up other types of work, or 'move West' as was the practice in early days. This what Ma's family had done when they came to Crane Run in their canvas-covered wagon.

313

- - - - - - - - - - - -

"Well, Grandpa, that's just what you and Grandma did when you moved to Ohio, wasn't it?"

"Yes, the home farm never would have supported all eight of us children if it had been divided among us. Perry farmed it for several years and also his own farm. The rest of us scattered in all directions."

"You weren't looking for a secluded farm like your grandfather was."

"No, we were looking for job opportunities. Many West Virginia people left the state during and just after World War II and went to Ohio where work was more plentiful. We were part of that movement."

"Many of these have been stories about the 'Horse and Buggy' days. Can you remember all the means of transportation we have talked about?"

"Well, Grandpa, you walked to Glenville that time to take your teacher's examination. And you walked to school, so walking would be one."

"Yes, walking would be the oldest method of transportation. Riding horseback was our next most common type"

"Wagons and sleds, and the boat you built."

"Your grandma has some stories about horses and here she comes with Ice cream and raspberries, so she must be ready to tell us her stories!"

- - - - - - - - - - - -

GRANDMA WOOD AND DOLLY

One day Grandma Wood rode their old mare, Dolly, over to Auburn to the store, about 5 miles distance. She planned to do her shopping first, stay overnight with friends she had not seen for awhile and return home the next day. That way she would have time to visit and get the news about people around Auburn that she knew, and in turn, relate the news of the Sinking Creek area. This was regular visiting practice in those days and was not considered 'sponging' or imposing on friends, to stop for a meal or to stay overnight, if not done too often.

After breakfast, the friends were getting around to their farewells, when someone came in from the barn with the exciting news that Dolly had a new colt stumbling and falling about in the stall with her. Without delay, all went out to inspect and welcome the new arrival.

Everyone agreed on one point. The colt would not be able to walk well enough to go home before the next day. This did not worry anyone, for there were things at the store they would like to look at together. And there were other neighbor women Grandma wanted to see, so the day and extra night passed all too rapidly.

The day-late goodbyes were taken the next morning and Grandma Wood hurried home as fast as the colt could toddle. She was anxious to show the colt to her family, and relate all the news she had learned at Auburn.

- - - - - - - - - - -

When we were attending school, which was about a 1 ½ miles each way, we thought it was a treat when in bad weather we were allowed to ride horseback to school. This did not happen very often since someone had to go along to take the horses back home. We sort of envied three of our neighbor children who walked about the same distance from the other side of the school. They got to ride much more often, because they had an old horse that all three could get on at once and ride to school. Then when they turned it loose, the horse would return home by itself.

The walking speed for horses is about 4 miles an hour, but not even that fast for farm horses. This gives the rider plenty of time to look about the countryside and do a little daydreaming along the way. Sometimes this leisurely procedure was unexpectedly disturbed.

Women were riding on sidesaddles at that time, and it was difficult to mount the horse without taking advantage of a stump or steep bank. Nearly everyone had an 'upping block' at a convenient place near the house, used for mounting horses by both men and women. Often this was a block of wood about 2 feet high with about half cut away to make a step about 1 foot high. Often a block of stone had 1 or 2 steps cut into it to get to the right height to get on a horse. We had a stile with a platform extending on each side of the fence so that a horse could be led up to either side of the fence to mount or dismount. The stile could also be used simply to get over the fence.

On one occasion, I was going to the store at Newberne, about 3 miles away, riding Old John, an awkward, clumsy farm horse. The road was muddy in the spring of the year, which was nothing unusual for that time of year and did not interfere with my enjoyment of the beautiful dogwood, service and redbud trees that were in bloom. My thoughts of new dresses, hats and yard goods at the store just ahead were interrupted suddenly, when Old John stumbled and fell in the mud, throwing me from the saddle, feet first into the muddy road. I did not fall down, but by the time Old John got back on his feet, I was well covered with mud. I cleaned my shoes as well as I could, but left the mud on my clothes, thinking that it could be removed much more easily after it had dried.

There was no upping block, so I led Old John over to the bank at the edge of the road, climbed back into the saddle and went on to the store.

Another time, I rode Old John to a Saturday afternoon meeting at the Union Church, about 3 miles down Sinking Creek below our farm. The road was good and we were about halfway there when Old John, who was walking along the edge of the road where it was smoother, suddenly stumbled and fell. I slid from the saddle and rolled down the hill and under the fence to safety as John followed close behind and lodged against the post and rail fence in such a way that he could not get up. Some men, who were working on an oil well across the creek in the bottom, came over and rolled Old John so he could get up. John seemed all right after his stumbling blunder, and since I wasn't hurt either, and my clothes needed only a little dusting off, we continued on our way to church. One of the men led Old John over to the bank at the upper edge of the road, which served as an upping block for me.

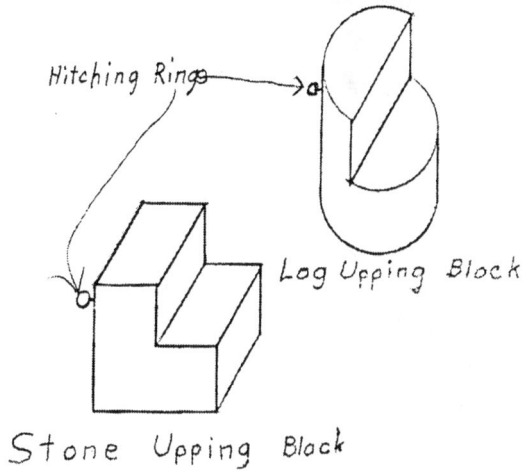

Hitching Ring

Log Upping Block

Stone Upping Block

Upping Blocks

- - - - - - - - - - -

When I was teaching beyond Auburn, about 7 miles away from home, my brother Page rode Old Beauty over to school so I could ride home. Page walked, taking advantage of short cuts along the way.

As I was riding along, Old Beauty slipped on some ice on a little bridge over a run, and fell. As she fell, I jumped clear and landed in the water up to my knees, getting the lower part of my dress wet. I remounted and rode on, but I was getting so cold that I stopped at Gluck's store in Auburn and bought a pair of stockings, which I put on in a back room of the store. I wrung the bottom of my dress as dry as I could and came out to the stove in the store, where I stood close to the heat, until my dress was dry. I was the only woman in the store at the time and told the men who were sitting around the stove what had happened. They thought I was lucky to be unhurt, and not any wetter than I was.

- - - - - - - - - - -

"Grandma, you sure had a lot of trouble with your horseback riding."

"Thank you for the ice cream. The raspberries taste like spring, even if they're from the freezer!"

"Grandpa, tell us more about sleds. There are kinds that don't need snow, aren't there?"

"And some were used either way. . . ."

- - - - - - - - - - - -

THE SLED

'Over the river and through the woods,
To Grandmother's house we go.
The horse knows the way, to carry the sleigh
Through the white and drifted snow. . ."

Such sleighs were built by experts with neat metal runners and bodies with comfortable good-looking seats, all attractively painted and pulled by beautiful high-spirited horses. I have seen two sleighs in our part of the country that would meet that description, but such sleighs were expensive and a rarity to be seen.

Children had homemade hand sleds which they used for riding, for pulling and hauling things, such as stove wood from the woodlot to the house, and for pulling the smaller children on when going to visit a neighbor. These hand sleds were used mostly when snow was on the ground.

We had a larger type sled, pulled by 2 or 2 horses, or by oxen, This type sled was a piece of equipment found on every farm. It was used for hauling all kinds of material, with or without snow on the ground. With 2 or 3 inches of snow, long hauling trips were more easily made.

One cold snowy winter, I delivered several hundred bushels of coal on such a sled, pulled by 2 horses. Each trip was 2 or 3 miles, and the sled carried as much as 50 bushels at a time. When stopping to let the horses rest, the sled would often stick fast and it was necessary to pull at an angle, or sidewise, to get the load

318

broken loose and started. I found it was better to make such stops on good snow and going downhill, if possible, to make starting easy. I have already told you of hauling lumber from Big Run, and tin roofing from Troy, for remodeling our house. This was on dry road, and was hard pulling for the horses. Lighter loads had to be taken.

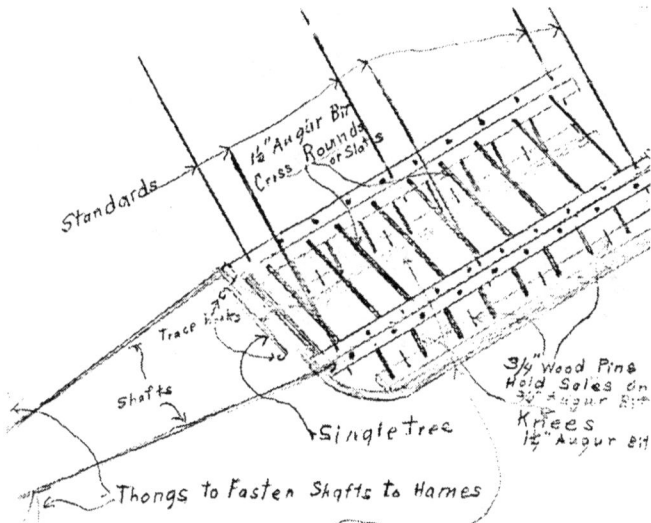

Standards

1½" Augur Bit
Cross Rounds or Slats

Trace Links

Shafts

Single Tree

¾" Wood Pins
Hold Soles On
¾" Augur Bit
Knees
1½" Augur Bit

Thongs to Fasten Shafts to Hames

Renewable Sled Soles of Poles

Sled as equipped above, for hauling hay, fodder, rails, posts, and poles. To haul corn, potatoes, and rock, a plank bottom laid on cross rounds with side boards against standards and end boards were used.

Slide for two horses and oxen were made longer and heavier equipped with tongue in place of two shafts.

One-Horse Sled

The sled soles would wear a long time on snow, but would wear off pretty fast on bare, gravelly ground with no sod, and faster yet on dry dirt roads. There were no paved roads in our part of West Virginia until after 1915 or 1920. Paved roads would have ground sled soles off even faster.

319

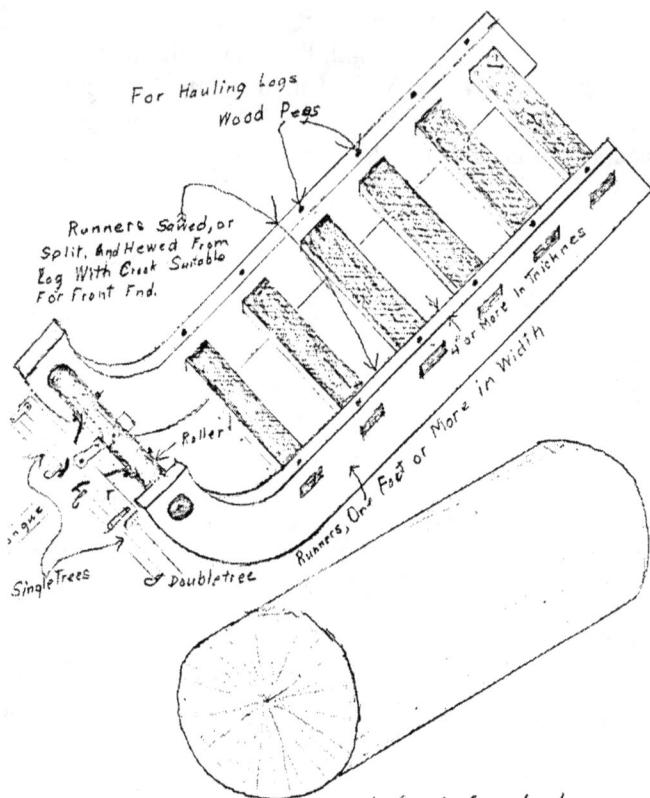

For Hauling Logs
Wood Pegs

Runners Sawed, or
Split, And Hewed From
Log With Crook Suitable
For Front End.

4" or More In Thickness

Runners, One Foot or More in Width

Roller

Tongue

Single Trees

Doubletree

Sled Benton Queen used to haul logs past our place to saw mill at Troy was like above sled.

Sled for Hauling Logs

The dirt roads developed mud holes in many places where the water did not drain off well, and in places where the water seeped in from the surrounding area. The road was only 6 or 8 feet above Cove Creek in several places. These always developed many mud holes in the clay ground though which the road ran. As the oil and gas industry developed, the movement on horse and ox drawn wagons, of all the equipment and supplies was far heavier than dirt roads would stand up under. Since this hauling was done in all kinds of weather, mud holes would develop and easily deepen until wheel hubs and wagon axles would drag. Just above the mouth of Big Run, a mud hole got so bad that it was dangerous to

320

put horses through it with a loaded wagon. The teams were unhooked from the wagons and driven around the mud hole to the other side, where two 2 or 3 long chains were hooked end to end to each wagon. Then enough horses were hitched to the chains to pull the loaded wagons through. Sometimes a block and tackle was used to get extra power in such conditions. It got so bad at this particular place that the road overseer hired George and me to take our team and haul rock to fill this and other places along this low stretch of road.

The neighbor farmer who owned the land along this road said we were welcome to any and all the rocks in the pasture fields or those that had been hauled off the meadow and piled here and there. We also got his permission to remove the fence at the bad place until we could haul in enough rock to make it safe to haul along the edge and complete the job. We picked up and hauled the loose rocks from his nearby pasture, but many more were needed, so we went across the creek and hauled several large piles of rock that had been piled about the edge of our meadow. This was the first time we had ever been paid for picking and hauling rock off our meadow, and was probably the first time the neighbor got his nuisance rocks picked up and hauled off, free of charge.

We still needed more fill, so we hauled gravel from the bar at the mouth of Big Run, about 100 yards away, to complete filling the dangerous mud hole. This spot gave no more trouble and was in good condition when the road was abandoned for a new location many years later.

We repaired many smaller places at the same time, but old and new mud holes were always a problem on dirt roads. Mud was everywhere in wet weather, and blinding dust in dry weather made travel disagreeable.

- - - - - - - - - - -

"I can see that talking about sleds, and rocks, and dust reminds your Grandma of another story."

"And this time she's bringing oatmeal cookies. I've been smelling them Grandma, and I hoped you were thinking up another story for us?"

- - - - - - - - - - -

321

DUST AND ROCKS AND SLEDS

Mama helped solve the dust problem for us girls by making us long coats of tan cotton material called dust protectors. We wore them to and from school and church. We would take them off on arrival and our clothes would be kept cleaner.

The problem with rocks was not as easily solved. Every spring, all of us children would have to help Dad pick up loose rocks in the meadows and load them on the two-horse sled. They were hauled off, and unloaded at the edge of the field, out of the way of the mowing machine. It seemed the rocks would freeze out of the ground in the winter and there were always plenty to haul away each spring. Especially plentiful were the rocks on newly seeded meadows after having been plowed and a crop of corn, followed by a wheat crop in which the grass had been sown.

It was no time at all until the sled was filled and ready for hauling and unloading. We children wore gloves to protect our hands, and too quickly, holes were in the finger of these gloves. Our fingers started getting sore. Then the gloves were put on backward for extended protection. If the rock picking was about done, we might get to stop and let the others finish, or perhaps get a new pair of gloves. Hands and backs of all of us were always tired by early afternoon, and we were frequently allowed to quit early, which was a treat and eagerly looked forward to. Rock picking was a spring chore on all farms that was never anticipated with joyful expectations.

The sled ride that I remember the best came at the start of the winter term of school, one year. Mayme and I were attending Normal School in Glenville that year, which was about 14 miles away. Dad took 10 or 12 of us back to Glenville in his two-horse sled. The sled was about 3 ½ feet wide, 12 or 14 feet long, and about 18 inches deep. Dad had put a lot of hay in the bottom. We wrapped up in blankets and sat in the hay, and kept snug and warm, arriving at school before noon. We had a lot of fun on that trip, laughing and singing on the way, and the time passed all too rapidly. Dad was able to make it back home before dark.

We would not have made such a trip by sled unless there was a good snow, except in an emergency.

"That sounds like the sleigh rides we have sometimes just for fun. We aren't really using them as a means of transportation. That was really a good way to get back to school."

"Have you ever heard of a 'Yankee Jumper?"

"No, that's a new one! Is that your next story, Grandpa?"

"Well, it's really an old one. . . . "

THE YANKEE JUMPER

The Yankee Jumper was a one-horse type of sleigh on which 1 or 2 people could ride. It was used mainly for fun, but wasn't widely or extensively used. It was made in the shape of a carpenter's sawhorse, but higher, about 36 inches in height. The legs were spread apart at the bottom about the same distance. A foot rest was fastened to the 2 legs on each side, 10 or 12 inches off the ground. Small poles, 18 or 20 feet long, were fastened to the bottom of the two legs on each side and shaved down thin enough on the top side in front, so the small end of each would bend up and fasten to the hames of the harness at the collar, acting as shafts. This served to pull and guide the Yankee Jumper, and to hold it back, going down-hill. This shaft-sled runner combination, caused the contraption to jump or slide over any obstruction in the road, adding to the fun and excitement of the ride, and also gave it the name, Yankee Jumper.

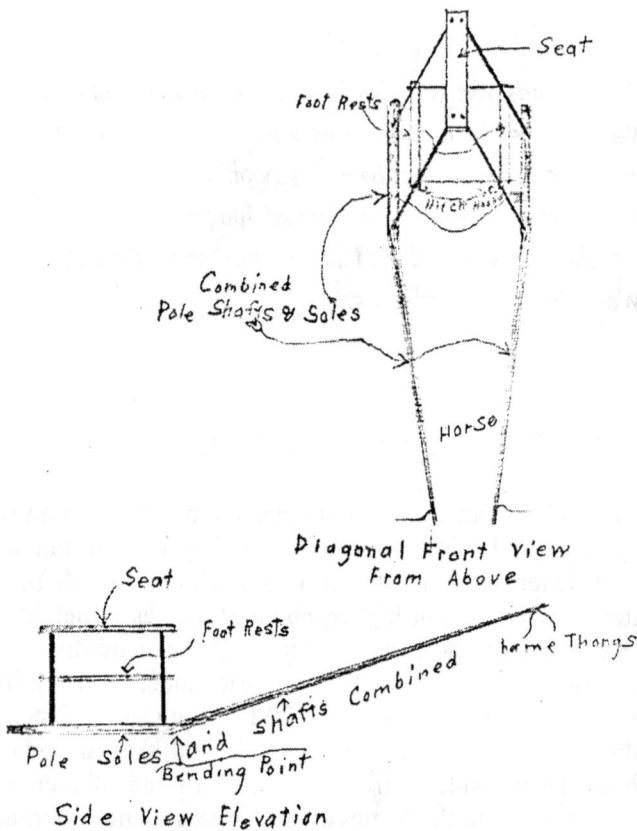

Seat

Foot Rests

Combined
Pole Shafts & Soles

Horse

Diagonal Front View
From Above

Seat

Foot Rests

shafts Combined

horse Thongs

Pole Soles and
Bending Point

Side View Elevation

Yankee Jumper

- - - - - - - - - - -

In addition to its many work uses, the two-horse sled was often used as a means of travel. Churches frequently held series of meetings extending as long as two weeks, variously called Revival Meetings, Protracted Meetings or simply, Big Meetings. Often extra preachers helped conduct these revivals, which were often held in the winter when the main farm work was over and all the people were free to attend both the night and day sessions.

When such meetings were held in cold snowy weather, people came out in their sleds as if for a sled review, with tassels,

324

jingle bells and all. Some had special seats on their sleds, others had the sled beds filled with straw, but all had lap robes and blankets to wrap up in so that all were warm and snug for the ride.

- - - - - - - - - - -

"Grandma says she has ridden the Yankee Jumper and that it's a very exciting ride. Now if we just had a horse, we could make one as soon as there's enough snow. Perhaps we could pull it with a snowmobile. "

"I think the snowmobile would be too fast. You wouldn't want quite that much excitement. Would you like to hear more about buggies?"

- - - - - - - - - - -

BUGGIES

We think of the animal-drawn wagon as used for heavy hauling for both short and long distances and for farm work, but it was also a means of travel and transportation as evidenced by the covered wagons and stage coaches used in the westward movement in the early days of this country.

The two-horse drawn hack, with two seats took the place of the stage coach in many parts of the country in hauling people and their luggage for hire at a regular fee.

The two-seated surrey, drawn by two horses (sometimes called a hack) and usually having a top lined with fringe, was a pleasure carriage, of a status similar to a Cadillac of Lincoln today. It was used for trips, visiting and pleasure drives, including shopping. Your Grandma says they had such a vehicle of which they were very proud.

The one and two horse single-seated buggies were widely used for pleasure and shopping. Many young men had beautiful buggies with fringed umbrella-tops in which they drove to see their girlfriends, and take them on pleasure drives. Heavy rains, muddy roads and blinding dust were conditions to be avoided on such drives, whether made in wagon, hack, surrey or fringed umbrella-top buggy.

It might be well for us to consider some of the dangers involved in the transportation system of the good old horse and buggy days. Fording the many un-bridged streams and creeks was hazardous under ordinary conditions, and became more dangerous at unfamiliar crossings and during periods of high water. One of the earliest fording accidents that I remember, involved a young neighbor man who lived about 1 ½ miles from us on Little Cove. He had been visiting 5 or 6 miles from his home and had started home. He came to an unfamiliar crossing and had been told that it was out of ride, but he attempted the crossing, which was not in the direct view of any house. He was a good swimmer, but he never reached home.

When friends came looking for him the next day, they found his horse some distance below the crossing, standing on high ground out of the high water. A day or two later, when the water ran down some, the young man's body was found a considerable distance farther downstream. This was a shock to the whole neighborhood as well to his family.

Another instance of horseback fording happened at the crossing just above our house when two of our nearest neighbors were going back home from the store and mill at Troy. They had crossed the creek safely just below our house, which was almost too deep. The rapidly rising water was well out of ride by the time they arrived at the upper crossing. They knew it was, but attempted the crossing in spite of their better judgment. One got safely across, even though the horse had to swim part of the way. The other horse swam also, but was washed downstream where the bank was high, yet the water was running over it. As the horse swam toward this water-covered bank, the rider sprang from the swimming horse to the bank safely. He had held on to the bridle reins. The horse fell back and went under water on his first attempt to climb out on the bank. On the second attempt, by the aid of his master pulling on the reins from the bank, the horse clambered to the bank. He was led, strangling and coughing, to high ground, but was unable to expel the water from his lungs and strangled to death in a few minutes after reaching dry ground. The neighbor was lucky and glad to escape, but it was a great loss to him, losing the horse. It broke his oilfield hauling team and cost him possibly about $500. to replace, since that was the selling price of a good horse at that time.

326

- - - - - - - - - - - -

There were other dangers. I once saw a farmer drive his two-horse wagon out on the road where he let the team stand while he went back to close the gate. At that time, the neighbor's dog chased a cat, both of them barking, growling and clawing at each other, across the road under the wagon at the horses' heels. The horses became frightened and started running toward their barn down the road a quarter of a mile. The wagon made so much noise over the rough road and rocks along the way, that the horses became more excited and ran all the faster. As they approached the turn-off to the barn, they were running at full speed. To make things worse, the neck yoke came loose from the front end of the wagon tongue. It began bouncing from horse to horse between them. As they approached the bridge across the run, the wagon tongue caught on the bridge floor and acted as a vaulting pole to throw the front end of the wagon into the air. At this point, the double-tree pulled loose, leaving the wagon in a crumpled mess at the bridge, while double and single-trees bumped the horses' heels. The neck yoke and whiffle-trees were bumping on their collars as they came to a stop before the closed barn doors.

When I got to the bridge and barn, the farmer had already arrived and was surveying the damage. He was all right and his team was also unhurt, except for a few bruises. The wagon fared worse, with a broken tongue and coupling pole, and a few broken boards in the wagon bed, which had been thrown clear of the wagon in the final pole-vaulting disaster. The farmer said there seemed to be nothing that he could not repair himself. For this, he seemed well pleased.

Surreys and buggies seldom had head-on collisions. They would sometimes hook wheels in meeting or passing and accomplish the same thing by upsetting one another, damaging both the buggies and passengers. There have been instances in which lone drivers have passed out, dropping the lines, unable to drive any longer. The faithful old horse or team continued the journey home safely with their unconscious driver. In many instances, the driver's life was saved by such a reliable team.

Too often, going to sleep or passing out while driving a team, was as dangerous as passing out at the wheel, when driving a car, and not to be recommended in either situation.

- - - - - - - - - - - -

"Well, Grandpa, at least you aren't going as fast in the buggy as in a car. Perhaps the stopping wouldn't hurt quite as much."

"That's true, but either way can cause damage. I told you some stories the other day about the use of Cove Creek in floating logs and crossties to market. Pa went along with a boat load of barrel staves once. . . ."

- - - - - - - - - - - -

PA'S LOG-BOAT TRIP TO PARKERSBURG

Since West Virginia is an inland state not bordering on any ocean, sea or lake, its water travel and freight movement was confined to small streams, creeks and rivers. From our farm, the log rafts were taken down Big Cove Creek, Leading Creek and the Little Kanawha River to market at Parkersburg on the Ohio River.

Pa told us of several trips to Parkersburg on rafts of logs, but one trip was a little different. It was on Brown's flat-bottom barge-like stave boat, which was guided in the same manner as rafts. This boat was about 150 feet long and 15 or 20 feet wide. It was loaded with several thousand barrel staves. Brown and his men had worked through the winter building the boat and getting out the barrel staves to be taken to market in it. That stave boat, together with the log rafts in the area that were being readied for the spring market, furnished an interesting topic of conversation during the winter, throughout the neighborhood.

Finally the boat was finished and completely loaded with staves, and together with several log rafts, all were ready and waiting for a spring rafting rise in the creek to get started on the way to market. In many instances the men hired to cut the logs during the winter, and to help make the boat and staves were paid part of their wages as the work progressed. The final payment was

328

when delivery was made to the mill company where the owners received full payment and could then pay off their workers.

Often neighbors would work together cutting and rafting logs, which they would then float to market, where they would sell them and divide the money among themselves, according to the number of logs and labor each had contributed. In this way, many in the neighborhood eagerly looked forward to marketing time and complete payment for both their material and labor.

Such a rafting rise began to develop one night in late April or early May. What appeared to be a general rain continued through the night and by morning, the creeks had begun to rise. The rain continued without letup and by noon, it was certain that a rafting, boat tide was coming. The men had assembled at their respective rafts, and made everything in readiness to shove off as soon as the creek was deep enough to carry the rafts safely over the shoals that lay ahead. The rain continued even harder and the creek came up faster. By mid-afternoon, the smaller rafts started shoving off first, careful to keep several hundred yards distance between each.

Brown's stave boat, on which Pa was working, was the last to shove off, since they thought it was heavier and would require deeper water than any of the log rafts. The river was rising rapidly and rain had increased to a downpour. There would be plenty of water indeed. The boat shoved off at a greater distance behind the last raft, since they were sure the extra weight and trimmer shape of the boat would cause it to develop more speed than the log rafts, if they were able to guide it in the main current of the river.

The boat, as well as all the rafts, was equipped with a heavy rudder at each end. The rudder was constructed of an 18 or 20 foot pole with a 12 or 15 inch wide board about 6 or 8 feet long, fastened to the big end to act as an oar to dip into the water. This rudder operated on a pivot so it could be lowered into the water to guide the boat in either direction. It was operated by men on the raft or boat in the same manner as rowing a boat.

The river-men were all glad to get started early in the afternoon, since it would give them time to get past some of the narrowest and crookedest part of Leading Creek before dark. Two or three men were kept busy on each rudder at both ends of the boat to guide it through the narrow places and around the creek turns. The straight stretches gave them time to rest and get their breath before they got to the next turn. By dark, they got down where other creeks emptied into Leading Creek, making it wider, deeper, and somewhat straighter. The heavy rain continued and the creek became higher and higher, running over its banks, flooding the low land along the way, and widening the deep, safe area midstream in which to guide the boat.

As darkness approached, the water was fast approaching flood proportions. This developed a new obstacle. The low limbs of the trees growing along the banks, and of those leaning far out over the creek, were getting in the way of operating the rudders. It was clear that this would be more and more of a problem, as the flood got higher. Things on the boat were tied down as best they could, as protection against those limbs.

Gradually, the stave boat overtook and passed one of the log rafts. The boat steered into the main current and the raft to one side in slow water. It had trouble getting around some crooks and had been slowed down before the boat came along.

Other rafts had come in from some of the side creeks so that there were more rafts in front and behind the boat than the ones that had left Troy together. No more passings were attempted after dark, since Leading Creek was too narrow and dangerous, even for side by side boating of raft and boat. The tree limbs raking of the boat and rafts got so bad that the rudders could not be operated. They were removed and tied down lengthwise in the middle of the boat or raft, so that the rudder board and pole formed a skid on which the limbs would slide over the boat more freely. This also made safer places for the men to lie down and hold tight while the limbs slid along the rudder poles. It was fortunate this was done, since it prevented any men from being raked overboard and lost in the darkness. There was little they could do in the darkness to guide the rudderless boat. It was a dangerous river trip indeed.

In more open areas, the men worked to loose the floating logs, brush and limbs from the front of the boat so it would float freely. Then they scurried back to their safe holding-on places, as they approached more tree-lined banks. There was one man who stayed too long, or got out too soon before the limbs had been passed. Two or three times he was knocked down by the limbs and was lucky to get to a safe place to hold on. Each time others warned him to be more careful. Then another heavy limb knocked him down and rolled him back over the boat as he yelled in pain for help. Several reached out and tried to grab him, but were unable to hold on to him, as the many branches dragged and rolled him past. Some were almost carried along with him. Back past the middle of the boat, someone from a better protected position grabbed and yanked him loose from the limbs and both held on tightly while the other branches passed over them. All drew a breath of relief in the darkness as they heard that he was safe. They all had plenty of breath left to tell the bruised man in no uncertain way, that they would tie him down and leave him there if he was ever the first one up and out after that. The dragging, rolling, bruising encounter had really impressed him, so much that they did not get the opportunity to tie him down.

When they floated out of Leading Creek into the Little Kanawha River, the expanse of water was wider and there was more space free of limbs in the middle of the river. The rain stopped and, as the dark clouds moved on, the night became somewhat less black, and objects stood out more distinctly in the darkness.

The boat was floating along near the right bank when a large tree could be seen almost directly in front of the boat. The boat was going to miss the tree on its right side and pass between the tree and the bank where it appeared wide enough. The tree proved to be a large black walnut tree that stood between the road and the river. The boat was actually floating down the road, and missing the tree only a few feet. The front end of the boat missed the big walnut tree, but had gone scarcely 50 feet when it hit the water-covered high bank at the side of the road and came to a grinding stop. Then the boat began slowly swinging toward the big tree, picking up speed as the rear end swung farther into the main river current. Either the boat would break in two near the middle, or the walnut tree would have to give way. All the men ran to the front end to be able to jump off the boat, should it start breaking up. All froze in their tracks as the side of the boat swung against the tree with a grinding sound. Then with a joyful gasp, they thawed from their tracks as the great walnut gave way with a loud crash as the swinging boat pressed it beneath the waves and floated free, on its way down the river.

Dawn followed quickly after the walnut tree incident and with came a gnawing, river sickness, brought on by the hardships of the night's travel. They were lucky to be nearing a small town

331

that sold a remedy that was guaranteed to cure such ailments, and enjoyed a reputation of fulfilling that guarantee. A man in a johnboat rowed out to the stave boat to assist in tying it up. The first tree was dead and snapped off. The second was a green tree and held fast. The cable stretched dangerously near the breaking point as the stave boat slowed to a stop and was then gradually pulled upstream by the stretch in the cable, until it came to a standstill, and gradually swung toward the river bank.

Everyone got off and hurried to the building where the cure for their stomach illness was being sold. The tables were filled with the many different appetizingly prepared dishes of that cure, ready for individual use as needed. After 18 hours on the river, the need was great.

Everyone returned to the boat, cured of their stomach trouble, and quickly repaired and mounted the rudder on each end of the boat for effective daylight use as they continued to Parkersburg. Only a few miles ahead was a long island with channels past on both sides where many rafts had been wrecked so badly that they had to be re-rafted before going further. Many felt that incorrect information had been given out as to how and on which side to pass, so that wrecks would happen and there would be extra work for some in the neighborhood, when they were hired to help with the re-rafting. The information they had received while eating was that with the high water, they would be safe to take either channel, since both were open and safe. Much to their relief, when they got to the island, they found that their information was correct and they passed in safety.

Late in the afternoon, the boat was towed to a docking space at the mill company where the staves and boat were sold at what they considered a good price. Mr. Brown immediately paid his men for helping on the boat, and also any back pay that was due them. Everyone stayed in Parkersburg overnight to see some of the sights and get a night's rest before starting back home the next day.

Pa and 2 or 3 others went into a hardware store to look around; where they saw an unusual looking saw hanging on the wall. It was 8 or 10 inches wide at one end, where double handles were fastened and sloped to 4 or 5 inches in width at the other end. It had large teeth on one side, its entire length of 6 or 7 feet, unlike any that the men had ever used in cutting timber. They wondered among themselves what kind of saw it was. Someone suggested they ask the clerk, but an old man with them, named "Pouncy,' objected, saying,

'No! We'll just wait around a bit. Some fellow will come in and ask and we'll find out what it is without anyone knowing we didn't know!' Sure enough, in came a young man, who asked, pointing to the saw we had just been talking about,

'What is that thing hanging up there?' The clerk answered,

'Oh that? That's an ice saw. We sell several of them to the ice house men around town to saw blocks of ice off the river to store in their ice storage buildings.' Old Pouncy walked slowly over and laid his hand heavily on the young man's shoulder, saying as he did so,

'Where have you grown up, young man, that you didn't know what an ice saw is or what it's used for?' without cracking a smile amid the chuckles and amusement that followed.

Later in the evening, Pa was impressed with a long train loaded with hogs. It slowly crossed the bridge over the Ohio River and picked up speed as it continued out of view toward the east. He wondered where so many hogs could be going, and what could be done with so many, and where could enough feed come from to feed so many hungry animals. As if in answer to his musings, another long train was crossing the same bridge from Ohio to West Virginia on its way in an eastward direction. This train was as long, but was loaded, not with hogs, but with corn, enough to feed many hungry hogs, and it, too, was coming out of Ohio.

Thus you see these down-stream trips to lumber markets at Parkersburg furnished incidents and experiences enough to keep the neighborhood conversation going until another marketing trip, as well as furnishing some extra money for the family.

JOHNBOAT TO GRANTSVILLE

A young man, who lived at Conings about 4 miles up Big Cove from our place, took and developed pictures throughout the area. He became a pretty good photographer. He took some pictures at our place and said he would have them ready to deliver before he moved to Grantsville, about 25 or 30 miles down-stream on the Little Kanawha River, where he would soon be opening a photography shop of his own.

We were surprised, one cloudy morning in early spring, to hear the bumping of oars and see a boat loaded with a trunk or two, some boxes, a table, chairs and other household goods, pull over to the creek bank and stop in front of our house. Even before he started toward the house, we recognized the young photographer coming to deliver our pictures. He said he wanted to open his shop early that spring at Grantsville before the roads were fit to travel over, so he and his brothers had built the boat bigger than usual in which to move. They had no trouble getting over the riffles on their way down from Conings and expected no difficulties on the remainder of their journey. They expected to finish their voyage the next day after staying overnight somewhere along the way. He and his wife were accompanied by one of his brothers who had come along to help row the boat and to help set up shop and get moved into living quarters.

We had no boat at that time and went down to the fence next to the creek to see them get in the boat, push off, and get going on their way again. The man near the middle used two oars, rowing, and the other, at the stern, used a paddle to guide and help propel the boat, which was necessary to make any progress, since the current was slow, except over the riffles. We children were all very much interested and followed along inside the meadow fence to watch them go over the old mill dam riffle, and guide their boat around the bend in the creek. The young man established his photography shop, which he operated successfully for many years.

- - - - - - - - - -

Flat bottom, sternwheeler boat service, powered with gasoline engines, was established and operated on the Little Kanawha River by 3 or 4 individuals, vying with each other for a share of the business. The operation was somewhat irregular, depending on the navigable supply of water in the river. The service was more dependable in the winter, except when the river was frozen over. In the summer, the water level was often too low. However water travel and freight movement were factors in the economy of that part of the county. Many students at Glenville Normal School had traveled from Gilmer Station, the only railroad connection in the county, to Glenville by train, river boat, and mud-road taxi service.

334

When I left for the Marines in World War I, I took the river boat to Gilmer Station to get the train to Charleston.

- - - - - - - - - - -

AIR TRAVEL

Air travel was of no commercial significance in our part of the country before the First World War. A few planes flew over, generally going to, or from county fairs, or other gatherings, where they took people for short flights, charging small fees. Exhibition flights were staged as extras by the management to draw crowds to such gatherings. The fees for riders helped defray expenses of the planes at such events.

- - - - - - - - - -

"That pretty much covers the kinds of transportation we used to have. I didn't ride on that railroad until I left for the First World War, and still haven't been on an airplane."

"Airplanes are pretty safe now, Grandpa. You'd really like seeing the countryside. It's even better than your view from that load of hay!"

"I'll take your word for it just now, but maybe next year.. Floods were big occasions in our lives, and we had them often. . ."

- - - - - - - - - -

FLOOD STORIES

Pa told about a thunderstorm that passed over our house that was of ordinary duration, but seemed darker and accompanied by much more thunder farther up the creek. About half an hour afterward, they heard logs bumping against each other up the creek, accompanied by an unfamiliar racket and noise. They ran out across the meadow to see what was going on. They were amazed and appalled to see the water rolling downstream in a front, 4 or 5 feet high, extending from bank to bank, carrying logs,

335

brush and trash along with it, all rolling along together. The logs, brush and trash served as a sort of moving dam, holding the water back. They had never seen anything like it before or since. There had been what is often called a cloudburst that put so much water in the creek at one time that it was like a dam bursting all at once, with a head of water pushed rapidly forward by the on-coming mass behind it. Such wash-outs happened infrequently, but were a danger to be guarded against, especially in our narrow valleys.

- - - - - - - - - -

There was a similar storm when we were growing up at home. It too, appeared much darker with more thunder up-stream from our place. The sun came out immediately after the storm. I went out to look for the rainbow which was often visible against the bluff. It was not as distinct as it usually appeared. While looking for the rainbow, something didn't seem to be right. The leaves and trash were floating to the left! Up Cove! Cove Creek was flowing backward up stream! I yelled to the other members of the family in the house so they could see what was happening. All of them were as amazed as I was at the sight. Pa said that something must be damming the creek below to cause that. The rest of us wondered if it was a miracle, or perhaps the world was coming to an end!

Some of us went down the meadow to the old mill dam riffle. There were no riffles. The water had backed up and was flowing quietly up-stream, getting deeper all the time. It was too deep to follow the road around the narrows to the mouth of Little Cove. We went by a path above the road, around the hill. As we got to where we could see up Little Cove, we could see it was at flood tide, overflowing its banks and shooting out across Big Cove at a depth of 8 or 9 feet, splashing on the opposite bank. The water from Little Cove was completely damming Big Cove to that height, with the water running both up and down Big Cove. More was going down stream than up, because it was lower on that side and ran away faster.

To see Cove Creek running backward was quite a remarkable sight and our whole family went down to watch. The creek kept backing up until the water became level. Because the fall in Big Cove was much less than in Little Cove, its flood water was longer

336

getting to the mouth of Little cove, thus allowing the damming effect, together with the temporary upstream flow. In a half hour or less, the flood waters arrived, reversing the flow to its normal direction, and bringing to an end all the marvelous excitement.

And yet, not all the effects disappeared so quickly. After both creeks had run down in a day or two, to their normal low-water stage, 2 horseback riders were fording the creek just at the point where both streams joined, the point where the damming had taken place. They were side by side a few feet from each other, when one rider's horse gradually entered deeper and deeper water and had to swim, which had never happened at this crossing before. The one rider had scarcely started chiding the other about getting into such deep water, when his own horse stepped suddenly into deep water. Both swam together to the opposite side in safety, except that both riders got wet in the process. The high water had washed out a deep hole in the crossing, over a man's head in depth. Barricades were put up on both sides of the creek with detour signs, to use crossings farther down-stream. Gradually, summer rises filled gravel and sand into the deep hole making the ford safe for use again.

- - - - - - - - - - - -

THE LANDSLIDE

Pa cleared part of a steep hillside for a cornfield when George and I were not yet big enough to be of much help in hoeing corn. There were 3 or 4 flat areas where the ground was not too steep to plow in preparation for planting and the crop could be cultivated after planting. Between the flat areas were steep banks that were too steep to get a horse over for plowing. These were cultivated by hand with broad hoes. It was a steep hillside, rising to a height of 4 or 500 feet above the level of Cove Creek. Many small slips had broken loose and settled down two or more feet. Some of these were holding fast, while others had slid down to the next flat. Still others had slid down to the creek at the bottom of the hill. On the lower flat, 250 feet up from the creek, the edge of the flat had slid away completely in places, looking like a piece of bread with the edge bitten off. On one of the biggest of these places, George and I had a play cornfield, near the steep edge. Pa told us that at one time, our play field was not near the edge, until part broke off in the big slip and slid into the creek.

The big slip had happened several years before, one very wet spring. It had been raining continuously for several days and the ground was soaked everywhere. In fact, people began to wonder if the rain would ever stop. The creek was at flood tide and over its banks a great deal of the time.

People were living in a house at the mouth of Big Run. When they went to bed in the evening, there was no danger that the creek would get up to their house during the night. But shortly afterward, they heard a crashing, sliding noise over toward the hillside, which they thought was just another slip, even though it seemed much louder than usual. They could hear water lapping against the house. When they went to the door to see what was going on, the water was all around the house, over the porch and within a few inches of running into the house. They started putting things up on chairs and beds, expecting the water to get higher. They knew there had not been enough rain to cause that sort of a flood. Excitement eased when the water seemed to have stopped rising. And they felt much better when they were sure it was falling. With water all around the house and falling, there was nothing to do but wait until daylight to find out what had happened.

Next morning, the creek was much lower and they could see a bare muddy area from the flat about 50 feet wide, extending to the creek with no trees standing. A big piece of that flat had broken loose, carrying trees and all with it. It had slid into the creek, filling it, and completely damming it from side to side. The flood waters quickly backed up behind the dam and around the house. It would have gone even higher, but it reached the top of the loose mud dam and ran over the bottom land around it. The loose, wet mud began washing out, together with some of the bottom bank on the opposite side, cutting a channel through, wide and deep enough to let the creek run through again. The new channel was pushed over about the width of itself away from the hill, cutting its new channel across the edge of the meadow on the other side.

Part of that slip has never all washed away and still holds the creek away from the hill, and through the deep water that served as our swimming hole for many years. It is still there, to be so used, if needed.

- - - - - - - - - - - -

THE RESCUE

Some years later, a cloudburst fell on the headwaters of Leading Creek, above Troy, forcing Leading Creek out of its banks in the highest flood that ever hit Troy. It forced many residents from their homes to high ground. There were no drownings, but many had to be removed from their houses in boats, since the water rose at night so rapidly, and without warning, that it was into the houses before many knew there was any flood danger at all.

One elderly couple, 75 or 80 years old, first learned of the flood when one of them dropped his hand over the edge of the bed into water nearly up to the bottom of the mattress. Their house had been built on a high foundation which was thought to be out of high water. It was already too deep around their house for them to wade out to safety. The water was rising rapidly in the one-story house, and there was no way to get into the attic. The house was in backwater and there was no danger of it being knocked from its foundation by rapid current and floating objects, but the rapidly rising water was then waist deep, as they stood on the bed yelling through the top part of the window for help.

A welcome answering call came to them from neighbors at the edge of the water in the distance, telling them to hold on, that help was coming. Two men would be out to get them in a boat. They were already holding on, and continued yelling until the men in the boat came to their window, helped them through the top part of the window into the boat, and took them safely to high ground and safety.

The two were talking to their sister and brother-in-law of the incident and said to them that they would be better off dead since they were both getting so old and no account. The answer to that statement was,

'Now, you know you don't believe that!'

'Oh yes! We do! We're no good any more.' came the answer,

339

'Then why did you both yell through the window for people to come and rescue you in a boat? You could have kept quiet and it would have all been over in a little while. We don't want to hear any more of your foolishness!' The argument stopped at that point.

- - - - - - - - - - -

"There, that's about enough high water stories for awhile."

"Yes, we'll probably dream about floods tonight, or landslides."

"Floods were very common along those small creeks. So many hillsides had been cleared of timber for farming. That made the rain run off them very quickly. A single day's hard rain would cause a rise in the creek. With a day or two more rain, the creek would be out of its bank. It was often over the meadow in front of our house, but never in the house."

"Grandpa, what years would you say these stories of yours took place?"

"I was born in 1897, so these stories covered the years from 1900 to 1917. Pa's stories were from 1870 to 1900, and Grandpa Lewis's, of course, took place during the Civil War, 1861-1865.

"There was another event that took place during the summer of 1914 in Europe, that affected our family more than we ever realized at the time. . ."

- - - - - - - - - - -

AND IN CONCLUSION

War was declared among the major powers of Europe, which was accompanied by immediate hostilities and battle losses. The nations not immediately involved, declared neutrality, and attempted to take no part on either wide, but many were gradually drawn into the conflict until the principal world powers became involved in what came to be known as 'The First World War.'

Prices of war supplies and goods of all kinds, including food supplies, went up and became scarce, even before the war assumed worked wide proportions.

An old man in our neighborhood, who was barely able to grow enough corn and garden supplies for the meager needs of his family of six, and bought salt, coffee and sugar from the store, expressed the feelings of many very well. I met him as he walked home from the store one evening, mumbling to himself.

"What is the matter, Lieu?" I asked, as we met.

"Prices have gone up! After I paid for the salt and sugar, I did not have enough left to get a pound of coffee. They weighed me out a half-pound of coffee! Said the war has caused prices to go up."

"Yes, I guess that is what has happened," I replied.

"I can't see why that war, away there, causes things to go up, away here," he answered. With scarcely a pause, he continued, "I told my woman to cook them coffee grounds over again!"

That was even before we got into the war.

- - - - - - - - -

In 1916, farmers were urged to double their production to be able to furnish more food for the people whose supplies were limited by the War in Europe. The farmers in our area attempted to that, and also for the added income it would bring them.

That same year, Woodrow Wilson ran for his second term as President; to a large extend on the cry, 'He has kept us out of war.' Scarcely had he been inaugurated than a declaration of war was made April 6, 1917 which was followed quickly by a draft registry of all men between the ages 21 and 31. All single able-bodied men were subject to immediate service as needed. Several enlisted in the armed forces in the early spring, although those under 21 had to have their parents' consent to enlist. I did not ask for this consent, but enlisted about a year later when I reached 21.

Production of food became more important after entering the war, to feed our own armed forces, in addition to continuing to furnish food and supplies for our allies. We raised bigger crops on our farm and rented extra land from a neighbor. In addition to our own work, George and I helped the neighbors with their work when we had time to spare from our own work. George did some oil field hauling with our team when time permitted, since oil and gas products became important in furthering the War Effort. This type of work was considered necessary and appropriate for men not yet called into the military service. Teaching and certain other work was more appropriate for women and married men, or those too old to be included in the draft. In this way I busied myself until I was 21, when I left home on April 22, 1918 to join the United States Marine Corps.

"So you can see that our lives were changed greatly by the war, whether we actually entered the armed forces or not. Pa was past 65 by this time, so George had to stay and do the farm work when I left. When I came back, we all went to school in Glenville, and never really lived and farmed at home any more."

"Grandpa, tell us about when you were in the Marines. Were you in any big battles?"

"Yes, I was in some big battles, but that's a story for another time. We've also survived the Roaring 20's, The Great Depression, World War II and our years in Ohio when we remodeled all those houses and apartments!"

"I bet you could draw a floor plan of each of those houses, couldn't you?"

"Yes, I could, but I don't think you'd be very interested in all those ways we changed kitchens."

"I hear Grandma is starting roses to take to Florida when you move there. Do you think she'll ride one of those three-wheeled bicycles?"

"I don't know about that. Neither of us ever had bicycles when we were young, so perhaps it's our turn. And just think, I'll soon have some Florida stories to tell you. There was this big alligator that lived across from our house. . . . ."

THE END
342

ABOUT THE AUTHOR

Thomas Bryan McQuain was born in 1897 near Troy, West Virginia, where he grew up on their family farm. The book covers the years between 1897 and 1917, when McQuain entered the Marines during World War I. His book, *To the Front and Back*, published by Heritage Books in 2005, relates his war experiences.

He graduated from Glenville Normal School and served as a teacher and principal, then builder and carpenter. He married Opal A. Morrison in 1922. They were the parents of four children: Miriam Ford Looker, Jesabel Linscott, Thomas McQuain and David McQuain. It was for the eleven grandchildren that this book was written in 1976. He died in 1988 and is buried in Ft. Myers, Florida, where he spent his retirement years.

Mr. McQuain also served in World War II and wrote of those experiences in the book, *My Second War*, which was privately printed and circulated.

Miriam McQuain Looker carefully edited the book for publication, leaving sentence structure and figures of speech as written by her father. Miriam spends her summers on one of the family farms near Troy, where the McQuain descendants gather each year.